I.B.TAURIS SHORT HISTORIES

I.B.Tauris Short Histories is an authoritative and elegantly written new series which puts a fresh perspective on the way history is taught and understood in the twenty-first century. Designed to have strong appeal to university students and their teachers, as well as to general readers and history enthusiasts, *I.B.Tauris Short Histories* comprises a novel attempt to bring informed interpretation, as well as factual reportage, to historical debate. Addressing key subjects and topics in the fields of history, the history of ideas, religion, classical studies, politics, philosophy and Middle East studies, the series seeks intentionally to move beyond the bland, neutral 'introduction' that so often serves as the primary undergraduate teaching tool. While always providing students and generalists with the core facts that they need to get to grips with the essentials of any particular subject, *I.B.Tauris Short Histories* goes further. It offers new insights into how a topic has been understood in the past, and what different social and cultural factors might have been at work. It brings original perspectives to bear on manner of its current interpretation. It raises questions and – in its extensive further reading lists – points to further study, even as it suggests answers. Addressing a variety of subjects in a greater degree of depth than is often found in comparable series, yet at the same time in concise and compact handbook form, *I.B.Tauris Short Histories* aims to be 'introductions with an edge'. In combining questioning and searching analysis with informed history writing, it brings history up-to-date for an increasingly complex and globalised digital age.

www.short-histories.com

A SHORT HISTORY OF THE WEIMAR REPUBLIC

Colin Storer

I.B. TAURIS
LONDON · NEW YORK

To Jenny with love.

Published in 2013 by I.B.Tauris & Co Ltd
6 Salem Road, London W2 4BU
175 Fifth Avenue, New York NY 10010
www.ibtauris.com

Distributed in the United States and Canada Exclusively by Palgrave
Macmillan, 175 Fifth Avenue, New York NY 10010

ISBN: 978 1 78076 175 6 (hb)
ISBN: 978 1 78076 176 3 (pb)

A full CIP record for this book is available from the British Library
A full CIP record is available from the Library of Congress

Library of Congress Catalog Card Number: available

Typeset in Sabon by Ellipsis Digital Limited, Glasgow
Printed and bound by T.J. International, Padstow, Cornwall

Contents

Acknowledgements

This was not an easy book to write. Condensing a topic as rich and multi-faceted as the history of Weimar Germany to a mere 75,000 words was no mean feat, especially when so much has already been written about it. Nevertheless, I have done my best to provide an introduction to the subject that will be accessible to both students and general readers. I hope I have succeeded.

I would like to thank Jo Godfrey who first suggested the project and who has provided much useful input and advice. Special thanks are owed to my colleagues at the University of Nottingham who provided encouragement and support, and to the staff at the University of Nottingham's Hallward library who dealt with my numerous inter-library loan requests quickly and efficiency. Finally, thanks, as ever, to all my friends and family – and especially to my partner Jenny – who have been unfailing in their encouragement and support throughout the writing of this book.

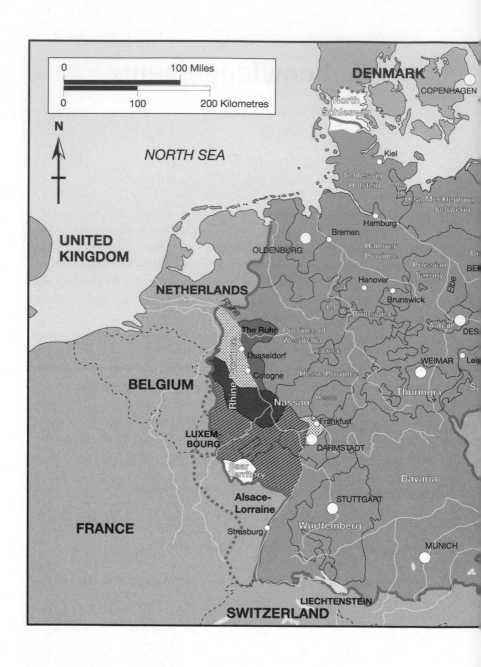

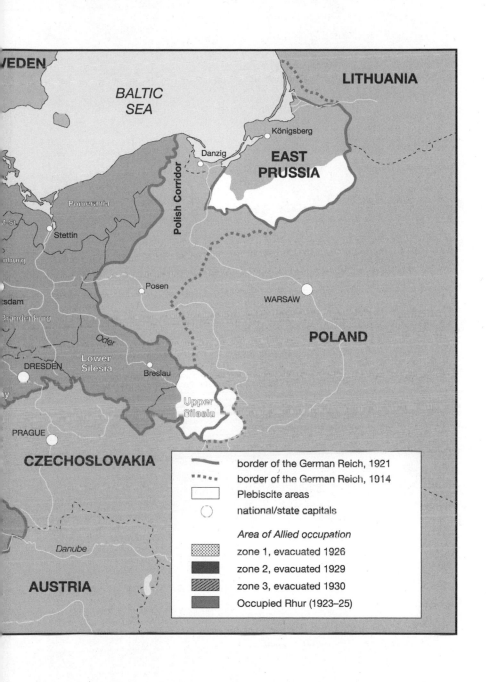

SWEDEN

BALTIC
SEA

LITHUANIA

Königsberg

Danzig

EAST
PRUSSIA

Pomerania

Polish Corridor

Stettin

nburg

Posen

WARSAW

POLAND

sdam

Brandenburg

Oder

DRESDEN

Lower
Silesia

Breslau

Upper
Silesia

PRAGUE

CZECHOSLOVAKIA

border of the German Reich, 1921

border of the German Reich, 1914

Plebiscite areas

national/state capitals

Area of Allied occupation

zone 1, evacuated 1926

zone 2, evacuated 1929

zone 3, evacuated 1930

Occupied Rhur (1923–25)

Danube

AUSTRIA

Introduction

PRUSSIA, GERMANY AND THE CRUCIBLE OF WAR

In many ways the Weimar Republic is still with us today. Its legacy is manifold, inspiring everything from television documentaries to cinema, crime novels, popular music and even comic books. Yet it also casts a darker shadow over contemporary politics and economics. It has become a byword for instability and has frequently been invoked by contemporary journalists and commentators in the wake of the recent world financial meltdown. In an age of global economic uncertainty, austerity and political and religious extremism, the troubled history of Weimar Germany seems more pertinent to modern western societies than at perhaps any other point in the last 80 years.

Yet even as contemporary events seem to mirror what we think we know about interwar Germany, a new generation of historians has been challenging the generally negative and deterministic view of the Weimar Republic that persists in both the popular and scholarly imaginations. For a long time historians tended to present a largely pessimistic view of the first German democracy, and all too often Weimar was regarded by historians and laymen alike as little more than the precursor of Hitler. This is hardly surprising considering that for a generation of Germans and, to a lesser extent, Anglo-American historians, the experience of dictatorship, world war and the Holocaust were the seminal traumas of their lives. To those refugees from Nazism who helped to shape our perception of interwar Germany, and for a generation of historians who sought to explain how the barbarity of the 1940s could have happened, the Weimar Republic was a weak and inherently flawed experiment, unloved by its people and doomed almost from the beginning by the circumstances of its birth. Later, for the 'New Left' of the 1960s (which was itself partly inspired by German theorists like Herbert Marcuse who had begun their careers in Frankfurt's Institute for Social Research in the early 1930s), the republic came to be seen as a missed opportunity, a chance to forge a Marxist middle way between soulless consumer capitalism and Stalinist totalitarian tyranny that was squandered or betrayed by moderate Social Democrats and bourgeois politicians. Such negative and deterministic perspectives continued to pervade the historiography of Weimar into the 1980s and 1990s and even works such as Detlev Peukert's seminal *Die Weimarer Republik: Krisenjahre der Klassischen Moderne* (1987)[1], which reinvigorated the study of Weimar Germany by viewing it as a focal point for the tensions inherent in modern industrial society, focused on the problematic notion of the 'crisis' of the republic.[2] Even the title of Eric Weitz's excellent (and generally more upbeat) 2007 study, *Weimar Germany: Promise and Tragedy*, has a melancholy and elegiac air, redolent of missed opportunities and hopes betrayed, which only underlines this sense of fragility and doom.

Nevertheless, recent research has to some extent proved a corrective to this negative and pessimistic perspective on Germany's first democratic republic. The 'cultural turn' in Weimar historiography, which was begun by Peter Gay and Walter Laqueur in the 1960s and 1970s, has both broadened and deepened our understanding of the Weimar Republic and begun to open it up from the narrow historical discourse that saw it as little more than a prelude to the Third Reich. More recently, a new generation of historians have shone a light onto previously neglected areas such as gender relations and popular culture in an effort to understand better how the traumas and trials of the Weimar period related to everyday life. In so doing they have not only often given voices to those who have for too long been overlooked by scholars interested in 'high politics' and the question of 'why did Weimar fail', but they have also challenged older narratives of an embattled democracy unloved by its citizens.

The primary aim of this book is to bring together much of this research, both old and new, and to provide those who are unfamiliar with this fascinating period of modern German history with an accessible introduction to the history of the Weimar Republic. To this end, it will examine both the politics and culture (broadly defined) of Weimar Germany and seek to place them in their wider historical and international context. In this way it is hoped that the reader will be presented with a more rounded portrait of the first German democracy, one which assesses it on its own merits and finds that, while it may not have endured in the face of extraordinary pressures, it still left a legacy of which it could be proud.

WEIMAR GERMANY IN CONTEXT

Historians tend to like their history to come in small, bite-sized pieces, divided neatly by period or country, all the better to structure school or university curricula, or books such as this. Yet all such divisions are, by necessity, artificial and arbitrary. History, as lived by its participants, is not episodic or clear cut. In a sense, the study of history is all about context. We can examine people, events, nations or whole time periods in exhaustive detail, but we can never fully understand their significance unless we appreciate their place in the bigger picture. Just as 'no man is an island', no historical event operates in isolation; each and every occurrence is just part of a larger whole, and it is only when we take a step back and view all the separate pieces in relation to each other that we get a full understanding of them.

This is perhaps particularly true in the case of Germany. Two of the central historical debates within the study of modern German history have been the extent to which continuities and common threads can be identified running through the development of successive regimes, and the degree to which the German journey towards becoming a modern liberal democracy took a 'peculiar' route that diverged from the more 'normal' road taken countries like Britain and France. Although this notion of a 'special path' (*Sonderweg*) towards modernity is not nowadays as influential as it once was, it is still important to us as students of the Weimar Republic because it seeks to see Germany's political and social development in a wider historical and international context. Briefly, the theory goes that the failure of liberal unification movements in the nineteenth century meant that the pre-modern aristocratic elite were able to maintain their hold on power, and Germany was thus prevented from developing the kind of civil society and political institutions that ensured stability and evolution towards democracy in Western Europe. The continuing influence of these old elites and the lack of strong democratic traditions and institutions are often cited as key reasons why democracy did not take root in Germany during the interwar period, so this theory has particular relevance to our examination of the Weimar Republic. But, in order to assess the merits of the *Sonderweg* thesis, we need to look back into German history and draw comparisons with developments in other nations.

This is equally true of many other explanations for the apparent 'failure' of the republic. One of the chief difficulties with much of Weimar historiography is that it tends to view developments in Germany in isolation from those taking place elsewhere in Europe. Again, this is a particular problem when looking at Germany. Internally divided and situated in the centre of the continent for centuries Germany was Europe's battleground. Surrounded by powerful neighbours and with an economy dependent on exports, Germany was perhaps more at the mercy of international developments than more other European state. This became particularly apparent after the First World War, when the reduction of its military, the obligation to pay reparations and its dependence on foreign investment severely hampered Germany's freedom of movement on the world stage. Furthermore, when viewed by itself or merely in comparison to older, established democracies like Britain or the USA, Weimar Germany does seem weak and unstable. But when compared to some of its close neighbours in the same period, it begins to look much more politically and economically robust. Similarly, when one considers Germany's path towards modernity in relation to the nations of Southern and Central Europe it begins to seem much less unique than it does if Britain or France are the benchmark.

THE RISE OF PRUSSIA

It is important to remember that at the end of the First World War Germany, as a single unified political entity, was still a relatively youthful country. Whatever the merits of the *Sonderweg* theory, it is certainly true that, compared to Britain and France, Germany came late to statehood. While its western neighbours were developing into modern nation–states, Germany remained, in the words of the Austrian Chancellor Prince Metternich, little more than 'a geographical expression'.[3]

Rather than being a single political entity, the territory that now makes up Germany was divided between a conglomerate of tiny autonomous states – principalities, dukedoms, bishoprics and free cities. Although self-governing, until 1806 all of these territories nominally owed allegiance to the Holy Roman Emperor, whose legitimacy rested on the claim to be the heir to the Frankish king Charlemagne who had been crowned 'Emperor of the Romans' by Pope Leo III on Christmas Day AD800. Nevertheless, the title was only formally agreed in 1512, an indication of the looseness of the political ties that held the Empire together. Its constituent territories (234 distinct states and 51 self-governing Imperial Cities in 1648) remained jealous of their individual powers and privileges, and the Emperor often found it difficult to impose his will on his subjects. Furthermore, although from the fifteenth century onwards every Holy Roman Emperor came from the ruling family of Austria, the Habsburgs, the title was not a hereditary one. Instead, the Emperor was elected for life by seven Elector–Princes who held considerable power within the Empire.

Strife between the various German states had been a common feature of the Middle Ages as the multitudinous prices, dukes and knights vied with one another for power and influence within the Empire, but from the sixteenth century the German-speaking lands were further fragmented by the Reformation. Henceforth, Germany was divided, not just politically but also by religion, as the followers of Martin Luther struggled with the Catholic Emperor and his allies. The result was a rough north–south confessional divide that to some extent persists to this day, further underlining the differences between the German states. The Peace of Augsburg of 1555 allowed the Princes to decide which denomination their state would adhere to, and also ultimately reaffirmed the independence of the princes, but this was not an end to the matter. Continuing religious tensions and challenges to imperial authority boiled over into open warfare in 1618 when the Emperor Ferdinand II sought to impose his will and his religion on his subjects.

The Thirty Years' War (1618–48) had a profound and enduring effect on the German lands and those living in them. For nearly three decades the armies of the great European powers and their allies rampaged throughout Germany laying waste to town and county and bringing with them famine, pestilence and misery. When the various states involved in the conflict finally fought themselves to a standstill, Germany, not for the last time, found itself at the mercy of its powerful neighbours. As at the Congress of Vienna nearly 200 years later, and the Paris Peace Conference a century after that, the Peace of Westphalia imposed on an exhausted and demoralized Germany a settlement that sought to balance the ambitions of the Great Powers while paying little regard to the desires of the Germans themselves. If anything, Germany was left more fragmented than it had been before; a weak and divided country which best served the interests of neighbouring states.

This enabled ambitious princes considerable scope to increase their power and influence not only in Germany, but in Europe as a whole. One of the more unlikely beneficiaries from the post-war settlement was the small, sandy, north German principality of Brandenburg–Prussia. This landlocked state with few natural resources and no defensible frontiers had managed to remain aloof from the religious conflicts of the sixteenth century, but had been drawn inexorably into the morass of the Thirty Years' War. Brandenburg was particularly hard hit by the conflict as its geographical position meant that Imperial, Saxon, Danish and Swedish armies rampaged back and forth across the Electorate, killing, raping and pillaging as they went. Disease ran unchecked through a population already suffering from famine and malnutrition, and many fled their homes in an attempt to avoid the horrors visited on the country by the war. The population of the Electorate halved between 1618 and

1648, and the economic and social dislocation brought about by the war further impoverished the already insolvent state.

All of this had a profound effect on the young Friedrich Wilhelm I (1640–88), later known as 'The Great Elector'. He was only 20 years old when he succeeded to the Electoral title and had spent much of his youth abroad, safe from the armies and epidemics that were raging through Brandenburg. Only Ducal Prussia, separated from the heartlands of Brandenburg by nearly 700 kilometres, had escaped the ravages of the Thirty Years' War, and from there the new elector set about reviving the fortunes of his domains with a single-mindedness and dedication that astounded his contemporaries. Determined to revive his state and ensure that it would never again be at the mercy of foreign powers, the Great Elector was to set in train a series of reforms that transformed not only his state, but the electoral office itself. By 1680 Brandenburg possessed an army with an international reputation, a small Baltic fleet, the beginnings of a modern bureaucracy and a thriving new technical and industrial base, thanks to the influx of protestant refugees from France. Perhaps most importantly, the Great Elector also bequeathed to his successors the notion that the army was central to Brandenburg–Prussia's survival and development and that as such the fates of the army and the state were inextricably linked. This was to have important and far-reaching consequences for both Prussia and Germany in the centuries to come.

Yet Friedrich Wilhelm's achievements were merely the beginning, the foundation upon which the edifice of Prussian greatness was built by three successive generations of Hohenzollern princes. While his achievements were perhaps less practical and substantive than those of his father, the Great Elector's son was instrumental in improving the international standing of his realm and to some extent liberating it from a subordinate position to the Austrian Habsburgs. Elector Friedrich III (1688–1713) sought to enhance the dignity and prestige of his House by seeking to exchange his electoral coronet for a crown, and, after protracted negotiations with the Emperor, he was crowned Friedrich I, King in Prussia, on 18 January 1701. This did much to raise Brandenburg–Prussia's status and, as his grandson conceded, proved to be 'a master-piece of politics: for the regal dignity rescued the house of Brandenburg from that state of servitude, in which the house of Austria had hitherto kept the princes of Germany'.[4]

Friedrich I was succeeded as elector and king by his son Friedrich Wilhelm I (1713–40), a 'strange mixture of duty and cruelty, high morals and boorish anti-intellectualism'[5], who was the archetypal, almost stereotypical, Prussian: he was Spartan to the point of meanness, obsessed with the army and always wore uniform in public. The army was the abiding obsession of his life, and under Friedrich Wilhelm military spending increased to 80 per cent of national income. Modern equipment, formation marching and precision drilling – including the now famous goose-step march – were introduced, as well as a new system of recruiting which reduced Prussia's reliance on foreign mercenaries. By the time of the death of the 'Soldier King' (*Soldatenkönig*) in 1740, the size of the army had more than doubled to 83,000 men. This gave Prussia the fourth largest army in Europe, with one person out of every 25 serving as a soldier (compared to one out of every 150 in France, a nation much larger than Prussia).

But it was, perhaps, the deal that Friedrich Wilhelm struck with his nobles which was to be his most enduring legacy for Prussia and later Germany as a whole. Like his grandfather, Friedrich Wilhelm faced concerted opposition to his policy of centralization from the Prussian nobility, who were fearful of losing their ancient powers and privileges. These *Junker* (the term is a corruption of *junger Herr* or *Jungherr*, meaning a young lord, but is roughly analogous with a country squire) wielded considerable political and economic power. Friedrich Wilhelm's ancestors had fought a series of battles with them as they sought to defend their rights and privileges against the centralizing tendency of the Hohenzollern rulers, but the 'Soldier King' took pains to make the aristocracy an integral part of his regime, thereby ensuring their loyalty to the state. Reversing his father's policy of promotion based on merit, he created the situation in which the officer corps was the sole preserve of the *Junker*. Henceforth, being an officer provided a nobleman with a fixed income, high social status, close links to the monarch and the opportunity to gain fame and glory on the battlefield. Under this new royal–military regime, generals took precedence over civilian ministers at court, and a rigid social structure modelled along military lines was developed. It was not for nothing that one of Friedrich Wilhelm's ministers, Friedrich von Schrötter, once quipped that 'Prussia was not a country with an army, but an army with a country'.[6]

In many ways the Prussian model of state and society that was established by Friedrich Wilhelm I was to endure well into the twentieth century. The place of the military at the centre of German political life and the continuing power and influence of the conservative *Junker* elite during the imperial and Weimar periods can be seen to have its origins in Friedrich Wilhelm's attempts to bring the Prussian aristocracy 'onboard' by giving them key positions at the heart of the political and military state that he created. By the middle of the nineteenth century the *Junker* had come to dominate the upper reaches of the Prussian (and later German) military and civil service, and were seen as the bulwark of the state; while the virtues of simplicity, thrift, dedication and diligence, as much as the vices of philistinism, cruelty and boorishness that were displayed by the 'Soldier King' were to be seen in later Prussian rulers from King Wilhelm I to President Hindenburg.

If Friedrich Wilhelm created the framework of the modern Prussian state, it was his son, Friedrich II, 'the Great' (1740–86), who did most to transform Prussia from a second-rate German state into a Great Power. In a series of wars between 1740 and 1779, Friedrich overturned his predecessors' close ties with the Emperor and challenged the Austrian Habsburgs' pre-eminence within Germany. By acquiring key strategic territories such as Silesia and West Prussia, he enlarged his kingdom by 66,000 square miles and over 3 million citizens, turning Prussia into a force to be reckoned with not just in Germany, but also in Europe. At the same time, he introduced a common legal system for all Prussia that remained in place almost unchanged for over a century, and encouraged Prussian manufacturing by offering exemption from taxes and conscription to factory owners and improving the infrastructure of the state. However, he never disguised his contempt for his subjects and was deeply conservative despite his espousal of Enlightenment ideals. A true 'enlightened despot', he acted to centralize all power in his hands, while at the same time continuing his father's policy of building up a loyal and efficient bureaucracy.

Despite the upheavals of the Austro-Prussian conflict that had been the feature of Friedrich's reign, Germany at the end of the eighteenth century seemed stable and well-ordered. In his last years Friedrich the Great, largely content with the conquests of his early reign, did nothing to rock the imperial boat, working closely with the other German princes to safeguard the institutions of the Holy Roman Empire (and with them the independence of the German states) from the ambitions of Emperor Josef II. If anything, the creation of a strong Prussia in the north in opposition to Austria in the south helped bring balance to the Empire. But, by the time of Friedrich's death in 1786, this apparent stability and continuity was about to be blown apart by the twin forces of revolution and nationalism.

GERMANY UNITED

Although traces of a developing German national consciousness – a sense of being German in a place called Germany – can be detected in the writing of the sixteenth and seventeenth centuries, it was only in the eighteenth century that such ideas began to be developed seriously. The wars of Friedrich the Great had already engendered an idea that it was glorious to die for the 'fatherland' – even if that fatherland was Prussia or Austria rather than 'Germany' – and this coincided with a gradual shift away from a top-down chain of feudal relationships in which loyalty rested with an individual or a dynasty towards a notion of loyalty to the institutions of the state and one's fellow compatriots. This stimulated thinking about German nationhood and led Johann Gottfried von Herder to develop his ideas about the relationship between language and nationality. In his *Treatise on the Origins of Language* (1772) and *Reflections on the Philosophy of History of Mankind* (1784–91), Herder argued that culture based on a common language and religion was central to the development of human history. He identified these cultures with 'peoples' (*Völker*) and believed that their national identity was expressed in their unique language and characteristics. This idea was deeply influential in shaping the way in which Germans saw themselves over the next century and a half, and never more so than during the wars against revolutionary France.

The outbreak of the French Revolution had profound consequences for the whole of Europe, but its effects were felt particularly keenly in Germany. The crushing defeat of both Austria and Prussia by French armies under Napoleon Bonaparte in 1805–6 overturned the status quo in Germany that had existed since 1648, not least through the dissolution of the Holy Roman Empire on 6 August 1806. By the terms of the Treaty of Pressburg, the number of German states was reduced to 39 through forced annexations and amalgamations, and all except Prussia, Austria, Pomerania and Holstein were compelled to join the Confederation of the Rhine, a loose association of French satellites that replaced the Holy Roman Empire. Meanwhile, Prussia was forced to sign the humiliating Treaty of Tilsit (July 1807) which reduced it to a shadow of its former glory by redistributing nearly half of its territory to France's German and Polish allies.

Defeat at the hands of Napoleon ushered in a period of soul searching in Prussia and Austria that culminated in a widespread acceptance of the need for reform amongst the ruling elites. Both states instituted wide-ranging civilian and military reforms, streamlining and modernizing their administrative and tax systems, introducing universal military service on the French model and opening the civil service and the officer corps to the middle classes. But above all, both states sought to co-opt the new ideas of nationalism as a means of rallying support behind their regimes. During the Wars of Liberation (1813–14) Prussian King Friedrich Wilhelm III (1797–1840) in particular made use of nationalistic sentiments and even committed himself (in the vaguest possible terms) to some form of united Germany in the future.

However, in the wake of Napoleon's defeat Germany found itself once again at the mercy of the Great Powers and the promised German nation state failed to materialize. Instead, much as had happened in the Peace of Westphalia, the *status quo ante bellum* was reaffirmed. A German Confederation (*Deutscher Bund*) made up of 39 sovereign states was established, with a Federal Diet made up of the (unelected) representatives of all the states and under the permanent presidency of Austria. In a sop to nationalistic feeling, this had, on paper, extensive powers to appoint ambassadors, negotiate treaties or raise a Federal army; in practice little could ever be agreed upon because a unanimous vote was required (which was virtually impossible to achieve due to the conflicting interests of the states). At the same time, Prussia's Great Power status was cemented once and for all by the acquisition of vast swathes of territory in the Rhineland in compensation for Polish territory lost to Russia. As a consequence, the population of the Kingdom of Prussia doubled overnight and it gained territory rich in resources and industrial capacity.

After 1815 a period of conservative reaction set in, and Central Europe was dominated by the Holy Alliance of Russia, Prussia and Austria, which pledged these three powers to act in concert to defend monarchism and Christianity from the threats of liberalism and nationalism. Nevertheless, German nationalism spread rapidly through Prussia and northern Germany, mostly in the form of choral societies that staged festivals and sang patriotic ballads. During this process nationalism became less youthful and radical, but also more closely linked to middle-class liberalism. However, German nationalists were divided over the question of how a German nation should be defined. According to the Prussian philosopher Johann Gottlieb Fichte, the nation was a product of culture and the collective will, and states and governments derived their legitimacy not from God, but from the people. The borders of states should therefore be based on nationality and their policies be dictated by the common good. This interpretation appealed to a nationalist movement driven by students, university professors and other intellectuals whose researches often supported their political aspirations. Yet this raised the problem of how much territory outside the boundaries of the German Confederation should be included in any future German state, as both Prussia and Austria incorporated a great deal of territory outside the *Bund*. The choice was between a *Grossdeutschland* (Greater Germany) that would incorporate the German-speaking parts of the Austrian Empire and be led by Catholic Austria, and a *Kleindeutschland* (Little Germany) that would exclude Austria, and be led by protestant Prussia.

Introduction

For much of the first half of the nineteenth century such questions remained purely academic, but in 1848 a combination of economic factors, famine caused by a series of bad harvests between 1845 and 1848, and growing frustration with the repressive conservatism of European politics led to an explosion of revolutionary fervour, and for a moment it looked as though the dreams of the liberal nationalists might become reality. Even before Viennese revolutionaries toppled the Austrian chancellor Metternich on 13 March 1848, a group of liberal nationalists had gathered in Heidelberg and issued a declaration calling for the establishment of a single German state under a constitutional monarchy. This call was heeded by like-minded liberals from throughout Germany and, at the end of March, 574 delegates from the various German states met in Frankfurt to agree on what form this new German state should take. This so-called *Vorparlament* (pre-parliament) prepared the way for elections to a National Assembly which convened in May. The Diet of the German Confederation was declared dissolved and the Habsburg Archduke John was appointed Imperial Regent, but the parliament was quickly overtaken by events. Despite his brief flirtation with German nationalism during the worst of the revolution in Berlin, Friedrich Wilhelm IV of Prussia (1840–61) refused the imperial crown when it was offered to him by the Frankfurt parliament. Furthermore, the delegates could come to no satisfactory answer to the question of where the borders of a united Germany should lie. As the German princes overcame the revolutionaries in their own territories and reasserted their authority during the autumn and winter of 1848–49, the parliament became increasingly out of touch with the political situation throughout Germany, and ultimately it was dispersed by force in May–June 1849.

The failure of the 1848 revolutions marked the end of attempts to unify Germany 'from below' by means of a popular movement, and the initiative shifted to the governments of the larger German states. Only through their action or with their consent could German unification be made a reality after 1848. Nevertheless, other, more practical moves had already been made towards laying the foundations for unification. These took the form of the development of the *Zollverein*, the Prussian Customs Union that allowed goods to be traded freely throughout Germany. By 1836 the *Zollverein* encompassed 25 states with a population of over 26 million people, and the establishment of what was in effect a German common market, coupled with moves to standardize weights and measures, laid the groundwork for future political integration by creating a unified German economic area. The simultaneous growth of railways and improvements in infrastructure across state borders also served to improve communications and bound the states more closely together.

The resultant economic boom of the 1850s created a much more assertive and self-confident Prussia, and when Otto von Bismarck was appointed minister president in 1862 the stage was set for a confrontation between the two leading German states. By orchestrating three Wars of Unification against Denmark (1864), Austria (1866) and France (1870–71), Bismarck was able to expand Prussia's territory, decisively eliminate Austria as a rival for the leadership of Germany and unite the German states in opposition to the old enemy, France. Riding on the crest of a nationalist wave, Bismarck convinced the mentally unstable and permanently hard-up Ludwig II of Bavaria to sign a letter offering the Prussian king, Wilhelm I (1861–88), the German throne. Thus it was that on 18 January 1871, 170 years to the day since Friedrich von Hohenzollern had been crowned as the first 'King in Prussia', the representatives of the German states gathered in the Hall of Mirrors of the Palace of Versailles to hear Bismarck proclaim Friedrich's great-great-great-grandson ruler of the German Empire.

On paper Bismarck's Empire was one of the most democratic in Europe, but in reality power continued to reside with the Prussian elites. Under the imperial constitution of 1871 power was divided between the central government and the 25 member states, which retained their own rulers, parliaments and administrations, with powers over direct taxation, education and public health. However, the Emperor, who was always the Hohenzollern King of Prussia, had extensive powers as head of the executive, civil service and armed forces. Day-to-day administration of government was in the hands of the Imperial Chancellor, who was appointed by the Emperor and had sole power of appointment of ministers. The bicameral parliament consisted of an upper house, the Bundesrat (the equivalent of the British House of Lords), made up of representatives of the federal states; and a lower house, or Reichstag (the equivalent of the House of Commons), elected by universal manhood suffrage. Neither house could initiate legislation, but the consent of both houses was required for a bill to pass into law, and the Reichstag had the power to approve or reject the federal budget. Legislation could be vetoed by the Bundesrat with a vote of 14 against, but Prussia dominated the chamber with 17 out of the 58 seats.

However, Germany's history of political fragmentation and the circumstances in which unification had been achieved left the new state with significant problems. One of its chief difficulties was that it suffered from what has been called a problem of identity. The German Empire was a confederation of four kingdoms (Prussia, Bavaria, Württemberg and Saxony), six grand duchies, five duchies, seven principalities, three free cities (Hamburg, Bremen and Lübeck) and the *Reichsland* (imperial territory) of Alsace-Lorraine. All of these constituent territories had long-established and differing traditions and identities, as well as their own political institutions, religious practices, ethnic makeups and, in some cases, languages. In this environment old loyalties – regional, social or confessional – endured. These divisions and Bismarck's attempts to deal with them, as well as the authoritarian political culture of the new Empire, had important consequences for the development of the German politics and society in the twentieth century. Campaigns against Catholicism and Socialism in the 1870s ultimately only served to solidify the separate identities of Catholics and the working class and provided a guaranteed constituency to the political parties that represented their interests: the Catholic *Zentrumspartei* (Centre Party) and the Social Democratic Party of Germany (*Sozialdemokratische Partei Deutschlands* or SPD). Both parties were to play a key role in the formation of the Weimar Republic, but the consequent identification of the republic with these groups, which within living memory had been regarded as fundamentally 'un-German', only added fuel to the sense that the post-war democracy was an alien imposition.

Bismarck's dismissal as Chancellor in 1890, and the determination of the young Kaiser Wilhelm II (1888–1918) to rule as well as reign, did nothing to smooth over the divisions within German society. While the political culture of the German Empire remained conservative and authoritarian, with political power in the hands of traditional elites – the aristocracy, the army, big business – there were significant forces at work in *fin-de-siècle* Germany that threatened to change the economic and social fabric of the nation for ever. The rapid expansion of German industry after 1871 had a transformative effect on population distribution and social relations within the Reich, while new class tensions between the emerging working class, the expanding bourgeoisie and the old, landed elites only exacerbated existing confessional, ethnic and regional divisions. At the same time, demands for rights for women, rebelliousness amongst the young and avant-garde cultural experiments were all interpreted as acute threats to the existing social, economic and political system. Most commentators came to believe that modern capitalism was undermining the very fabric of society and, as international tension rose, the German people began to feel increasingly uncertain and embattled.

THE CRUCIBLE OF WAR

Many of the great turning points of German history have come as the result of conflict. The Thirty Years' War helped shape modern Germany and facilitated Prussia's rise to dominance; Friedrich the Great's wars transformed his state into a European power of the first rank; the wars against Napoleon stimulated German nationalism; while the Wars of Unification unified Germany under Prussian leadership. But if war was responsible for creating Bismarck's Empire, it also brought about its destruction. Bismarck's plans for Prussian expansion had been limited solely to the creation of a Prussian-dominated German state, and he had no desire for further foreign policy adventures. However, his successors took a different view. From the 1890s onwards, the feeling grew that Germany was being denied its legitimate rights as a Great Power by jealous rivals who sought to contain it in continental Europe. At the same time, the delicate system of alliances developed by Bismarck in order to avoid the nightmare scenario of Germany being surrounded by hostile powers began to break down, and by 1904 Europe was split into two mutually hostile camps divided by rivalry and distrust.

It was in this poisonous atmosphere of international suspicion and ever-increasing tension that the heir to the throne of the Austro–Hungarian Empire, the Archduke Franz Ferdinand, was assassinated during a state visit to the recently acquired province of Bosnia–Herzegovina on 28 June 1914. The murder of the heir to the throne of one of Europe's Great Powers shocked the world, and was both a blow and an opportunity for Austria–Hungary. The Austrians had lost their future head of state, but the assassination provided them with a chance to crush neighbouring Serbia once and for all. Within a month Austria had issued an ultimatum to Serbia and, when its terms were not met, Austria declared war. However, Serbia was not without allies. Russia was pledged to support and protect the Serbs, and duly mobilized its armies against Austria. In response, Austria's ally, Germany, declared war on Russia. Two days later, it also declared war on Russia's ally, France. The next day, 4 August, German troops crossed the Belgian frontier on their way to France, and in response Great Britain declared war on Germany. Within days what had initially seemed to be a regional crisis had escalated into a general European conflict, and the First World War had begun.

The Germans greeted news of the outbreak of war with a spontaneous outpouring of patriotic feeling, as did the peoples of all the combatant nations. The conflict was seen as a chance to settle old scores, to challenge the existing international order that had belittled and ignored Germany's ambitions, and to escape the monotony of modern life and win fame and glory on the battlefield. Moreover, the war was an opportunity to suspend, if not transcend, the divisions of class, confession and party that divided Imperial Germany, and recreate the (largely imagined) sense of *Volksgemeinschaft* (national community) of the Wars of Unification. On 4 August, Wilhelm II addressed the crowds from the balcony of the royal palace in Berlin, declaring that he no longer recognized parties, only Germans. Such sentiments were mirrored in the Reichstag, where the party leaders responded to the Kaiser's rhetoric by declaring a political truce, the *Burgfriede*, for the duration of hostilities. War credits necessary to finance the conflict were passed unanimously, and even the SPD, who had held vocal anti-war demonstrations in the last week of July, joined in the patriotic fervour and declared their support for the war.

Once war had been declared, it was essential that Germany acted quickly to get its troops into the field. Facing enemies in both the east and the west, Germany put its faith in the so-called Schlieffen Plan which envisioned a massive assault through Belgium into northern France, encircling Paris and defeating France in six weeks. The German armies would then be free to turn and face Russian forces which, it was assumed, would be slower to mobilize due to the Russian Empire's vast size. But in the event, the attack into northern France was held up by stiffer than expected resistance, and the German advance faltered and then stalled in the face of an Anglo-French counterattack along the river Marne in September 1914. As a result, German troops were ordered to dig into defensive positions along the river Aisne. There then began a 'race to the sea', as the Allies and the Germans each sought to outflank one another, leading to the construction of a 400-mile-long line of trenches and fortifications that stretched from the border with Switzerland to the North Sea. By December, the Western Front had stagnated into a static war of attrition – the war of movement in the west was at an end, and with it any German hope of a quick victory. Germany was confronted with precisely what it had tried to avoid, a war on two fronts for which it was not prepared militarily, let alone socially and economically.

Meanwhile, the war in the east was also not proceeding according to plan. The Russians had mobilized more quickly than expected, and launched twin offensives into Austrian Galicia and East Prussia in August 1914. In military terms this was not a serious development, but the effect of the invasion on German morale was significant, and threw the Kaiser and his advisors into a panic. Wilhelm prevailed upon his generals to transfer a further two army corps to the east to stem the Russian advance. These forces were under the overall command of 67-year-old Paul von Hindenburg, who had been called out of retirement in order to smash the Russian invasion. Together with his chief of staff Erich Ludendorff, Hindenburg annihilated the invaders at the Battles of Tannenberg and the Masurian Lakes. The Russians lost over 250,000 men during the course of these battles, while German losses were about one tenth of that number. Hindenburg became a popular hero, and was rewarded with promotion to the rank of Field Marshal and command of the entire eastern front.

With the failure of the Schlieffen plan and with it any hope of a quick victory, it soon became apparent that modern mechanized warfare would impinge on the lives of those left at home to an unprecedented extent. From the start, war production and the Allied blockade put huge strains on the German economy. Banks and export industries were badly disrupted, while Germany's ability to import essential raw materials and food stuffs was severely curtailed. As a consequence, the state was required to step in at an early stage in order to ensure that the troops at the front continued to be supplied with sufficient quantities of ammunition. As the war continued it became increasingly clear that the free-market economy was not capable of meeting the needs of the war effort, and the government was forced to intervene in the economic life of the nation. As more and more elements of the peacetime economic and political order were subordinated to military needs, the power and influence of the General Staff grew. By the time that the popular heroes of the eastern front – Hindenburg and Ludendorff – were appointed heads of the General Staff in 1916, Germany was arguably governed by the 'silent dictatorship' of the *Oberste Heeresleitung* (Army Supreme Command or OHL) which increasingly used its influence on the Kaiser to exert control of the appointment of ministers, veto reform and introduce legislation to militarize society.

As the war dragged on, rising casualties and the falling standard of living led to an increasing feeling of disillusionment and war-weariness. Under pressure from their constituents, the parties of Left and Centre began to press for a negotiated peace, while repeated attempts to break the stalemate on the Western Front met with failure. Ultimately, the attempt to starve and terrorize the enemy into capitulation through a strategy of unrestricted submarine warfare only served to draw the United States into the conflict in April 1917, a development that more than offset the collapse of Tsarist Russia the same year and doomed Germany to defeat. In March 1918, the High Command made its last desperate throw of the dice by transferring troops from the east to launch a massive offensive against the British and French in the hope of bringing an end to the war before the Americans could arrive in any numbers. Despite an unprecedented 40-mile advance that saw Paris menaced for the first time since August 1914, the spring offensive had ground to a halt by July. Lack of reserves and equipment meant that the Germans were both unable to capitalize on their initial successes or withstand the Allied counterattack which began on 18 July. Under pressure from the better equipped and better fed Allies, worn out by four years of warfare and facing fresh American troops in many sections of the front, the German defensive line first buckled and then broke. By the end of September the Germans were in full retreat, and the deteriorating military situation, combined with growing unrest at home, convinced the High Command that the war was effectively lost.

On 7 November a fleet of cars bearing large white flags and carrying German plenipotentiaries, led by the Catholic politician Matthias Erzberger, crossed the Western Front. They were met by Allied troops and taken through the ruined landscape of northern France to a railway siding in the forest of Compiègne, where they were confronted by the representatives of the Allies, led by Marshal Ferdinand Foch. Given the stark choice between agreeing to the Allied terms and seeing Germany invaded, Erzberger and his companions had no choice but to sign an armistice at 5 am on 11 November 1918. Six hours later the guns fell silent and the war was at an end. But by the time the armistice was signed revolution had already broken out back in Germany, sparked by a naval mutiny at Kiel on 3 November. The revolution quickly spread to Hamburg, Bremen and Berlin, while a separate uprising led to the declaration of a Bavarian republic in Munich. By 9 November the Social Democrat, Friedrich Ebert, had become chancellor, a republic had been proclaimed in Berlin and the Kaiser had been forced to abdicate, bringing an end to the Hohenzollern Empire that Bismarck had brought into being almost half a century before, and ushering in a new phase in German history.

Timeline

1918

28 January	Beginning of a week-long nationwide series of strikes.
21 March	Beginning of German spring offensive on the Western Front.
18 July	Allied counterattack begins.
8 August	'The Black Day of the German Army': British forces break through German lines.
29 September	Army High Command calls for an immediate armistice and formation of a civilian government.
3 October	New government under Prince Max von Baden formed. Armistice negotiations opened with President Wilson of the USA.
3 November	Austria–Hungary surrenders. Naval mutiny in Kiel.
9 November	Proclamation of the Republic. Kaiser Wilhelm II abdicates. A new government under Friedrich Ebert formed.
10 November	Ebert–Groener Pact, by which the army promises to defend the government against the threat from the extreme Left in return for political autonomy.
11 November	Armistice comes into effect on the Western Front.
15 November	Stinnes Legien Pact between big business and trade unions.

16–21 December Congress of Workers' and Soldiers' Councils.
29 December   USPD withdraw from the Council of People's
               Representatives.
30 December–   Founding congress of the German Communist
1 January   Party (KPD).

1919
5–12 January   Spartacist uprising in Berlin.
19 January   Elections for the National Assembly.
6 February   National Assembly opened in Weimar.
13 February   Dissolution of the Council of People's
               Representatives. Phillip Scheidemann becomes
               chancellor of SPD–DDP–Centre coalition. Ebert
               elected Reich President by the National
               Assembly.
21 February   Bavarian Minister President Kurt Eisner
               assassinated.
3–10 March   'Bloody Week' in Berlin as second wave of left-
               wing unrest crushed.
7 April–1 May Short-lived Soviet Republic in Munich.
21 June   Scheidemann government resigns to be replaced
               by a new administration under Gustav Bauer.
28 June   Treaty of Versailles signed.
11 August   Weimar constitution ratified by the National
               Assembly.

1920
13–17 March   Kapp Putsch in Berlin.
March–April   Communist uprisings in Central Germany and
               the Ruhr defeated by government troops.
6 June   Reichstag elections result in losses for the DDP
               and an upsurge in support for right-wing
               parties.
21 June   A 'bourgeois' coalition under Konstantin
               Fehrenbach formed.
4 December   Split in the USPD. The 40,000-strong left wing
               of the party votes to merge with the KPD.

1921

23 March	Beginning of Communist 'March Action'.
29 July	Hitler becomes chairman of the NSDAP.
26 August	Matthias Erzberger assassinated.
4 November	SA established.

1922

21 January	Walther Rathenau becomes Germany's first Jewish foreign minister.
16 April	Treaty of Rappallo signed with the USSR.
24 June	Rathenau assassinated.
18 July	Law for the Protection of the Republic is ratified by the Reichstag.
24 September	The right wing of the USPD merges with the SPD.
22 November	Shipping magnate Wilhelm Cuno becomes chancellor.

1923

11–16 January	Franco–Belgian invasion of the Ruhr.
13 August	Resignation of the Cuno government. Gustav Stresemann becomes chancellor.
26 September	'Passive resistance' called off. A state of emergency declared.
21–23 October	Communist uprisings in Hamburg, Saxony and the Rhineland.
29 October	Elected government of Saxony and Thuringia deposed.
3 November	The SPD withdraws from the government.
9 November	Attempted 'Beer Hall Putsch' in Munich.
15 November	Introduction of the *Rentenmark*.
30 November	Stresemann steps down as chancellor and is replaced by Wilhelm Marx.

1924

4 May	Reichstag elections result in a swing away from the moderate parties to the Communists and Nationalists.

| 1 September | The Dawes Plan is introduced. |
| 7 December | Fresh Reichstag elections provide modest gains for the government parties and the SPD. The period of 'relative stabilization' begins. |

1925

15 January	The DNVP joins the government for the first time.
24 February	The NSDAP is refounded.
28 February	President Ebert dies.
26 April	Paul von Hindenburg is elected Reich President.
15–16 October	Locarno Treaties signed.

1926

8 September	Germany joins the League of Nations.
9 October	Hans von Seeckt forced to resign as head of the Reichswehr.
10 December	Stresemann is awarded the Nobel Peace Prize.

1927

| 29 January | The DNVP joins the government for the second time. |
| 16 July | New law providing universal unemployment insurance is passed. |

1928

20 May	Reichstag elections result in a swing from the DNVP to the SPD.
29 June	Formation of the 'Grand Coalition' under Hermann Müller.
20 October	Alfred Hugenberg becomes leader of the DNVP.

1929

1–3 May	'Bloody May' riots in Berlin between communist demonstrators and SPD-controlled police.
7 June	Publication of the Young Plan.
3 October	Death of Gustav Stresemann.

28–29 October	Wall Street Crash.
22 December	Referendum on the Young Plan.

1930

12 March	Reichstag ratifies the Young Plan.
27 March	Fall of the Grand Coalition and appointment of Heinrich Brüning as chancellor.
30 June	Withdrawal of Allied troops from the Rhineland.
16 July	The Reichstag dissolved by presidential decree.
14 September	Reichstag elections result in Nazi electoral breakthrough.

1931

July	Banking crisis in Germany.
11 October	Formation of the Harzburg Front.

1932

10 April	Hindenburg re-elected in the second round of the presidential elections.
13 April	Ban on the SA introduced.
12 May	Wilhelm Groener resigns as defence minister.
30 May	Resignation of Heinrich Brüning. Franz von Papen becomes leader of a 'government of national concentration.'
4 June	Reichstag dissolved.
16 June	Ban on the SA lifted.
20 July	Illegal dissolution of the elected government of Prussia.
31 July	Reichstag elections see the NSDAP become the largest party.
13 August	Meeting between Hindenburg and Hitler. Hitler refuses the offer of the vice-chancellorship and demands to be appointed chancellor.
12 September	Reichstag dissolved following a vote of no confidence in Papen.
6 November	Reichstag elections see the NSDAP lose 2 million votes but remain the largest party.

2 December	Papen resigns. General Kurt von Schleicher becomes chancellor.

1933

4 January	Secret meeting between Papen and Hitler.
28 January	Schleicher resigns.
30 January	Hitler is appointed chancellor.
1 February	Reichstag is dissolved.
27–28 February	Reichstag Fire. The Law for the Protection of People and State suspends civil liberties and effectively bans the KPD.
5 March	Reichstag elections return a narrow majority for the NSDAP–DNVP coalition.
23 March	Enabling Act grants the new government sweeping emergency powers.

1

YEARS OF CRISIS, 1918–23

Considering what came afterwards, it is perhaps significant that the Weimar Republic came into being almost by accident. The proclamation of the republic on 9 November 1918 was not the result of a detailed political programme or a long hard-fought campaign, but a reaction to events and an attempt to divert the people's energies from a more radical course. Yet the fact that democracy was thrust upon the German people should not mislead us into thinking that Weimar was, as has been so often asserted, 'a republic without republicans'. In fact, as recent research has shown, there was a surprising degree of consensus over the constitutional settlement of 1919, which incorporated both many of the long-cherished ideals of the liberals and social democrats, and the desire of the conservatives for a strong executive. Nevertheless, there were still those in Germany who opposed the new regime, and a sizable minority on both the Left and Right to whom the republic itself was anathema. These forces determined to use whatever means they could to overturn the constitution, making its early years ones of turmoil in which the moderate parties struggled for stability in the face of extremist pressure. This led them to make some fateful compromises which were to have far-reaching implications for the fate of the republic.

THE DOMESTIC IMPACT OF THE WAR

By the autumn of 1918, Germany and its allies stood upon the brink of collapse. Four years of total war had sapped their manpower and morale, and only deepened existing social and political divisions. As casualties mounted and conditions on the home front deteriorated, the fragile political consensus reached in 1914 began to crack and the government faced growing opposition on the streets and in the Reichstag. The final straw was the realization that the war was lost and all the suffering and hardship had been for nothing. When this became clear, the political edifice created by Bismarck nearly half a century previously began to crumble, leaving anarchy and uncertainty in its place.

Together the Central Powers lost over 4 million men during the hostilities. Of the 13 million Germans who marched off to war between 1914 and 1918 around 2 million never came home at all, while of those who did return 4.2 million did so bearing the physical wounds of their wartime experience. Even those who escaped physical harm carried psychological scars, and few returned from the front unaffected by what they had seen and done. Roughly 19 per cent of the adult male population were direct casualties of the war.[1] As more and more men were thrown into the meat grinder of the trenches, as the quantity of rations and quality of equipment deteriorated and news of wartime shortages on the home front filtered through to the fighting men, morale began to suffer. While discipline amongst soldiers at the front on the whole remained strong, behind the lines it was a different matter. One in ten men transferred from the eastern front in 1917 deserted while in transit, and by September the Berlin police estimated that there were around 50,000 deserters in the capital alone. By the summer of the following year as many as 100,000 men had deserted, while mutinies broke out in Ingolstadt, Munich and Würzberg.[2]

These ominous signs of military unrest were mirrored by growing dissatisfaction on the home front. Before the war Germany had imported around one third of its food, and with the Allied blockade in place no amount of rationing or *Ersatz* (substitute) foods could solve the problem of shortages and high prices. The nutritional value of the German diet plummeted and cases of malnutrition and rickets soared, especially amongst children. During the so-called 'turnip winter' of 1916–17 an early frost destroyed most of the potato crop, forcing the majority of the population to survive on a diet of turnips.

Few Germans actually starved to death, but many were desperately hungry and the search for food and fuel became a full-time occupation for many older women. In this the Germans were more fortunate than their allies. By 1918 the Austro–Hungarian food supply had broken down completely and famine had gripped the Empire. Between 7 and 11 per cent of civilian deaths in the Austrian capital Vienna were as a result of starvation, and people were expiring in their homes or dropping dead in the streets.[3] In both Vienna and Berlin a flourishing black market grew up, which only increased public anger and exacerbated existing social tensions. The middle classes viewed those who relied on state and charitable assistance as freeloaders, while the poor resented this attitude and felt humiliated by their dependence on handouts. However, both groups reserved their greatest anger for the wealthy, whose lifestyle seemed unaffected by the war.

All this had a radicalizing effect on the German population, leaving both men and women more independent, less pliant and deferential, and determined to challenge social convention and live life to the full. Women and adolescents increasingly moved into the labour force to take the place of men conscripted into the army, creating a huge pool of unskilled workers who laboured in poor conditions for low pay and had little to lose from striking. At the same time, the feeling that society was in a state of flux – which had been a nagging concern in pre-war German culture – was exacerbated by the conflict, and old political loyalties were eroded. Already deeply divided between reformist and revolutionary wings, the Social Democratic Party split in April 1917 over their continued support for the war effort, and 42 breakaway Reichstag deputies formed the *Unabhängige Sozialdemokratische Partei Deutschlands* (Independent Social Democratic Party or USPD) which demanded an immediate end to the war and a radical programme of social and political reform. This schism was further widened by the Russian Revolution, which seemed to offer a model of radical action to those on the Left of the labour movement, especially with the trade unions and Majority Social Democrats (MSPD) cooperating with the state.[4] At the same time, the Centre Party responded to the mood of their constituents and took up the popular cause of a negotiated peace, while the

29

embattled bourgeoisie, fearful of defeat and revolution, retreated to the Right and adopted even more extreme positions in the face of widespread opposition and uncertainty.

These developments created a dangerous and highly combustible mood within Germany that threatened to explode at any moment. A year before the end of the war, there was a dramatic indication of the growing public hostility towards the imperial regime when between two and three thousand Berliners went on strike in protest over cuts in the bread ration and the regime's vague promises of domestic reform after the war. The unrest quickly spread throughout the country and was largely orchestrated not by the official trade unions, but by radical elements within the labour movement such the Revolutionary Shop Stewards (*Revolutionäre Obleute*) in Berlin and unaffiliated radicals in other industrial cities. The demands of the strikers were both economic and political: lower food prices and higher wages, but also an end to the war, the restoration of civil liberties and domestic political reform. In this instance the trade unions and MSPD were able to reassert their authority and bring about a peaceful end to the strikes, but this was only a temporary truce in the struggle between government and workers.

Labour Unrest, 1913–19

Year	No. of strikes	No. of workers (in millions)	Working days lost (in millions)
1913	2464	0.323	11.76
1915	141	0.015	0.04
1917	562	0.668	1.86
1919	3719	2.132	33.08

Source: Geoff Layton, *From Bismarck to Hitler: Germany 1890–1933* (London, 1995), p. 68

Industrial unrest flared up again in January 1918 when a week-long strike broke out following similar disturbances in Vienna and Budapest. Up to 1 million German workers downed tools, with around 500,000 striking in Berlin and many more coming out in sympathy in Cologne, Hamburg, Danzig, Leipzig, Nuremburg and Munich. The demands were similar to those made a year earlier, but there were now calls for solidarity with striking workers elsewhere in Central and Eastern Europe which sounded dangerously like the kind of rhetoric used by the Russian Bolsheviks. Furthermore, this time the MSPD found itself unable to rein in the strikers, and, in a foreshadowing of events at the end of the year, they were forced to ride the tide of popular dissatisfaction and place themselves at the head of the movement for fear of losing the support of the working class once and for all. This being the case, the government hit back, imposing martial law, placing factories under military control, declaring a state of siege in Berlin and banning the Social Democratic newspaper *Vorwärts*. Nevertheless, a strike on this scale and for this duration was an ominous indication of the public mood, and contained clear signs that the social changes wrought by the war would have a significant impact on political events.

REVOLUTION FROM ABOVE AND BELOW

This was the situation when, on 29 September, the High Command informed the Kaiser that the war was for all intents and purposes lost. The failure of the German spring offensive, the Allied breakthrough on the Western Front on 8 August 1918 – Ludendorff's 'black day of the German Army'[5] – and the collapse of Bulgarian and Austro–Hungarian forces on the Macedonian front in September, brought home to the High Command that its final gamble had failed and that an immediate surrender was essential to prevent invasion and social collapse. Believing that the Allies would deal more leniently with a civilian government, and wishing to pass the ignominy of surrender to someone else, Hindenburg and Ludendorff suddenly dropped their resistance to domestic reform and recommended that the Kaiser institute a programme of political reorganization. To this end, the moderate Prince Max von Baden was appointed chancellor on 3 October and for the first time two Social Democrats – the co-chairman of the SPD Philipp Scheidemann as minister without portfolio and the trade unionist Gustav Bauer as labour minister –

were included in the cabinet. There followed three weeks of frantic attempts at reform which have been characterized as a 'revolution from above'. The Prussian 'three class' voting franchise[6], which had been introduced in 1849 and had long been a *bête noire* for the Left, was abolished; the personal prerogatives of the Kaiser (and in particular his powers to appoint ministers) were curtailed; and it was announced that henceforth the chancellor and the government would be accountable to the Reichstag. However, the practical effects of the reforms were limited by the fact that they were not widely publicized, and that the Reichstag almost immediately adjourned pending new elections. This was to have important consequences in the months that followed, as it meant that parliamentarians had little influence over subsequent events, leaving the fate of Germany in the hands of a small coterie of power brokers drawn from the ranks of the army, the old elites and labour movement.

At the same time, the revelation that Germany was surrendering unconditionally after four years of struggle and sacrifice destroyed the people's confidence in the imperial government once and for all and unleashed a dramatic backlash against the existing regime. By the end of October Germany was a powder keg just waiting to explode. The spark that lit the fuse of revolution was the decision by right-wing officers amongst the High Seas Fleet (which had played little part in the war aside from the indecisive Battle of Jutland in 1916) to order the *Kriegsmarine* to put to sea for a final suicidal confrontation with the Royal Navy. When news of this impending *Todeskampf* (suicide offensive) leaked out it led to a mutiny at the naval base at the Baltic port of Kiel, and on Sunday 3 November more than 20,000 sailors and dockworkers gathered at a local park in a show of solidarity with the mutineers. The demonstration was met with force and seven people were killed and 29 injured when military police opened fire on the protestors. However, this only served to further radicalize the sailors, and the next day the whole of the Third Squadron of the fleet mutinied. Armed sailors then marched ashore and occupied the military prison, freed their comrades and then took over other strategic buildings. When soldiers from the local garrison were sent to put down the revolt they merely fraternized with the mutineers and went over to

The beginning of the November Revolution: Anti-war demonstrations at Kiel, 4 November 1918 (Bundesarchiv Bild 183-R72520 / CC-BY-SA).

their side. By 6 November the disturbances had escalated, with dock-workers joining the rebels and the establishment of Workers' and Soldiers' Councils along the lines of those set up during the Russian Revolution of 1917.

This was at first more of a spontaneous protest movement than a revolution. The Kiel mutineers were not trying to topple the government – if anything they saw themselves as defending it against reactionary elements within the officer corps. Nevertheless, once news of the disturbances at Kiel and the initial heavy-handed attempts to crush it leaked out, the discontent that had simmered beneath the surface for so long exploded into a full-blown revolution that quickly spread throughout the Reich. Across the country strikes were held, mass demonstrations staged and Workers' and Soldiers' Council established. This was followed by the occupation of public buildings and freeing of political prisoners, but there was little bloodshed: in most cases the authorities lost their nerve at the first sign of unrest and either fled or handed power to the councils. This was what happened in Bavaria, where anti-war demonstrations in Munich on 7 November led to the establishment of Workers' and Soldiers' Councils. That night the king fled Munich and the new 'Revolutionary Parliament' nominated the left-wing journalist Kurt Eisner as minister president. Within 24 hours, and without a shot being fired, the old regime in Bavaria had collapsed and power was in the hands of a scruffy-looking middle-class intellectual who claimed to represent the interests of the working classes.

So far the revolution had been a relatively bloodless affair, but there was deep concern that this could change at any moment. Hitherto the leadership of the SPD, with the help of the councils, had been able to maintain a reasonable amount of good order, but with radical forces within the labour movement – foremost among them the *Spartakusbund* (Spartacus League), a radical splinter group loosely affiliated with the USPD set up by Karl Liebknecht and Rosa Luxemburg in January 1916 – agitating for further change, the Social Democratic leader Friedrich Ebert and his comrades were uncertain as to how much longer popular dissatisfaction with the government could be held in check.

Matters came to a head on the morning of 9 November when the revolution reached the capital. By noon, news reached the Chancellor that large columns of workers were making their way to the city centre. Under pressure from the crowds outside, Prince Max felt that he had no choice but to act and issued a proclamation announcing the abdication of the Kaiser and crown prince and the formation of a regency. Meanwhile, a delegation of the SPD executive had arrived at the Chancellery to demand that they take over the government in order 'to preserve law and order'. Prince Max was only too happy to comply and willingly handed power to Ebert, whose first act as chancellor was to call on the protestors to leave the streets.

However, this appeal, like the declaration of the Kaiser's abdication, was too little too late. By one o'clock hundreds of thousands of workers had reached the city centre and, early in the afternoon, Karl Liebknecht and his supporters occupied the Imperial Palace, hauled down the imperial standard and replaced it with the red flag. Liebknecht then appeared before the dense crowds milling about between the palace and the Reichstag and delivered a fiery speech in which he proclaimed the formation of a Soviet republic. At roughly the same time, Phillip Scheidemann addressed the crowd in the hope of persuading them to disperse. Speaking from a window in the Reichstag, he announced the formation of a 'labour government to which all socialist parties will belong', exhorted the masses to 'stand loyal and united' and ended his oration with the words 'Long live the German Republic!'[7]

Scheidemann believed that this was a decisive moment in the revolution, the point at which the crowds turned away from radicalism and the idea of a democratic republic became 'a thing of life in the brains and heart of the masses'[8]. Yet this assessment smacks of wishful thinking. The republic still had a long way to go before it became a reality. That Ebert recognized the precarious nature of his position is evidenced by the precautions that he proceeded to take to ensure that, having gone this far, the revolution went no further. Even as the MSPD entered into feverish negotiations with the Independent Socialists in order to deliver the promised 'labour government', he never formally relinquished the title of Imperial

Phillip Scheidemann proclaiming the Republic from the window of the Reichstag, 9 November 1918. (Bundesarchiv, Bild 175-01448 / Unknown / CC-BY-SA).

Chancellor and as such remained head of the traditional organs of the state.

After much internal debate, the USPD agreed to enter into a coalition with the MSPD on the condition that only socialists be included in the cabinet (thus dashing Ebert's hopes of a cross-party government of national unity), that the government declare that all power resided with the councils and that elections to a National Assembly be postponed until the revolution had been consolidated. Reluctantly Ebert agreed, and, on 10 November, the Council of Peoples' Representatives (*Rat der Volksbeaufragten*) was formed. This was in effect a new government outside the traditional power structure of the imperial state and was made up of three representatives of the MSPD – Ebert, Scheidemann and Otto Landsberg (an SPD Reichstag deputy from Magdeburg) – and three members of the USPD – Hugo Haase, Wilhelm Dittmann and the Revolutionary Shop Steward Emil Barth – with Ebert and Haase as co-chairmen.

With the formation of this council a two-tier system of government came into operation for the next eight weeks – the Council of Peoples' Representatives and the Workers' and Soldiers' Councils on one hand, and the more traditional apparatus of the state (the civil service, the army, etc.) on the other. Ebert maintained that the council was merely a caretaker government, and that all decisions relating to the long-term constitutional settlement would be put off until after elections to National Assembly could be held. At the same time, he used his position as chancellor to try and establish a functioning relationship with the middle-class parties and civil service in order to ensure the orderly demobilization of the army, continuation of food supplies and a smooth transition to a peacetime economy. All this was contrary to the USPD's insistence that the councils were the embodiment of the revolutionary will of the people and as such had a mandate to implement a radical social programme including the nationalization of industry, the break-up of the old landed estates and the radical democratization of the army, civil service and judiciary.

The scene was set for a clash between the radically different visions of state and society espoused by the two wings of the labour movement, but Ebert's ability to impose his authority on the country was enhanced when, on the evening of 10 November, he received a telephone call from General Groener at Army Headquarters in Spa. Groener offered the new chancellor the army's support in return for a promise to resist bolshevism and preserve the independence of the military. Ebert's agreement to this suggestion has been seen as a betrayal of the revolution, and it is true that the so-called Ebert–Groener Pact ensured that the army, particularly the officer corps, would remain largely unchanged and retain a degree of their former power and independence from the civilian authorities during the Weimar period. However, while Ebert's decision to do a deal with the army has often been roundly attacked by historians on the Left, to interpret it as a betrayal is to fundamentally misunderstand the nature of the November Revolution. Rather than betraying the revolution 'it is . . . possible to detect in the MSPD's strategy a consistency and clear-sighted realism which delivered pretty much what was intended from the outset.'[9] Ebert and his Social Democratic colleagues never desired a complete transformation of German society – indeed, the Chancellor was heard to comment that he hated the revolution 'like sin'[10] – and once the monarchy had been toppled they consistently sought to guide Germany along a moderate course. Nor was there much appetite amongst the population in general for the radicalism of the far Left – the mass of soldiers, sailors and workmen's demands were for peace, bread and democratization, not social revolution. While it is true that on the whole the middle classes and the moderate socialists exaggerated the threat from the Left – there was, after all, no disciplined revolutionary party like Lenin's Bolsheviks in Germany, only the small band of intellectuals who made up the Spartacists – it is also true that historians have had a tendency to exaggerate the degree to which the new government's accommodation with Groener signalled a shift to the right. Ebert's government was not pernicious in intent. When one considers that they lacked any other means to impose their fragile authority on the capital, let alone the country as a whole, Ebert's compromise with Groener begins to look less like a betrayal of the revolution and more like 'a reasonable precaution to protect his government against violence from the extreme Left.'[11]

Ebert's position was further strengthened by two events. Firstly, on 15 November, the trade unions under Karl Legien came to an agreement with employers, represented by the industrialist Hugo Stinnes. The so-called Stinnes–Legien Agreement saw the employers' associations recognize the legitimacy of the unions and agree to the introduction of an eight-hour working day, in return for an agreement to abandon calls for the wholesale nationalization of industry. This did much to satisfy the long-held grievances of the working classes and dampened enthusiasm for a more radical socio-economic programme. At the same time, elections to the councils produced a victory for the moderates who favoured Western-style parliamentary democracy over Soviet communism. When over 500 delegates (299 for the SPD, 101 USPD, 25 liberals and 75 without party affiliation) representing the councils from all over Germany met at Berlin's Busch Theatre on 16–21 December 1918, they were easily persuaded that any momentous decisions about Germany's future should be put off until after the election of a National Assembly. Despite some fiery rhetoric about the nationalization of key industries and the democratization of the army, on 19 December the Congress voted in favour of the proposal that all power should be left in the hands of Ebert's government until elections on 19 January 1919.

THE CHALLENGE FROM THE LEFT

By December 1918 it looked as though the revolutionary energies of the proletariat had been channelled along the moderate liberal-democratic course favoured by Ebert and the MSPD leadership, but events over the Christmas period proved that the revolution was far from over. On 23 December the Peoples' Naval Division (500 sailors from Kiel who it had been hoped could be used as an elite force in defence of the new government) refused to evacuate the royal palace where they had been quartered since arriving in the capital in November. Barricading themselves in the royal stables, they resisted peaceful attempts to persuade them to leave, and a regular army division was ordered to expel them by force. On Christmas Eve government troops bombarded the palace with artillery, but the sailors stayed put. The next day the government, fearful of a widespread reaction against their hardline tactics, backed down, while a crowd of Spartacists briefly occupied the *Vorwärts* offices. The clash with the People's

Naval Division, and the decision to use force against them in particular, brought to a head the tensions between the USPD and MSPD members of the Council of People's Representatives, and on 29 December Haase, Dittmann and Barth resigned from the government.

The withdrawal of the USPD from the council also provided the MSPD's spokesman on military and colonial matters, Gustav Noske, with an opportunity to play the role of strong man in the growing atmosphere of political and military crisis. Noske accepted the post of Minister for National Defence with the words 'You can count on me to re-establish order in Berlin. Someone must be the bloodhound. I am not afraid of the responsibility.'[12] His first move was to appoint the aristocratic reactionary General Walther von Lüttwitz as commander-in-chief of Berlin, and to provide the government with a better means of defending itself.

Whatever Groener might have promised Ebert on 10 November, the regular military establishment was 'almost completely incapable of taking action to suppress unrest within Germany.'[13] Once it became clear that the war was actually over, the overriding concern of most soldiers was to get back home as quickly as possible and, rather than wait to go through the long and laborious process of being officially demobilized, they simply left their units and headed for home. Those soldiers who did stay with their units, especially those who had been stationed behind the lines, became a menace to the public, stealing food and equipment and selling them on the black market, refusing to obey orders, intimidating the local population and getting involved in violent clashes with fellow soldiers returning from the front.

Under these circumstances Ebert's government turned to irregular paramilitary forces in order to maintain any sort of order and defend itself from the radical Left. This idea has been attributed to General Groener's adjutant, the future chancellor and *éminence grise* of late Weimar Germany, Colonel (later General) Kurt von Schleicher.[14] But some such voluntary paramilitary detachments had already come into being. After the November Revolution a wave of volunteerism and 'self-help' flooded across the country, resulting in the formation of a variety of *ad hoc* paramilitary groups ranging from revolutionary 'red guards' to republican 'self-defence regiments' and middle-class

Einwohnerwehren (home guards).[15] Among the first was the 1,500-strong *Eiserne Brigade* (Iron Brigade) under Colonel von Roden, which was raised by Noske in November 1918 from loyal naval officers in Kiel. Independently and on his own initiative, General Ludwig von Maercker formed the *Freiwillige Landesjägerkorps* (Volunteer Rifleman's Corps) which was led by experienced officers and non-commissioned officers (NCOs) who had seen front-line service, and was open to any man who had completed basic training, but rejected overtly political (i.e. anti-republican) volunteers and required all members to take an oath of allegiance to the Ebert government. Other units sprang up, phoenix-like, from the ashes of the regular army in the winter of 1918–19: General von Hoffmann brought a division of horse guards, General Held formed a unit from the 17th Infantry Division, while General von Hulsen raised an 11,000-strong force in Potsdam. All these followed the precedent set by Maercker, with a senior officer (sometimes a General, but more often a Colonel, Major or Captain) announcing his intention to form a *Korps* to like-minded colleagues who then occupied a barracks or similar building to use as a base and begin recruitment and training. Recruitment was initially by word of mouth, but soon newspaper advertisements and lurid recruiting posters began to appear appealing to Germans to stand up and defend their country from bolshevism.

These volunteer units quickly became collectively known as *Freikorps*, after the irregular volunteer formations that had joined the Prussian Army during the Wars of Liberation against Napoleon. This title was at once descriptive – the volunteer units were 'free companies' of irregular troops outside the normal military hierarchy – and a political statement. By adopting the mantle of the *Freikorps* the volunteers were positioning themselves as defenders of the Fatherland against foreign encroachment – be that in the form of French or Polish invasion or in the form of the 'alien' ideology of communism. Yet, with their lack of regular military discipline and propensity for extreme and sometimes indiscriminate violence, many of the post-war *Freikorps* were perhaps more similar to the *Landsknechte*, sixteenth-century German mercenaries famed for their military prowess and freebooting brutality, than to the patriotic volunteers who fought against Napoleon.

Recruiting poster for the Freikorps Lützow drawing explicit links
between the right-wing paramilitaries of post-war Germany and the
nationalist volunteers of the nineteenth-century Wars of Liberation
(Bundesarchiv, Plak 002-007-128).

The rapid proliferation of these units and the zeal with which
they went about their work have often been seen as evidence of the
brutalizing effects of war that bequeathed a culture of political
violence to Weimar Germany. But it would be a mistake to think
that paramilitary violence was a peculiarly German phenomenon in
the interwar period. The armistice and the subsequent Treaty of
Versailles might have ended the conflict on the Western Front, but
the bloodshed continued in Central and Eastern Europe and the
Middle East, as various factions battled for dominance or gave vent

to long-standing ethnic animosities in the power vacuum left by the collapse of the Austro–Hungarian, Russian and Ottoman Empires. German paramilitaries maintained strong links with similar groups in Austria and Hungary, 'supporting each other with arms and logistics in the hope of bringing about the downfall of the republican regimes and communist movements of Central Europe.'[16] Indeed, the *Freikorps* were just part of 'a fairly homogeneous transnational milieu of predominantly middle- and upper-class political radicals characterized by youth and war-induced militancy', who shared a common experience of war and defeat, revolution, unfulfilled personal and national ambitions, opposition to western democracy and a fear and loathing of the Slavonic world (which was seen as being the origins of almost everything they despised) that bordered on the pathological.[17]

At the same time, the war had unleashed a tide of nationalist and economic discontent and 1919 saw a global wave of strikes, demonstrations and uprisings against the established order. There was a very real fear amongst western leaders that the foundations of capitalism and liberal democracy were being shaken and might give way. Thus the allied governments were perfectly prepared not only to encourage the new German government to make use of right-wing paramilitaries to stave off the threat of Bolshevik revolution, but to employ their own paramilitaries to combat nationalist unrest in Ireland and elsewhere.[18] Thus, the political violence that was unleashed upon the German population in the years between 1918 and 1923 was far from being unique and can indeed be seen as conforming to a wider regional, European, and even global, trend towards violence and unrest.

With his troops in place, Noske attempted to dismiss Berlin's police president, the left-wing USPD member Emil Eichhorn (who was widely suspected of having helped the Peoples' Naval Division during their confrontation with the government). This move was greeted with mass demonstrations on 5 January. Seizing their opportunity, the newly formed Communist Party of Germany (*Kommunistische Partei Deutschlands* or KPD), under the leadership of Karl Liebknecht and Rosa Luxemburg, established a revolutionary committee and issued a proclamation deposing Ebert and announcing a new revolutionary government, while armed Communists occupied key buildings in Berlin.

Noske rose to the occasion with alacrity and, working from a makeshift headquarters in the Luisenstift girl's school, unleashed his *Freikorps* upon the insurgents. On 10 January a detachment of soldiers was sent to secure the suburb of Spandau where the Spartacists threatened to take the local munitions works. The following day, 1,200 young officers, cadets and students attacked the Belle–Alliance Platz (Berlin's publishing district) with overwhelming force, using flame throwers, machine guns and artillery to drive the Spartacists out from their positions behind makeshift barricades. By Wednesday 15 January the revolt was all but over and the Communist leaders had fled into hiding. However, this did not save them from vicious reprisals. On 16 January it was reported in the *Berliner Zeitung* that Liebknecht and Luxemburg had been arrested and taken to the Eden Hotel, headquarters of the Garde Kavallerie Division. There they had been beaten and interrogated before being bundled into separate cars. Liebknecht, already bleeding profusely from a head wound, was taken to the Tiergarten, told to get out of the car and then shot in the back. Luxemburg was clubbed over the head before being shot and dumped into the Landwehr canal.

But this was not an end to the violence. On 6 February the United Worker's Council for the Ruhr, fearing that the government would move against them after an earlier clash over the expropriation of the region's coal mines, ordered a general strike. When *Freikorps* moved in, an autonomous republic was proclaimed and coal shipments to the rest of Germany suspended. On 3 March the KPD published an appeal for a general strike in Berlin, signalling 'Bloody Week', a second wave of revolutionary unrest in the capital which left up to 15,000 people dead and 12,000 injured after nine days of savage street fighting. This was followed by a series of violent confrontations in Gotha, Halle, Dresden, Brunswick and Leipzig between March and May 1919, as General von Maercker was dispatched to pacify central Germany.

Meanwhile, the assassination of Kurt Eisner, and the wounding of his Social Democrat rival for leadership of the revolution, Erhard Auer, on 21 February 1919, had thrown Bavaria into turmoil. With the two dominant personalities in Bavarian social democracy out of action, the country descended into anarchy. The newly elected Provincial Assembly broke up in disorder, what was left of the cabinet fled to Bamberg and a general strike was called in Munich. The power vacuum was filled by an unlikely group of anarchists and intellectuals led by the essayist and poet Erich Mühsam and the 25-year-old expressionist playwright Ernst Toller. They had no practical experience of politics, and their government, if it can be called that, added an element of farce to the Bavarian Revolution absent elsewhere in Germany. The Minister of Finance, Silvio Gesell, wanted to abolish money, and the Foreign Minister Franz Lipp (who had recently been released from a psychiatric hospital) declared war on Switzerland and telegraphed Lenin complaining that his predecessor had absconded with the key to the ministry toilet.[19] Finally, after only six days, this short-lived regime collapsed in the face of an attempted putsch by Republican Guards. The radical working class in Munich repudiated the Bamberg administration and a *Räterrepublik*, a Republic of Councils, was declared. The Russian Communist, Eugene Levine, who had been dispatched to Munich by Liebknecht and Luxemburg to set up a Bavarian Communist Party, seized control of this new body and managed to recruit a 10,000-strong Red Army which immediately began requisitioning food, property and cash and rounding up their political opponents.

Initial attempts by the SPD-led government in Bamberg to retake the capital met with humiliating failure, and Minister President Johannes Hoffmann was forced to appeal to Berlin for military assistance. Noske was only too happy to oblige and on 27 April a 30,000-strong force of *Freikorps* entered Bavarian territory. Dachau was taken two days later, and as the government forces approached Munich the leader of the Red Army ordered that the 100 or so bourgeois hostages being held in the capital's jails be massacred. On 1 May the *Freikorps* entered the city virtually unopposed and unleashed a week-long White Terror on the city in retribution for the supposed excesses of the Soviet regime. At least 10,000 'Reds', including Levine and the anarchist theorist Gustav Landauer, were murdered before the bloodletting was over. Finally, on 7 May, the commander of the government forces General von Oven reported to his superiors that Munich had not only been 'pacified', but also 'cleansed'.[20]

Despite the wave of violence that was sweeping the country, elections to a National Constituent Assembly had been held on 19 January. These produced a resounding victory for the MSPD and their moderate allies in the Centre and liberal parties, and gave a popular mandate (and with it legitimacy) to Ebert's provisional government. The Assembly convened on 6 February, not in Berlin but in the sleepy Thuringian town of Weimar. The decision to meet there was based on considerations that were both practical and ideological. On the one hand, by convening the first elected body of the new republic in Weimar the government was consciously distancing the new regime from Prussian militarism and conservatism and evoking the spirit of the Enlightenment and German Romanticism. However, there were also very practical reasons for not attempting the serious business of drafting a constitution in the Reich capital: 'Red Berlin' was still considered much too dangerous, and Weimar was much smaller and easier to defend than the Prussian capital.

Ebert was elected president on 11 February, and Scheidemann became chancellor of a coalition made up of the moderate left-leaning parties. The first major tasks facing the National Assembly were to transform the temporary armistice of November 1918 into a permanent peace treaty, and to formulate a constitutional framework for the new republic. The debate over the Treaty of Versailles

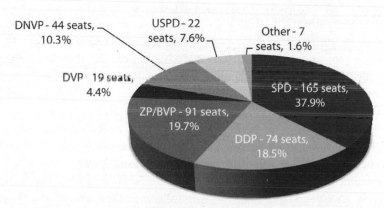

DNVP - 44 seats, 10.3%

USPD - 22 seats, 7.6%

Other - 7 seats, 1.6%

DVP - 19 seats, 4.4%

SPD - 165 seats, 37.9%

ZP/BVP - 91 seats, 19.7%

DDP - 74 seats, 18.5%

National assembly election results, January 1919.

(see Chapter 4) exposed the divisions in German society over the peace terms and led to the collapse of the republic's first government after only 130 days, with the withdrawal of the DDP from the cabinet, but ultimately Germany had no choice but to sign the treaty on 28 June 1919. Meanwhile, between February and July a 25-man committee of experts led by the eminent jurist Hugo Preuss, and including such luminaries as the sociologist Max Weber, the leading liberal politician Friederich Naumann and the historian Friedrich Mienecke, worked on a constitution for the republic. On 31 July the constitution was approved by a vote of 262 to 75 and it was signed into law on 11 August 1919.

THE THREAT FROM THE RIGHT

By the spring of 1920 it seemed as though the political situation was stabilizing, while an end to the Allied blockade meant that the economic situation was also improving. With rising employment and more food in the shops, labour disputes and demonstrations fell and the government began to feel secure for the first time since November 1918. With the formation of a regular army, the Reichswehr, on 1 October 1919, the government began to feel that the continuing existence of the paramilitary *Freikorps* was not only unnecessary but potentially dangerous to their position, and they attempted to disband the volunteer corps. The result was a violent backlash that plunged Germany into a renewed cycle of political violence.

Many volunteers had joined up because their prospects in civilian life were limited, and now once again demobilization brought the prospect of unemployment and social isolation. At the same time, the decision to demobilize the *Freikorps* brought to a head pre-existing tensions between certain sections of the old officer corps and the government. While the politicians and diplomats believed that military power had been decisively vanquished and that the key to a revision of the Treaty of Versailles was economic revival and negotiation with the Western Powers, a hard core within the officer corps interpreted the signing of the treaty as an attack on the army which 'demonstrated that the republic was anti-military.'[21] This suspicion seemed to be confirmed by the attempt to demobilize the

Friedrich Ebert, co-chairman of the MSPD and first President of the Republic, photographed in 1922 (Bundesarchiv, Bild 146-2004-0097 / CC-BY-SA).

volunteer forces that had done so much to defend the new regime from the threat posed by the extreme Left, and led some dissatis fied officers to make common cause with a small number of right-wing conspirators who were already plotting to overthrow the republic.

The demobilization of the *Freikorps* proved the perfect opportunity for these plotters. In disbanding the paramilitaries the government provided their opponents with a ready-made army of malcontents who owed allegiance to no-one but their officers and were prepared to use violence to achieve their aims. On 13 March 1920 Hermann Erhardt, a former naval captain who had carried over the brutal discipline of the *Kriegsmarine* to his *Freikorps*, marched his men through the Brandenburg Gate and seized control of Berlin. When Noske demanded that the military crush the putsch, the generals informed him in no uncertain terms that 'Reichswehr units would not fire on other Reichswehr units.'[22] With no troops to defend them the cabinet fled to Dresden, pausing only to urge the working classes to 'Go on strike, put down your work, stop the military dictatorship' and 'fight with every means for the preservation of the republic.'[23] The conservative politician and co-founder of the Fatherland Party, Wolfgang Kapp was declared chancellor by the rebels, and General von Lüttwitz was appointed commander-in-chief of the army. However, the coup lacked significant support even amongst conservatives and senior army officers. The working classes heeded the government call for a general strike, the Reichsbank refused to issue money without the proper authorization and civil servants refused to carry out the orders of the putschists. After just four days the coup collapsed and Kapp fled in panic.

Nevertheless, the abortive putsch failed to produce a reaction against the Right. In the Reichstag elections of June 1920 the SPD and DDP's share of the vote roughly halved, while the Independent Socialists and Nationalists saw their support blossom. This was the first instance of what Richard Bessel has termed 'a defining characteristic of Weimar politics', the tendency of the electorate to punish those 'parties that had accepted governmental responsibility, and thus responsibility for necessarily unpopular decisions', in the polls.[24] In fact, the most immediate consequence of the Kapp Putsch was the revival of the threat from the Left. Passive resistance to the attempted coup spilled over into a left-wing insurrection in the Ruhr, as militant workers responded to the call for a general strike to defend the republic with their own political demands. Unlike the previous uprisings in Berlin in January and March 1919, the *Märzrevolution* (March Revolution) was well organized and carried out by around 50,000 well-armed and disciplined members of the 'Red Army of the Ruhr', who rapidly succeeded in defeating detachments of police, volunteers and units of the Reichswehr to take control of Germany's largest industrial region. However, the victory of the Communists was short lived. After a 12-day truce between the insurgents and government forces collapsed, General von Watter led a combined force of regular army units and paramilitaries into the Ruhr on 2 April. This 'surge attack' was as violent and bloody as the suppression of the Munich Soviet the previous year, with one

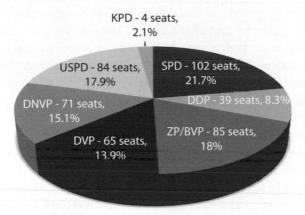

Reichstag election results, June 1920.

estimate suggesting that 1,000 'Reds' were killed in the first two days of the operation.

Such indiscriminate violence against the Left by paramilitary forces has traditionally been seen by historians as evidence of both the 'betrayal' of the revolution by the Social Democratic leadership and of widespread hostility towards the new republic on the Right. Yet more recently some scholars have successfully challenged the view of a vast stratum of resentful upper- and middle-class Germans opposed to the new regime.[25] While many in the officer corps, the civil service and the judiciary had no love for the new republic, the vast majority of them were willing to work towards their aim of restoring Germany to its former glory within the legal framework provided by the Weimar constitution. Conan Fischer draws comparisons with the French Third Republic, where conservative and monarchist forces were relatively reconciled to the new moderate republicanism and a 'functional loyalty', if not love, for the republic developed over time. He argues that similar examples of 'functional loyalty' can be seen in Weimar Germany, as in bureaucratic resistance to the Kapp Putsch.[26] Elsewhere, the ultimate aim of certain sections of the officer corps might have been the restoration of the monarchy or the overturning of the Versailles settlement, but they recognized that, for the time being at least, a broad-based liberal

Colin Storer

parliamentary republic was the only means of preventing Germany sliding into anarchy and civil war, and the best way for it to regain its strength after the trauma of revolution and defeat. That this was the case is demonstrated by the readiness of the Army Command to support Ebert's government and the passivity of civil servants during the Putsch.

Nevertheless, the threat from more radical elements within right-wing opposition to the republic did not disappear after the failure of the Kapp Putsch. Indeed, the ridiculously lenient sentences handed down to the ringleaders of the coup (of the 775 army officers who participated in the putsch, only six were dismissed and von Lüttwitz was allowed to retire on a full pension) meant that many of the core conspirators remained at large. These were able to join the welter of right-wing secret societies, paramilitary organizations and *völkisch* groups that proliferated in the early days of the republic. One contemporary commentator identified at least 59 such groups committed to the overthrow of democracy, but this should not lead us to conclude that the republican system faced concerted and coherent opposition from the Right. These groups were often isolated and of limited numbers, without common goals or strong leadership, and they frequently changed their names or disbanded and then reformed in order to circumvent official prescriptions on their activities.

After the destruction of the *Räterrepublik* and the White Terror that followed, Bavaria became the heartland of the German Right, the centre of a Central European network of counter-revolutionaries. Under the rule of a conservative clique made up of Gustav Ritter von Kahr, the Reichswehr commander General Otto von Lossow and the chief of police Colonel Hans Seisser, the authorities turned a blind eye to the activities of right-wing organizations banned by the federal government in Berlin, while official funds were syphoned off to help the anti-republican cause. Among the political refugees who found succour in the south was Captain Ehrhardt, who, shielded by sympathetic landowners and the local chief of police, established his Organization Consul in Bavaria in 1921. There followed a 14-month campaign of politically motivated murders which had two aims: to mete out 'justice' to the 'traitors' who had betrayed Germany in November 1918 in the manner of the medieval *Femegerichte* (tribunals that had administered swift and brutal justice in times when no official judicial system existed), and to provoke a left-wing uprising which could then be crushed by the resurgent Right and lead to the establishment of a military dictatorship. It is estimated that these 'Feme' killings accounted for around 350 political murders between August 1921 and June 1922. The majority of victims were civil servants who were prepared to work within the republican system, informers and former members of the Organization Consul, but Ehrhardt also set his sights on prominent republican politicians.

By far the most high-profile of these killings were those that began and ended the campaign: the assassinations of the government ministers Matthias Erzberger and Walther Rathenau. Hated by the Right for his part in the 1917 peace resolution and the armistice negotiations as much as for his public declaration of Germany's need to fulfil its obligations under the Treaty of Versailles, Erzberger had already survived one assassination attempt, but his opponents finally caught up with him during a holiday at the Badenese spa resort of Bad Griesbach. On 26 August 1921, while out for a walk with one of his Centre Party colleagues, he was attacked by a Nationalist death squad. Erzberger suffered a total of 12 gunshot wounds and did not survive the attack, while the assassins, Heinrich Tillessen and Heinrich Schultz, returned to Munich to be spirited away to Hungary where they were sheltered by sympathetic counter-revolutionaries and where the right-wing government refused to extradite them.[27]

The murder of Erzberger was followed by that of the USPD party chairman Hugo Haase, who was gunned down on the steps of the Reichstag, and an attempt on the life of the former chancellor Philipp Scheidemann. But the attack which caused the most public outrage and forced the authorities to take drastic action against the 'Feme' was that on the serving foreign minister, Walter Rathenau. Already a hated figure for the Right due to his Jewish ancestry and his advanced political views (which involved the formation of a European free-trade area), Rathenau further earned their ire as foreign minister by pursuing *Erfüllungspolitik* (the policy of fulfilment) with the Allies and signing the Rapallo Treaty with the Soviet Union. On the morning of Saturday 24 June 1922, Ratheau left his home in the Berlin suburb of Grunewald to make his way to his office in Wilhelmstrasse. A little after 11 o'clock his car was overtaken by another containing a group of right-wing assassins, who sprayed Rathenau's vehicle with small-arms fire before throwing a grenade through the window. The Foreign Minister suffered wounds to his head and chest and by the time a doctor could be summoned he was dead.

However, far from leading to a left-wing insurrection or a growth of nationalist feeling, the effect of the assassination was to precipitate a great outpouring of popular disgust at the murderers, and support for the republic in the form of mass demonstrations organized by the trade unions, democratic parties and republican associations. Indeed, such was the public anger at the crime, that the Organization Consul decided that it was politic to suspend its campaign of political violence and lie low for a while. But Rathenau's murder had more profound consequences than merely bringing to a halt the campaign of nationalist violence. It enabled the supporters of parliamentary democracy to seize the moral high ground from the anti–republican Right – who had hitherto portrayed themselves as the true patriots and defenders of the 'German spirit' while lambasting their republican opponents as traitors, the 'November Criminals' who had stabbed the army in the back in 1918 – and associate them with murderous extremism. At the same time, Rathenau was quickly transfigured into a republican martyr, a man who had selflessly given his life in the service of the republican state and the German people. In more practical terms the murder of Rathenau finally galvanised the Reichstag to take measures against the threat from the Right and led to the passage of the Law for the Protection of the Republic on 18 July 1922. This not only prohibited extremist organizations and established special courts to deal with cases of political violence, but also, much like contemporary anti-terror laws, prohibited the language and imagery of extremism.[28]

Nevertheless, 1923 brought fresh problems for the new republic, which in turn revived the threat from both the Left and the Right. With the collapse of the currency (see Chapter 3) and the population crying out for an end to the economic crisis, the conditions seemed right for anti-republican forces at either end of the political spectrum to mount renewed challenges to the democratic political

The chief conspirators behind the Munich Beer-Hall Putsch posing
before their trial in spring 1924. General Ludendorff stands at centre-
right, next to Hitler (Bundesarchiv, Bild 102-00344A / Heinrich
Hoffmann / CC-BY-SA)

order. With growing left-wing unrest in the Ruhr and central Germany,
and right-wing forces massing in Bavaria, President Ebert declared
a state of emergency and handed extensive powers to the military.
In Saxony and Thuringia where the Communists had entered into
a coalition government with the SPD in October and begun recruiting
'proletarian hundreds', the army did not hesitate to depose the
elected government and replace it with a State Commissar appointed
by Berlin, but they refused to act against right-wing forces in Bavaria.

This provided a previously obscure local politician with the opportunity to make his first bid for power in November 1923. Inspired
by Mussolini's infamous 'March on Rome' the previous year, Adolf
Hitler and his chief lieutenants hatched a plot to first seize power
in Munich and then use this as a starting point for a 'March on
Berlin'. On the evening of 8 November 1923, the Nazis surrounded
Munich's Bürgerbräukeller and succeeded in taking State Commissioner von Kahr and his fellow triumvirs hostage. However, despite

an auspicious beginning the attempted coup soon descended into farce. After proclaiming the start of the 'national revolution', Hitler left the Bürgerbräukeller and the hostages were released. The triumvirs promptly went back on their promises of support and rallied police and troops to oppose the Nazis. On the morning of 9 November it was decided that the putsch should continue, and at noon the massed ranks of Nazi stormtroopers began to march on the War Ministry. When they reached the Odeonzplatz they found their way blocked by armed police, who ordered them to halt before firing a single volley at the marchers. Faced with real bullets, the Nazis broke and fled. Hitler, along with other leading figures like General Ludendorff, was arrested, while the remainder of the Nazi leadership fled abroad.

Aware that Hitler could expose the anti-republican sympathies and paramilitary activities of many prominent regional politicians, the Bavarian state government managed to persuade the Reich authorities to hold his trial not at the Reich Court in Leipzig, but before a special People's Court in Munich. In the event, the proceedings were a travesty. Presided over by a judge with well-known nationalist sympathies, the court allowed Hitler to insult witnesses for the prosecution and subject the court to lengthy political tirades. Ludendorff's involvement in the attempted coup was suppressed and the old man acquitted, while Hitler himself was sentenced to a mere five years in prison, despite the fact that his treasonable actions were punishable by the death penalty. This trial, more than any, other exposed the 'biased standards of the Weimar judiciary'[29], which was much more lenient towards right-wing suspects in cases of political violence than those on the Left. Of the 400 murders with an obvious political motive that were committed in Germany between 1918 and 1922, 354 were carried out by right-wing killers and 22 by left-wingers. Of the perpetrators of these 22 killings, 17 received harsh sentences, including ten sentenced to death. Of the 354 right-wing murderers, 326 went completely unpunished. The average jail sentence for a left-wing political prisoner was 15 years. For a right-winger it was four months.[30]

Nevertheless, 1923 proved the high-water mark for political turmoil in the republic. Thereafter, as the currency stabilized and foreign investment stimulated the moribund economy, the democratic state settled down into a period of relative stabilization. Yet the difficult circumstances of its birth left the republic with a bitter political legacy that would continue to dog it throughout its lifetime, and made it more difficult to reconcile both the extreme Left and the radical Right to the republican system. Even so, Germany was by no means unique in facing such challenges in the aftermath of the First World War. Established regimes across Europe and throughout the world experienced labour unrest and revolutionary upheavals in immediate post-war period which were greeted with a ferocious backlash from the authorities and/or right-wing elements. Not only Germany and other defeated nations such as Austria and Hungary, but also victorious powers such as Italy and the British Empire, as well as the new nations of Central and Eastern Europe, suffered prolonged periods of paramilitary violence as different factions attempted to influence the political direction of these states through the use of force. At the same time, although the armistice of 11 November 1918 marked a ceasefire on the Western Front, elsewhere the bloodshed continued unabated. Civil war raged in Russia and the Baltic States and broke out in the Irish Free State shortly after it had achieved independence from Britain in 1922. Elsewhere, cross-border skirmishes, armed interventions and outright war were as influential as the peacemakers in Paris in drawing the territorial boundaries of post-war Eastern Europe and the Middle East.

In comparison to some of these conflicts, the political upheaval in Germany does not seem particularly unusual or severe. Despite the use of the term 'civil war' by both contemporaries and historians to describe the disorder and violence that followed the November Revolution, there was no coherent or unified plan for an armed insurrection amongst the radical Left, and what violent clashes took place tended to be small-scale skirmishes rather than pitched battles. Political violence in post-war Germany tended to be reactive – after the Spartacist Uprising of January 1919 the government and right-wing militias, fearing an armed uprising from the Left, sought to use force to bring order to and impose their political will on the country, which in turn further radicalized the Left who fought back when placed under this pressure. Nevertheless, it is important to remember that the vast majority of Germans chose to express their political preferences through peaceful demonstrations or strike action rather than violent confrontation. True, such demonstrations could turn violent, especially in the overheated and sometimes hysterical political climate of the early 1920s, but the fact remains that those doing the shooting were always in the minority.

All of this should lead us to question some of the commonly held assumptions about the early days of the Weimar Republic. Certainly these were 'years of crisis', both in the fact that they were marked by violence and turmoil, but also in the more positive sense that this very uncertainty and upheaval meant that the future was open, and anything – good or bad – could emerge. What did result from this was not a restoration of the monarchy, a military dictatorship or a Bolshevik Workers' State, but rather a moderate parliamentary democracy that enjoyed a high level of popular support. That the overwhelming majority of Germans voted for the parties of the 'Weimar Coalition' in the elections to the National Assembly in January 1919 – the first national elections since 1912 – demonstrates a broad popular support for the type of moderate parliamentary democracy proposed by the MSPD and the liberals. Even amongst the bastions of the old imperial system – the army and the civil service – the majority were willing to accept and work within the new system. Many in the officer corps took a pragmatic view, recognizing that a broad-based liberal parliamentary republic was the only means of preventing Germany sliding into anarchy and civil war, and that defeat and the collapse of the monarchy offered opportunities for military reform. Similarly, within the bureaucracy, conservative and monarchist forces were relatively reconciled to the new moderate republicanism and a 'functional loyalty', if not love, for the republic developed over time. Indeed, the Prussian civil service was instrumental in defeating the Kapp Putsch, and the Foreign Office rapidly recognized that Germany's best interests were serviced by working in collaboration with the republic rather than in opposing it. Similarly, the public outrage that followed the murder of Rathenau and the support for the republic during the Ruhr Crisis suggests that commitment to the new democracy was more than skin deep.

2

THE STRUGGLE FOR MODERATION: WEIMAR POLITICAL CULTURE

In many ways the difficult circumstances in which the Weimar Republic came into being set the tone for its later development. Born out of a humiliating military defeat and a traumatic period of revolution and political violence, the proclamation of the republic on 9 November 1918 was itself an *ad hoc* move, an attempt to take ownership of the revolution and divert the revolutionary fervour of the people from a more radical course. Unwanted and unloved even by those who had proclaimed its existence, it was a 'republic without republicans' which suffered from a lack of legitimacy. It was able to muster temporary support from those who regarded it as the least-worst option for Germany, but it was never able to elicit any real affection or commitment from its citizens. On top of this, the political ruptures of the 'years of crisis' left German politics and society deeply and irreconcilably divided and, combined with the flaws and compromises inherent in the new constitution, doomed it from the start.

This is the interpretation of Weimar democracy that has largely been favoured by historians for much of the past 80 years. While there is much truth in this – war and revolution, not to mention the deeply divided society and authoritarian political culture of the empire, did bequeath a bitter legacy to the republic, while the constitutional settlement that emerged in 1919 was a far from perfect compromise between differing visions of the new state – it does not tell the whole story. In particular, recent research which has ranged beyond the traditional focus on political parties and Reichstag debates has called into question our long-held notion of a 'republic without republicans', to argue that what emerged during the Weimar period was a distinct political culture (or cultures) that, at least until the onset of the Great Depression, proved surprisingly robust.

THE WEIMAR CONSTITUTION

The Weimar constitution was intended to embody advanced principles of democracy and borrowed heavily from the experience of Britain, France and the United States. At the same time, it sought to provide a degree of continuity with the past. As such, it was a compromise between advanced liberal–democratic thinking and a more traditionalist and conservative political culture that had been inherited from the empire. At the same time, the experience of the November Revolution left many fearful of mob rule and convinced that a strong guiding hand was needed, especially in times of national crisis. Thus the framers of the Weimar constitution sought to devise a document that would reconcile 'a truculent bourgeoisie and an insurgent working class, both of which had been alienated from the state by the war and its aftermath.'[1] The result was a state based on the notion of class compromise that sought to incorporate the popular demand for democracy and freedom, while at the same time protecting the vested interests of important groups within German society.

Unlike the constitution of 1871, which was 'a contract among monarchs', the Weimar constitution began with a declaration that power ultimately resided with the people. Like the empire, the republic had a bicameral parliament made up of a directly elected lower house (the Reichstag) and an indirectly elected upper house (the Reichsrat) selected by the elected assemblies of each of the federal states (*Länder*). The Reichstag was elected every four years by all Germans over the age of 20 through a system of proportional representation. This meant that political parties were 'granted seats in proportion to the percentage of the popular vote they received.'[2] However, this electoral system also meant that it was difficult for

The heart of Weimar democracy: the Reichstag in session, August 1927
(Bundesarchiv, Bild 102-04640 / CC-BY-SA).

any single political party to gain an overall majority in parliament, making the formation of weak coalition governments the norm (there were 20 different governments in the 15-year lifespan of the republic, ten of them between January 1919 and May 1924, and only three of which could command a majority in the Reichstag). At the same time, it also enabled small single-interest or extremist parties, many of whom were fundamentally opposed to the republican system of government, to gain representation in the Reichstag and hinder the work of the government.

The head of government, the Chancellor, was appointed by the President, but it was expected that he command a majority in parliament as parliamentary approval was needed to pass legislation. Furthermore, while the Chancellor chose his cabinet, this was subject to approval by the Reichstag, and the Chancellor and his ministers were required to resign if they lost a vote of no confidence. Legislation could be proposed by any member of the Reichstag and was passed by a simple majority vote in the lower house. These bills were then passed for approval to the upper house. The Reichsrat had the power to veto legislation, although the lower house could overrule the veto if a two-thirds majority of deputies voted in favour of doing so. Thus, while theoretically the *Länder* had little power over national legislation, the fragmented nature of Weimar party politics meant that, in effect, bills vetoed by the upper house frequently died. In unusual circumstances (if the proposed legislation was particularly controversial or would have a serious impact on foreign affairs) the President could decree that a proposed bill should be presented to the public as a referendum before it could be passed into law. Constitutional amendments could be proposed by any member of the lower house in the same way as other legislation, but required a clear two-thirds majority in the Reichstag to be passed.

While the Chancellor was responsible for the day-to-day running of the country, the ceremonial and political roles of head of state were exercised by the President. Most politicians on the Right were wary about giving too much power to parliament, and the presidency was therefore intended as a political counterbalance to the Reichstag. The President of the Republic was directly elected by universal suffrage for a seven-year term (the exception was the first president, Friedrich Ebert, who was elected by the National Assembly rather than by a popular poll due to the precarious political situation, and died before his seven-year term had expired), and held extensive executive powers above and beyond the legislature. The president had the final say on military matters as supreme commander of the armed forces, held the power to convene and dissolve parliament and (very much as the Kaiser had done) had powers of appointment and dismissal over the Chancellor and the Reich government. Furthermore, Article 48 of the constitution allowed the President to suspend civil rights and rule by decree in the event of 'public order and security' being 'seriously disturbed or endangered', and to order the use of force to compel state governments to fulfil their obligations under the constitution or federal law.[3] Any German citizen aged 35 or above was eligible to stand for election as president as long as they were not a member of the Reichstag at the time. In the event of parliament losing confidence in the President, the Reichstag could force a referendum on his 'recall' before the expiration of his term in office. To do this a vote of no confidence had to be passed by a two-thirds majority in the lower house (Article 43).

As well as setting out the institutional structure by which the republic was governed, the Weimar constitution also enumerated the rights of German citizens and attempted to meet the demands of the people for legislation to offset some of the social and economic disparities in German society. The constitution established a Supreme Court on the American model, which was supposed to be above politics and to which citizens could appeal in the event of disputes with the state. It also guaranteed certain fundamental civil rights – equality before the law (Article 109), the right to free speech and assembly (Articles 114, 118 and 123), equality for women (Article 109), economic justice (Article 151) and the right to strike (Article 159). It also established a welfare state (Article 161) that took the system of unemployment benefit, sickness insurance and old-age pensions, first introduced by Bismarck in the 1880s, even further and, for the first time, enshrined in law the principle that it was the role of the state to assist the less fortunate in society (a principle which would be built upon by the republic's post-war successor). Primary education was made compulsory and the Reich government, state assemblies and local communities had joint responsibility for ensuring its provision. The franchise was extended to include all women over the age of 20 and give them parity of voting rights with men, a year before this was achieved in the United States, while in Britain and France women could not vote on an equal footing with men until 1928 and 1944 respectively.

The Weimar constitution achieved much that was ahead of its time: it established a parliamentary democracy and introduced a welfare state, guaranteed fundamental human rights and attempted to address some of the political and social problems that had bedevilled Germany under the *Kaiserreich*. But it failed to heal the deep divisions within German society: industry, land and public services were left unreformed and in private hands, while the armed forces, civil service and universities continued to be dominated by the conservative upper and upper-middle-classes whose commitment to the new republic was lukewarm at best. This can be blamed on the fact that the constitution had, by necessity, to be a compromise between differing political forces and sought to provide stability and security for the German people as whole. Those on the Left could not push for more radical social and economic reforms without risking prolonging the violence and uncertainty that had gripped Germany since November 1918. Nevertheless, the republic's founders were, to some extent, guilty of wishful thinking: 'the SPD leadership hoped that structural change would follow in the wake of legitimate constitutional reform'[4], but in the event little fundamental change was accomplished without state intervention to assist in breaking down vested interests in big business, the landed estates, the army and the judiciary. The exception that proved the rule was Prussia, which became an unlikely bastion of republicanism for much of the Weimar period. While at a national level many imperial officials remained in post, the same could not be said in Prussia. Under Social Democrat Minister President Otto Braun, and Interior Minister Carl Severing, 'regional and local government . . . saw many monarchist officials replaced by republicans . . . the police force reformed, illicit military and paramilitary activities suppressed and all manner of right-wing extremists pursued with increasing conviction.'[5]

Furthermore, the new republic suffered from a certain degree of constitutional uncertainty – did ultimate power lie with the representative assembly of the people or the popularly elected head of state? The liberal intellectuals who had formulated the constitution had attempted to create a political system that reconciled their ideal of a democratic *Volksstaat* (citizen state) with the conservative desire for a state where power was concentrated in the hands of a strong executive. The result was a system with a 'strong' presidency that was, in theory at least, tempered by parliamentary checks and balances. This tension between these 'two radically different visions' has been see as 'the underlying fault line of the Weimar Republic.'[6] Although initially there was thought to be no contradiction here, with hindsight it is easy to see in the system of proportional representation used to elect the Reichstag, or in the emergency powers given to the President under Article 48, the roots of Weimar's later political fragmentation and slide into dictatorship. Yet, whatever its flaws, the electoral system was decided upon for the best of motives, with the intention of making parliamentary elections as democratic as possible. Similarly, it is easy to detect echoes of the imperial authoritarianism of the past or the totalitarian tyranny of the future in Article 48, but it is important to note that it was not the provision of emergency powers themselves that led to dictatorship, but the method and spirit in which they were used. Article 48 was used frequently during the republic's 'years of the crisis' as a means of enacting legislation quickly and safeguarding the republic on occasions when the ordinary legislative process was too cumbersome – indeed, these powers were used no fewer than 63 times during the Ruhr Crisis and hyperinflation of 1923 alone. But, when invoked by President Ebert during this period, Article 48 was used in the way in which those who wrote it had intended: as a short-term measure to defend the republic and the German people at a time of public disorder. However, when the President was a figure who was, at best, ambivalent towards the very idea of republicanism and democracy, as was the case after 1925, Article 48 became instead a means to circumvent the Reichstag and revive the authoritarian political culture of the old imperial elite.

THE WEIMAR PARTY SYSTEM

The political culture of the Weimar Republic, like German society as a whole, was deeply fragmented and dominated by several hostile subcultures based on ideology, class and confession. All of Weimar's political parties fitted into one or another of these with little or no crossing of boundaries. Although the language of social unity was often deployed, and despite the fact that more than one of these factions aspired to become a *Volkspartei* (people's party) that would transcend traditional loyalties, each party remained wedded to its particular vision of state and society and drew its support mainly from established social milieus, making little effort to expand its appeal beyond their core constituencies. At the same time, many of them regarded the new republic as a temporary polity, a *Notbau* (temporary construction) as Friedrich Meinecke

Colin Storer

called it[7], which would sooner or later be replaced by a new political system based on their own ideological vision of what that state should be.

Despite the fact that most German political parties re-organized themselves in the winter of 1918–19, there was considerable continuity in the party system between imperial and republican Germany. Of the nine main political parties operating under the Weimar Republic, five were identical to or had evolved out of the main political factions of the Imperial Reichstag (see Appendix 1). Many of the individuals who came to dominate Weimar politics had entered the Reichstag before the war and enjoyed political careers spanning the Wilhelmine and republican periods (Ebert had entered the Reichstag in 1912 after over a decade in local politics in Bremen; Scheidemann had been active in politics since 1883 and was elected to the Reichstag in 1903, the same year as Matthias Erzberger; and Gustav Stresemann was elected as a representative of the National Liberal Party in 1907). This provided a high degree of continuity between the political classes of the empire and the republic.

Nevertheless, the experience of war and revolution had a transformative effect on German politics and society, breaking traditional political loyalties and forging new ones. As we saw in Chapter 1, the war and revolution led to a split in the labour movement that transformed the SPD from the sole political representative of the German working class into just one of three (two from 1922) political parties espousing Social Democratic and Marxist ideals. Similarly, although the reordering of the political establishment in 1918 initially seemed to offer an opportunity for the two wings of nineteenth-century German liberalism to overcome their differences and forge a united liberal party, differing visions of the state and the annexationist position of the leader of the National Liberals, Gustav Stresemann, ultimately meant that the 'bourgeois centre' entered the Weimar period even more fractured than it had been under the empire. And while the various parties of the Wilhelmine Right had more success in overcoming their differences and forming a single political grouping, the revolution and collapse of the old order only served to intensify the process of radicalization that had already begun during the war.

The SPD entered the Weimar period as the strongest of Germany's political parties with a clear ideological vision and an established organizational base. By the early twentieth century, the SPD was the largest political party in the world with over 1 million members and, despite the emergence of two rival Marxist parties after 1917, it carried over much of this support into the Weimar period as the result of a working class long socialized and 'indoctrinated' to see the Social Democrats as their natural political champions. The SPD were consistently the single largest party in the Reichstag between 1912 and 1932, and their experience of wartime cooperation with the state and 'bourgeois' parties stood them in good stead after 1918 as champions of the new republican order. Nevertheless, the commitment to an orthodox Marxist ideology meant that even many within the SPD, the party that had done more than any other to bring the republic into being, saw the liberal–democratic order as merely a step on the road towards a Utopian socialist future. Its status as the champion of the working classes caused the party to always see itself as an outsider, and this prevented it from collaborating fully with those who did not share its ideological position. For this reason it withdrew into opposition in 1923 and remained there until 1928. This meant that the largest party in the Reichstag was more often than not outside the governing coalition (even if it did extend its informal support or tolerance to the government of the day), thus weakening the government and denying the SPD the chance to gain credit among voters for the relative stability and prosperity of Weimar's middle years.

Elsewhere on the Left, the more radical independent socialists (USPD) lost their direction and cohesion after the war and foundation of the republic. United only in their opposition to socialist support for the war, once peace came they lost much of their *raison d'être*. The formation of the German Communist Party (KPD) highlighted the ideological divisions within the USPD and, in October 1920, the party split and the majority joined the Communists, while the rump of the party limped on for another two years before rejoining the SPD.

Much more ideologically and organizationally robust was the Communist Party. From its inception, the KPD remained fundamentally opposed to parliamentary democracy and wedded to the goals of bringing about revolution and the establishment of the communist Utopia. Not only the bourgeois parties but also the 'reformists' and 'opportunists' in the moderate Left were branded as class enemies, and anyone who deviated from the party line (as dictated from Moscow) was ruthlessly purged from the party. Nevertheless, in the first years of the republic there was considerable division within the KPD over what tactics would best achieve their ends. The influence of those within the party who favoured violent revolution was still strong, as demonstrated by the March Action of 1921 and the uprisings in Thuringia, Saxony and the Ruhr in 1923, but the KPD was increasingly under pressure from its Soviet masters to forego direct action and engage in a united front with the SPD while at the same time pressing for greater socialization. This became the official party line with the appointment of Ernst Thälmann as leader in 1925, an event which brought the German Communist Party firmly under the control of Stalin. From then on the party pursued a policy of the 'concentration of forces', which implied 'awaiting a future struggle . . . whilst proclaiming itself not reconciled to the republic, continuing to contest elections with some success and playing an opposition role in the Reichstag, as well as working inside the trade unions.'[8] Nevertheless, this failed to gain them a mass following, especially as the violent tactics of the early 1920s had alienated the majority of the working classes. The KPD's core constituency remained the unskilled working class and the ranks of the unemployed, and they signally failed to reach out to the majority of the German working class (even during the worst days of the Depression when their predictions of the inevitable collapse of capitalism seemed to be coming true, the Communists still lagged behind the SPD and the Nazis in terms of electoral support). This, together with the inflexibility imposed from Moscow, severely hampered the KPD's ability to either capitalize on the opportunities presented by the Great Depression or to mobilize resistance to the Nazi threat after 1929.

If the political Left remained divided between two parties that espoused radically different methods of achieving the same ends (the liberation of the working class and the creation of a socialist society), the centre ground was even more fragmented. An attempt in 1918

Political fragmentation: Communist, Nazi, Catholic Centre, Socialist and other campaigners display their party's election posters during the Reichstag elections of July 1932 (Bundesarchiv, Bild 102-03497A / Unknown / CC-BY-SA).

to merge the two main liberal parties of the imperial era came to nothing, and German liberalism remained divided on roughly the same lines as it had been during the *Kaiserreich*. On the one hand, the German Democratic Party (DDP) espoused a belief in progressive social policy and support for the republic combined with a desire for a more centralized state and a commitment to revise the Treaty of Versailles. On the other hand, the German People's Party (DVP) was more ambivalent about the republic, initially favouring a constitutional monarchy instead, and championed unrestricted private enterprise. Both these parties competed for middle-class votes with the Catholic Centre Party, whose internal ideological divisions were more than made up for by its strong confessional identity which gave it broader electoral support, and the right-wing DNVP. As the economic and political situation worsened in the late 1920s, the liberal parties found it increasingly difficult to survive as their traditional supporters abandoned them in favour of parties who offered more radical solutions to Germany's problems. The death of Gustav Stresemann in 1929 left the DVP leaderless and bereft of its greatest electoral asset, while the defection of key supporters to the host of middle-class splinter parties that emerged in the late 1920s (the Business Party, the *Deutsche Bauernpartei*, etc.) forced the DDP to rebrand itself as the more nationalist State Party in 1930, in an attempt to stave off electoral eclipse.

In contrast, the political Right seemed much more cohesive and clear in its goals. For most of the Weimar period, right-wing opposition to the republic was focused on the German National People's Party (DNVP), an amalgamation of the old Conservative and Free Conservative parties with the Pan-German League, the Christian Social Party and the racist *Deutschvölkische Partei*. Yet although the Right managed to carry out the kind of merger that eluded the liberals, the DNVP remained deeply divided in terms of both ideology and support, encompassing every shade of right-wing anti-republican opinion from monarchist landowners and army officers to anti-socialist businessmen, lower-middle-class nationalists, conservative Christians and racist extremists. Indeed, the old Conservatives under Count von Westarp only joined the DNVP reluctantly, and maintained their own separate organization throughout the Weimar period (breaking away completely in 1930 to form the Conservative People's Party, KVP), while the various nationalist clubs and societies who made up the majority of party activists resisted any attempt to impose central control on them. It has been suggested that what held the DNVP together was its commitment to a restoration of the monarchy[9], but it is perhaps more accurate to see the unifying principle behind the party as a shared hostility towards the republican system. Although the party's programme explicitly called for the 'renewal of the monarchy erected by the Hohenzollern', there were also many within the DNVP who were as ambivalent towards monarchism as they were towards the republic.

As the second-largest party in the Reichstag after 1924, the DNVP was divided between those who were prepared to constitute a loyal opposition within the republican system and those who remained implacably opposed to democracy. Although it joined the government twice (in 1925 and 1927), the DNVP was engaged in an internal struggle between these factions throughout the middle years of the republic, which was only resolved with the election of the dictatorial press magnate Alfred Hugenberg as party chairman in 1928.[10] Under Hugenberg the party shifted towards the Right and made the disastrous decision to bring the Nazis into a 'National Opposition' against the Young Plan, a move which ultimately only served to improve the fortunes of the NSDAP who increasingly picked up support from those who had once given their loyalty to the Nationalists.

Even further to the Right than the DNVP, and even more implacably opposed to the republic, were the host of Nationalist and anti-Semitic (*völkische*) groups that emerged in the wake of the war and revolution. Many had their origins in pre-war nationalist pressure groups such as the Pan-German League or the wartime Fatherland Party, but others emerged in the wake of the revolution to espouse a radical new vision of state and society that blended extreme nationalism or Prussian conservatism with a vague socialism based on the comradeship of the trenches. There were at least 15 of these groups in Munich alone in 1919, and throughout the 1920s these societies waged 'a broad cultural war' against 'the socialist and republican Left' through mass demonstrations and political agitation.[11] Out of this welter of anti-republican extremist societies emerged a group that, by 1933, could genuinely claim to be a mass movement.

Founded in Munich in 1919 the *Deutsche Arbeiterpartei* (German Workers Party or DAP) sought to bring nationalism and anti-Semitism to the working masses by combining them with an ill-defined socialism. It was soon joined by Adolf Hitler, an embittered Austrian who had fought in a Bavarian regiment during the war and subsequently been ordered by military intelligence to keep an eye on the activities of groups such as the DAP. Under Hitler's influence the party added the words 'National Socialist' to its name and adopted a 25-point programme that called for the radical revision of the Treaty of Versailles, the establishment of a strong central authority under a single leader and the implementation of radical socialist, corporatist and racialist policies.[12] By 1921 Hitler had displaced

Anton Drexler as leader, and the party had acquired its own newspaper, the *Völkischer Beobachter*, and developed a paramilitary wing mostly made up of former *Freikorps* men dubbed the *Sturmabteilung* (Storm Detachment or SA). Nevertheless, for much of the Weimar period the NSDAP remained a marginal and regional force within Weimar politics. Despite a strong following in Bavaria, by 1924 the Nazis could only contest national elections as part of the *Völkischer-Block*, a short-lived anti-Semitic electoral alliance between the Nazis, the German Racial Freedom Party (*Deutschvölkische Freiheitspartei* or DVFP) and the National Socialist Freedom Movement (NSFB). Even after Hitler's release from prison in December 1924 and the refounding of the party in 1925 with a commitment to achieve power through legal means, National Socialist electoral performance continued to be poor. They attracted little support during Weimar's middle period and won only 12 seats in the Reichstag elections of 1928. What dramatically altered their fortunes was the onset of the Great Depression. This new economic crisis allowed the Nazis to present themselves as a radical alternative to the more established parties who seemed unable to bring rising unemployment under control, and they picked up support from both unemployed workers and middle-class voters who feared loss of status and a communist takeover. By 1932 the party had displaced the SPD as the largest single party in the Reichstag, and was being considered as a possible coalition partner by the right-wing Chancellor Franz von Papen.

Weimar therefore had a deeply divided political culture in which several of the foremost political parties were fundamentally opposed to democracy itself. The smooth functioning of the democratic system was made even more difficult by the deep ideological divisions and strong class and cultural identities of the various political parties, which only made finding consensus and common ground more difficult – a serious problem in a political system where coalition government was the norm. Nevertheless, as we shall see, these divisions were not as insurmountable as it is often thought. Although some groups never became reconciled with the republican order, during Weimar's middle years it was possible for different parties to overcome their differences and work together, while even some of those who were opposed to democracy became prepared to engage in constructive opposition.

EXTRA-PARLIAMENTARY POLITICS

Weimar Germany was a deeply divided but also a highly politicized society. The highly fragmented nature of German politics and the strong class and confessional loyalties that intersected with political affiliations tended to blur the boundaries between the political and non-political. Under the Weimar Republic seemingly ordinary and innocuous acts could take on a political significance, especially during periods of heightened tension in the early 1920s and after 1929. Furthermore, despite (or perhaps because of) the horrors of the Great War and the trauma of defeat, Weimar Germany remained a highly militarized society, and armed uniformed militias were a signif icant feature of Weimar political culture, especially once the republic entered its final, terminal, period of crisis and instability after 1929.

The parliamentary caucus was only a small part of the organization of each of Weimar's political parties. This tends to be true of all political parties, but was particularly the case in Germany. The federal nature of the Weimar state meant that each party had to maintain a large and complex organizational structure designed to enable the group to mobilize support and contest elections at municipal, regional, state and national levels. At the same time, the strong ideological, class and confessional identities of many of Weimar's political parties meant that they had extensive parallel organizations designed to mobilize supporters. These included sporting, social and educational groups, as well as youth organizations and paramilitary 'defence' leagues. This was particularly true of parties like the SPD and Centre, whose identities were rooted in particular sections of the community and who played a role above and beyond that of mere political representation for their constituents.

This was by no means a new development. The experience of persecution under Bismarck in the 1870s and 1880s had been an important factor in the development of both working class and Catholic identity, and the SPD had made extensive use of social organizations as a means of circumventing the Anti-Socialist Law.

In many ways, the struggle against state persecution enabled the Social Democrats to develop a 'parallel society for industrial workers . . . within which Marxism became a sort of secular religion lived out in daily life both in the workplace and in private life.'[13] Likewise, the Centre Party's status as the political wing of German Catholicism meant that it maintained strong links with the Catholic trade union movement, churches and youth groups that blurred the lines between the political and non-political. And while these two parties might have had the strongest ties to extra-parliamentary organizations, they were far from being alone. The DDP also had strong links with the liberal Hirsch–Dunker trade unions, while the KPD and Nazis had their own youth organizations that helped to ensure ideological uniformity and foster party loyalty.

At the same time, the polarization of society and the violent political clashes of the 'years of crisis' bequeathed to the republic new kinds of political activism. After 1918, politics increasingly moved out of parliament and closed political meetings and onto the streets, as the middle classes adopted the political tactics of the labour movement – public demonstrations, strike action, etc. – in order to make their feelings felt. Similarly, in the chaotic political situation of 1918–19, supporters of both the Left and Right had voluntarily taken up arms to defend their vision of state and society from the perceived threats of 'Bolshevism' and counter-revolutionary monarchism. At the same time, the 'myth of war experience' was used to legitimize violence, and led to a glorification of combat amongst both veterans and those too young to have seen action. Political violence came to be seen as both a rite of passage and a means of proving their masculinity for many young men, while membership of a paramilitary body provided them with a sense of belonging. All these factors led to the development of the Combat Leagues (*Wehrverbände*), paramilitary organizations affiliated with Weimar's political parties that acted as instruments for exerting political pressure on opponents through the symbolic occupation of public space and violent confrontation.[14]

Growing out of the *Freikorps* movement, the anti-republican rightwing Combat Leagues were Weimar's oldest and most dangerous paramilitary organizations. Foremost among these was the Nationalist veterans association, the *Stahlhelm*. From about 2,000 members spread across 30 local chapters in 1920, this organization grew to over 100,000 members and 300 chapters by 1924 as its ranks were swelled by former *Freikorps* men. It also became increasingly political and, although it maintained its independence from any single party, under the leadership of Franz Seldte and Theodor Duesterberg it developed links with the conservative DNVP, campaigned against the Young Plan and joined the right-wing Harzburg Front in 1931.

The murders of high-ranking Cabinet ministers such as Erzberger and Rathenau, and the lukewarm response of the courts (see pages 45–48), led some on the moderate Left to the conclusion that the only way that the republic could be defended was for grass-roots activists to organize themselves into their own paramilitary defence force. Thus the Social Democrat, Otto Horsing, together with party colleagues and representatives from the Centre and DDP founded the *Reichsbanner Schwarz–Rot–Gold* in February 1924 as an unofficial republican defence force. This had its roots in the republican self defence units which had been formed in April 1923 to oppose any attempt by either the Communists or Nationalists to take advantage of the instability caused by the Ruhr Crisis and hyperinflation. However, the *Reichsbanner* was founded with a wider political aim, 'to finally allow the republicans to assert the kind of presence in the public sphere that for many years only their enemies had commanded.'[15] Ostensibly unaffiliated with any single political party, this group nevertheless rapidly became the paramilitary wing of the Weimar Coalition with strong links to the socialists and the trade unions and, by 1930, was more or less the paramilitary arm of the SPD. At its height in 1926 it had over 3 million members, and from its foundation until it was disbanded by the Nazis in 1933 it never had fewer than one million active members, making it Germany's largest paramilitary force.

In response to the formation of the *Reicshbanner*, the KPD formed its own paramilitary wing, the *Roter Frontkämpferbund* or Red Front Fighters League (RFB). This largely grew out of the so-called 'Proletarian Hundreds', armed formations of workers raised by the SPD and KPD in Thuringia and Saxony during the crisis of 1923. By

1925 it had a membership of 40,000 divided between 558 local branches in cities throughout Germany. Although it maintained that it was independent of the Communist Party, the RFB helped to protect communist politicians and meetings from attack from right-wing thugs, and played a key recruiting role for the KPD. By 1927 it had 111,000 members, but the figure increased further as the Depression set in and political disputes were increasingly played out in the streets.

These left-wing paramilitary groups were in many ways a response to the political violence unleashed by the radical Right. In the early days of the republic such attacks came from the *Freikorps* and the *Feme*, but after 1929 right-wing political violence mainly came from one source: the National Socialist *Sturmabteilung* (SA). Founded in 1920 as the Nazi's sporting club, the 'Brownshirts' (as they became known due to their distinctive uniform of army-surplus tunics intended for soldiers serving in Africa and the Middle East) were originally intended to be a uniformed guard for high-ranking Nazi leaders, but as time went on it became increasingly apparent that it was politically useful to have a gang of thugs who could intimidate opponents and respond forcefully to those who did not agree with the Nazis' message. The dissolution of the *Freikorps* swelled the ranks of the SA in the early 1920s, and former regular soldiers and *Freikorps*-men such as Hermann Ehrhardt, Ernst Röhm and Franz Pfeffer helped transform the SA from a disparate group of 6,000 men in 1926 to a disciplined force of 60,000 by 1930. However, as the membership of the SA grew so did its independence and influence. Always the refuge of the most violent and socialistic members of the Nazi Party, the SA was deeply unhappy about the strategy of attempting to gain power through legal means, but tension was lessened somewhat by Hitler's decision to blend political activism with paramilitary violence after the elections of September 1930.

A REPUBLIC WITHOUT REPUBLICANS?

As we have seen, there was considerable continuity between the political parties and personalities of the empire and republic. Weimar's political class was largely homogenous in terms of age, education, political experience and social background, which meant that despite their ideological differences, German politicians of the Weimar era worked surprisingly well together. Furthermore, while the electoral system did lead to a high turnover of governments, the ostensible weakness of Weimar's proportional representation was, to some extent, offset by the continuity of individuals making up successive cabinets: over a period of 15 years and 19 different cabinets the 223 ministerial posts were filled by just 79 politicians, of whom 19 per cent held office five times or more. Otto Gessler (DDP) became defence minister on the removal of Noske in March 1920 and remained in post until June 1928, serving in 13 different cabinets regardless of the party affiliation of the Chancellor. Heinrich Brauns (Centre) had a similar ministerial career, and Gustav Stresemann (DVP) served twice as chancellor in 1923 before becoming a successful foreign minister until his death in 1929. This indicates that under normal circumstances Weimar's political class were prepared to compromise and developed ways to work within the system, leading to a degree of continuity in policy, at least until the final crisis of 1930–32.[16]

Moreover, if we take levels of political participation as a measure, it becomes clear that Germans were not as alienated from the republican system as is often thought. Weimar's citizens joined political parties and associated social, youth and paramilitary organizations in large numbers, and were involved in various forms of political activism. Electoral turnout under the empire had been high, and it continued to be so under the republic, with 60 to 80 per cent of the population voting in both regional and national polls. This should be compared with electoral turnout under the post-war Federal Republic, which only exceeded these proportions in 1972, or the 61 per cent turnout in the UK general election of 2010. This suggests that German voters in the early twentieth century were no less politically engaged or more alienated from the democratic system than their post-war descendants or modern Britons, and indicates that, rather than being a politically immature nation with weak democratic institutions and traditions, Weimar Germany in fact had a thriving political culture in which contested elections and intensive electioneering were the norm. Rather than being estranged from or indifferent towards the republic, the vast majority of the German people 'positively participated in the republic and to a greater or lesser degree . . . reaped the benefits of the welfare state.'[17]

Similarly, we must question the persistent assertion that the majority of those who participated in the democratic process and a sizable number of those who openly declared their support for the republic were fair-weather friends, so-called 'rational republicans' (*Vernunftrepublikaner*) who supported the democratic state for want of anything better. That there was no public appetite for either a restoration of the monarchy or a more radical left-wing state was amply demonstrated by the overwhelming support for the moderates during the November Revolution and subsequent elections to the National Assembly. This was underlined repeatedly during the 'years of crisis' by the lack of popular support for violent attacks on the republic and its politicians from both the Left and the Right. The assassinations of Matthias Erzberger and Walter Rathenau in particular provoked a tide of outrage and revulsion and led to mass demonstrations in support of the republic. As the aristocratic diarist Count Harry Kessler noted on observing a pro-government demonstration in Berlin's Lustgarten the day after Rathenau's murder: 'the bitterness against Rathenau's assassins is profound and genuine. So is adherence to the republic, a far more deeply rooted emotion than pre-war monarchical "patriotism" was.'[18] And it was not just the faceless masses who demonstrated a more genuine commitment to democracy than has sometimes been suggested. Even amongst the ranks of the army, civil service, judiciary and big business, who have traditionally been seen as at best ambivalent towards the republic, there were some important and influential individuals – such as the state secretary for the foreign office Count von Maltzan and the industrialists Peter Klöckner and Paul Silverberg – who argued that the republican settlement was the best deal for Germany. Finally, the fact that even in 1932 the pro-republican *Reichsbanner* was the largest of Germany's paramilitary associations with over one million members indicates that even at its darkest hour the republic was able to muster considerable support from its citizens.

At the same time, it is clear that the oft-repeated assertion that Weimar lacked legitimacy in the eyes of its citizens and failed to develop unifying myths and symbols with which the population could identify, needs to be reassessed. While it is true that for many on the Right the republic was seen as fundamentally 'un-German', a foreign imposition, inspired by internationalist political creeds such as socialism and completely alien to Germany with its long tradition of monarchy[19], its supporters were able to counter such assertions with their own appeals to German history and tradition. In an interesting inversion of the *Sonderweg*, some republican commentators saw Bismarck's empire as 'a withered side branch on the tree of our people'; while as the heir to the liberal nationalism of 1848 the Weimar Republic was 'a fundamentally legitimate and appropriately national form of state'.[20] Furthermore, the authorities consistently sought to link the republic with 'events of national, historical and cultural importance' as part of a 'deliberate strategy to embed the young democracy into a tradition of German culture and history.'[21]

Despite the long insistence that the Weimar Republic lacked a political symbolism of its own which left it at a disadvantage *vis-à-vis* its conservative Nationalist and Communist opponents, the republic was in fact better at developing such symbols than the imperial regime it had replaced. After 1870 Bismarck was personally indifferent towards the creation of national symbols, being more concerned with enacting legislation to create practical national institutions such as a national bank or a single currency. The black–red–white colours of the Hohenzollern monarchy had only been formally adopted as the German flag in 1896, there were no nationwide national holidays and the empire never managed to agree on a national anthem.

In contrast, the republican authorities acted quickly to address the issue of shared national symbols for the new state, establishing the federal art office (*Reichskunstwart*) at the Ministry of the Interior in October 1919 with the express task of replacing the old symbols of the monarchical state (everything from the national flag and coats of arms to coinage and postage stamps to national monuments and the staging of state occasions) with those more appropriate for the democratic republic. Like the framing of the constitution this was a difficult balancing act between continuity and innovation: on the one hand the new democratic republic wanted to distance itself from the trappings of the authoritarian empire, while on the other it recognized that tradition and precedent play an important role in legitimizing such symbols. To this end, the German eagle, which became the state symbol of the republic, was reminiscent of the heraldic symbol of the Prussian monarchy; the black–red–gold flag of the liberal revolutionaries of 1848, which had connotations of both democracy and nationalism, was adopted as the national colours; and the *Deutschlandlied* (with words written in 1841 set to a tune written in 1797) was officially recognized as the national anthem in 1922. These decisions were not uncontroversial and were the subject (like almost everything else) of bitter arguments between the Left and the Right, but the very fact that the republic treated so seriously the issue of finding national symbols that expressed the ethos of the state and with which it citizens could identify, demonstrates that they were not as blind to the necessity for 'symbols and fantasy' in politics as some contemporaries and historians have suggested.[22]

Meanwhile, under the auspices of Edwin Redslob, the *Reichskunstwart* worked hard to develop a framework of national symbolism and political theatre that would foster a sense of community and togetherness, both seen as hallmarks of the republican state.[23] Through a number of set pieces of national theatre heavy with republican symbolism – such as the official funerals of Walther Rathenau (1922), President Ebert (1925) and Gustav Stresemann (1929), the inauguration of President Hindenburg (1925) and the annual Constitution Day celebrations – the authorities sought to provide focal points for a new form of republican patriotism based on notions of 'personal sacrifice for the sake of democratic principles and ideals rather than on race.'[24] Despite the fact that this was never officially adopted as a public holiday – the Reichsrat approved the measure, but it was never passed by the Reichstag – Constitution Day (11 August) became increasingly significant as an opportunity to celebrate republican aims and ideals. From modest beginnings in 1921, this evolved into a genuinely popular expression of republican patriotism that involved widespread social events as well as official ceremonies. One of the highlights of the celebrations in Berlin was a torchlit parade through the city centre consisting of the *Reichsbanner*, the trade unions, the German Association of Civil Servants,

Republican militarism? The massed ranks of the Reichsbanner march through the Brandenburg Gate in Berlin on the tenth anniversary of the Weimar Constitution, 11 August 1929 (Bundesarchiv, Bild 102-08216 / Unknown / CC-BY-SA).

the Jewish War Veteran Organization, local choirs and other civic groups, numbering 12,000 in 1927 and rising to 30,000 a year later.[25] For the celebration of the tenth anniversary of the adoption of the constitution in 1929, hundreds of thousands of people turned out to mark the occasion in Berlin alone while the provinces reported similar crowds.[26] So established had the occasion become that even though the celebrations had to be scaled down due to public spending cuts during the Depression, Constitution Day remained a fixture of the public calendar until the Nazis abolished it.

Thus, the 1920s saw the emergence of a type of republican patriotism founded on notions of community, togetherness and self-sacrifice. This recognized the battle for national unification of the nineteenth century and the more recent violent struggles for democracy, as well as the hardships and losses of the First World War. Yet it also suffered from the fact that it had to try to 'render abstractions perceptible to the senses.'[27] This was a difficult but not impossible task and one to which the republican authorities and parties of the Weimar Coalition responded with alacrity. The establishment of the federal art expert shows that they recognized the importance of symbols in popularizing this new kind of nationalism, and that they understood the need for both continuity and change in designing such symbols for the new state. At the same time, the political theatre of great national occasions such as the state funerals of Ebert and Stresemann, or the annual Constitution Day celebrations, provided a forum for the display of these symbols to a mass audience who, on the whole, responded more positively than has traditionally been recognized.

Similarly, we need to revise the notion that German democracy was weak and ineffective, blighted by a lack of democratic institutions and traditions. Although the power and influence of the Reichstag and the political parties had been limited during the imperial era, Germans had nevertheless had nearly 50 years' experience of universal male suffrage and participatory politics. During this time, Germany had developed 'genuinely competitive and representative political parties'[28] and a political class who continued to dominate German politics into the Weimar period. Until the onset of the Great Depression, the Reichstag and other institutions of the democratic state mostly functioned well. What is more, most of Weimar's citizens proved happy to, at best, demonstrate their active support for the republican system of government and, at worst, work constructively within its framework. If we take membership of political organizations and electoral turnout as measures of democratic health, Weimar Germany looks much more robust than many modern liberal democracies. And as Anthony McElligott has pointed out, 'even at the height of the multiple crises in 1932, roughly one third of electors voted for parties that either explicitly or generally favoured the constitution, and a further fifth supported parties that, while not explicitly pro-democracy, nevertheless were not openly fighting the republic'. It is therefore clear that 'To assert that the Weimar Republic was a "republic without republicans" is simply wrong.'[29]

3

THE GREAT INFLATION AND
WEIMAR ECONOMICS

As early as the third century BCE it had been noted that 'there is nothing new under the sun.'[1] Recent events such as the Zimbabwean hyperinflation of 2008–9, the global banking crisis, credit crunch and subsequent recession have evoked the spirit of the Weimar Republic's economic instability in the minds of many. A quick trawl of the internet offers up numerous online commentators (of various levels of economic expertise) giving dire warnings that the North American and European economies are treading the path followed by Germany in the 1920s. Yet even if news reports of runs on banks, rising prices, unemployment and international intervention to rescue defaulting European economies stir memories of the troubled economic situation in interwar Germany, any such modern crises pale in comparison to those of the 1920s. So traumatic were the experiences of hyperinflation and depression that they have become embedded in German collective memory and culture. There are still people alive today who can remember the hardships caused by the collapse of the German currency, and they and those like them have passed on their memories to subsequent generations, with the result that few Germans have not heard (perhaps apocryphal) stories of worthless paper marks being carried in wheelbarrows (in one oft-repeated account the wheelbarrow is stolen and the money left behind)[2] or the hunger and suffering that the inflation and depression engendered. These anecdotes remain powerful today, so how much more powerful must they have been when they were still fresh in the memory?

The extent to which the collapse of the republic was a consequence of economic or political factors has been hotly contested. While some historians argue that political decisions were ultimately responsible for the violent economic fluctuations of the period, others take the view that Germany's problems were essentially the result of uncontrollable economic forces. Similarly, there has also been much debate as to whether Germany's economic troubles were at root the consequence of an invidious international position, or whether it was essentially internal factors – and in particular the excessive power of either organized labour or big business – that were to blame for hyperinflation, economic stagnation and depression. As we shall see, Germany was not unique amongst European nations in facing acute economic difficulties in the aftermath of the First World War. The collapse of the Austrian krone in 1921–2, to give just one example, was just as spectacular as that of the mark and preceded the nadir of Germany's hyperinflation by almost a year. Furthermore, the origins of the dramatic collapse of the German currency in the middle of 1923 and consequent economic and political crisis, like those of so many of the problems that the republic faced, are to be found in events that occurred and decisions that were taken long before the collapse of the monarchy.

GERMANY'S FIRST ECONOMIC MIRACLE

Economics had played an important role in the unification of Germany and in securing its place amongst the Great Powers. Prussian prosperity – rooted in the growing industrial might of its Rhenish and Silesian provinces – was instrumental in helping it to surpass Austria in their struggle for the mastery of Germany, while the *Zollverein* helped lay the economic and political foundations for a German nation state. After unification, the state continued to subsidize the development of infrastructure (especially railways and canals), while the creation of a single currency in 1873 and the foundation of the Reichsbank in 1875 helped to create an integrated financial system. At the same time, Germany experienced a 'double revolution' of intense industrialization and a population boom that ultimately led to it challenging Great Britain for the mantle of Europe's leading industrial power. Between 1895 and 1911 German industry grew by an average of between two and five per cent per year, inflation was low (less than 1 per cent) and there was almost no unemployment. Industries such as steel, machine tools and chemicals led the way, and companies such as Siemens, AEG, BASF and Krupp benefitted from an influx of capital investment, a focus on research and development and a highly educated workforce which enabled them to become world leaders in their fields. By 1914 German gross domestic product (GDP) was larger than Britain's and nearly double that of France.

However, if economics helped to unify Germany politically, it also helped to ensure that it remained divided socially. Rapid industrial expansion after 1870 brought with it profound social problems and 'has been viewed by historians as a source of a distinctly crisis-ridden modernity.'³ As in other European countries, industrialization profoundly altered the ways in which people lived and worked, rapidly creating a huge urban working class which was largely at the mercy of employers. At the same time, the prosperity generated by the first German economic miracle (*Wirtschaftswunder*) was very unevenly distributed. In 1911 the top 10 per cent of Prussian society owned 63 per cent of wealth, while many ordinary Germans languished in poverty. For the working classes insecure, short-term employment

German Population Growth, 1870–1910

Population (in millions)		
Year	Total	Per cent in towns over 2,000
1871	41.1	36.1
1880	42.2	41.1
1890	49.4	42.5
1900	56.4	54.4
1910	64.9	60

Source: Geoff Layton, *From Bismarck to Hitler: Germany 1890–1933* (London, 1995), p. 11

Comparative output of heavy industry, 1870–1910 (in millions of tons)

a) Coal

Year	Germany	UK
1871	37.7	119.2
1880	59.1	149.3
1890	89.2	184.5
1900	149.5	228.8
1910	222.2	268.7

b) Steel

Year	Germany	UK
1871	0.14	0.41
1880	0.69	1.32
1890	2.13	3.64
1900	6.46	4.98
1910	13.10	6.48

Source: Geoff Layton, *From Bismarck to Hitler: Germany 1890–1933* (London, 1995), p. 11

Comparative gross domestic products of the Great Powers, 1914 (in billions of dollars)

Austria–Hungary	France	Germany	Italy	Russia	UK	USA
100.5	138.7	244.3	91.3	257.7	226.4	511.6

Source: David Stevenson, *With Our Backs to the Wall* (London, 2011), p. 420

was the norm. As people left the countryside in search of work in the new industrial enterprises, the populations of the towns and cities swelled, leaving many workers and their families living in appallingly overcrowded and unsanitary conditions. As late as 1913, 30 per cent of Berliners lived with five or six people to a room. In these conditions disease was rampant and, although death rates declined as wages and living conditions improved in the 1890s, some urban areas had infant mortality rates of up to 40 per cent, even in the 1910s.

Faced with such squalor and insecurity, German workers survived as best they could through seeking personal improvement, looking for ways (both legal and illicit) to supplement their income and by forming mutual aid networks with co-workers. Recognizing that as individuals they were weak but possessed great potential bargaining power if they acted collectively, German workers, like their fellows in other industrialized nations, began to form trade unions in the 1860s. By the 1890s three distinct (and often mutually antagonistic) strands of trade unionism had developed: the socialist 'Free' Unions who had close ties with the SPD, the Christian (or Catholic) Trade Unions affiliated with the Centre Party and the left–liberal 'Hirsch–Dunker' unions (named after the two liberal reformers who founded the umbrella organization in 1868).

The growth of unionism and social democracy were alarming developments for many at the top of German society. In order to combat the perceived threat from the Left, Bismarck adopted a carrot and stick approach throughout the 1880s, outlawing the SPD on the one hand while introducing a policy of 'state socialism' designed to offset some of the inequalities of industrial society on the other. While the introduction of health insurance (1883), accident insurance (1884) and old age and disability insurance (1889) did little to detach support from the SPD (which flourished underground during the period of the Anti-Socialist Law), they did provide a much needed safety net in which employers paid contributions to help those too ill, old or infirm to work. These measures laid the foundations of the German welfare state and, together with the gains won through collective bargaining between unions and employers and an economic upturn in the 1890s, led to an improvement in living and working conditions for many Germans. Real wages rose by around 80 per cent between 1871 and 1913, while the working week decreased from a 72-hour norm in the 1870s to an average of 57 hours or less in the first years of the twentieth century.

WAR FINANCE AND INFLATION

This period of growth was brought to an abrupt halt by the outbreak of war in 1914. It is true to say that none of the combatant nations fully appreciated the strain that the conflict would place on their economies when they entered the war. However, in Germany the problems were made worse by geography and politics. Although the Saar basin, Alsace and Silesia provided key materials such as coal and iron ore, Germany was still reliant on imports of many essential raw materials to keep its industry going, particularly in wartime. However, British command of the seas and Germany's geographical position in the centre of Europe meant that the Entente powers were able to put in place a very effective blockade that severely limited not only Germany but also its Austro–Hungarian allies from importing food and other essentials. Similarly, political considerations prevented the government from seeking to cover the costs of the war by taxing the population.

When war broke out in 1914 everyone expected a short conflict and, rather than risking raising import prices and antagonizing the population by increasing taxation, the government gambled on winning the war and using the reparations payments extracted from their defeated foes to pay off their debts (a calculation also made by France). Between September 1914 and September 1918 the authorities issued nine six-monthly war loans (*Kriegsanleihen*) in which ordinary Germans were invited to invest with the promise of a return of five per cent after ten years. Until 1916 the money gathered was sufficient to meet the state's short-term liabilities. But as Germany's military fortunes waned, fewer and fewer Germans were prepared to invest in war bonds and expenditure began to outstrip revenue. In response the government introduced a war profits tax and a turnover tax, but continued to cover less than 20 per cent of total war expenditure through taxation. By 1917 military spending was taking up over half of gross national product (GNP), compared to only three per cent in 1913, while at the same time national income was falling. In an attempt to bridge the gap between income and expenditure the government sold their debts to the Reichsbank in return for cash (the monetization of public debt), precipitating a dramatic rise in the amount of paper money in circulation.

Until 1914 Germany, like other European nations, had limited the amount of paper currency in circulation by maintaining a gold standard in which one paper mark was worth a single gold mark and could (in theory at least) be exchanged for gold on demand. The Reichsbank was obliged by the Bank Law of 1875 to hold enough gold to cover one third of the issue of paper notes. But as the war progressed, Germany, like the other combatant nations, increasingly sought to circumvent such restrictions, leading to a further massive increase in the amount of paper money in circulation. At the same time, Germany was exporting gold bullion – twice as much as Britain – in order to finance the import of much needed food and war materials. As a result, the national debt ballooned to 150 billion marks (compared to an annual national debt of about five billion before the war) with the German government owing 1,600 million marks to the Netherlands alone. Unlike the currencies of the Allied nations, the value of the mark fell precipitously and Germany emerged from the conflict with a currency worth roughly half its 1914 value.

Thus defeat found the German economy, like the German population, exhausted. Although Germany had been more successful at mobilizing its economy than its allies and was not, unlike Austria, facing full-scale economic collapse and mass starvation in the autumn of 1918, it had been far less effective at organizing its war economy than Great Britain. Shortages caused by the Allied blockade and economic dislocation caused by wartime mobilization of men and resources, not to mention the fiscal consequences of the decision not to finance the war through direct taxation, all played a part in bringing about the fall of the Hohenzollern dynasty and the creation of a parliamentary republic in the winter of 1918–19.

FROM INFLATION TO HYPERINFLATION

The new government found itself in the unenviable position of having to sort out the economic and financial mess left by their predecessors at the same time as facing political opposition and economic pressure from both Left and Right. Industrial and agricultural production had to be restored to their pre-war levels, the looming fiscal crisis caused by wartime inflation had to be dealt with, the expectations for a more equitable system of industrial relations and social life raised by the November Revolution had to be met, and demobilization and a return a peacetime economy had to be managed. Although all the basic factors that had contributed to German economic success in the pre-war period were still in place, four years of warfare had dramatically reduced the size of the population and thoroughly disrupted normal economic life. On top of this, the new republican regime faced a huge bill not only for pensions owed to more than 800,000 wounded veterans, 530,000 war widows and 1.2 million orphans, but also to cover the costs of the ambitious new welfare state promised in the Weimar constitution.

Essentially, the economic legacy of the war left the Weimar Coalition with two options: increase taxation or cut government spending. In the precarious political situation after the war neither option was attractive (some might say practicable) as they would both serve to alienate the population and lead to further hardships and social unrest. In the end, the democratic politicians now leading Germany opted to do neither. In the immediate aftermath of the war the government felt compelled to adopt a policy of full employment in order to stave off labour unrest, a policy that Niall Ferguson has termed paying 'reparations to the working classes'[4]. In order to pay for this the government chose to lower taxation and allow the national debt to grow, in the hope that people would have more money to spend and that this would stimulate demand and create employment. The hope was that this deficit financing would overcome the problems of demobilization by creating jobs as well as helping to cover the costs of new welfare projects. However, an essential part of this policy was allowing inflation to continue.

Matters were made even worse by Germany's international situation. While the confiscation of its overseas colonies and the reduction of its army and navy presented the German government with opportunities to save money, these were more than offset by the loss of around 13 per cent of Germany's pre-war territory, including key industrial areas such as Silesia and Alsace (and the consequent 16 per cent fall in coal production and 48 per cent drop in the production of iron ore). Furthermore, Germany was compelled to make recompense 'for causing all the loss and damage to which the Allied and Associated Governments and their nationals have been subjected to as a consequence of the war imposed upon them by the aggression of Germany and its allies'[5], which included war pensions and the costs of the occupation of the Rhineland. This imposed yet another drain on already stretched government finances at a time when the state was still struggling to come to terms with the economic fallout of the war. The result was that the politicians of the moderate Left had their hands further tied over economic policy: if they raised taxes to finance the massive public spending necessary to fund the transition to a peacetime economy and build the welfare state, then their political opponents on the nationalist Right would accuse them of taxing Germans to finance Allied reparation demands. It seemed much more politic to attempt to persuade the Allies that Germany was unable to pay and to seek a renegotiation of the amount and schedule of payments, while at the same time 'exporting economic grievances'[6] by blaming Germany's economic woes on the Treaty of Versailles and the reparations payments alone. Indeed, some historians have suggested that the civil servants and businessmen who directed Germany's reparations policy in the early 1920s were responsible for encouraging the public to see in reparations the key to Germany's economic woes – thus directing attention away from indicators showing that inflation had its roots in domestic factors – and perpetuating the myth that only with the abolition of the indemnity could Germany return to economic stability and prosperity.[7]

Nevertheless, to some extent the inflation helped to stimulate Germany's post-war economy. The decreasing value of the mark allowed canny businessmen to borrow in order to purchase raw materials, manufactured goods or industrial plant and then pay back the loan when it was worth a fraction of what it had been a few months before. This ensured that until the middle of 1922 the rate of economic growth was high and unemployment virtually disappeared. Low taxation also helped to stimulate demand and Germany managed the move to a peacetime economy more smoothly than some other European nations who were suffering less from inflation.[8] Indeed, Carl-Ludwig Holtferich has gone so far as to argue that deficit financing was an inspired and successful policy that enabled the Weimar Republic to compete effectively with other European economies which went into recession in 1920–21 and had much higher rates of unemployment (17 per cent in Britain in 1921 compared to Germany's 1.8 per cent).[9]

However, this growth was merely a prelude to the inevitable crash. The government's policy of deficit financing could not be sustained indefinitely. Even during the period of apparent growth and prosperity there were clear indicators that all was not well. Economic growth and full employment barely masked the rising tensions in German society caused by the government's economic policy. Price controls on agricultural goods alienated farmers, while rent controls created a housing shortage in the big cities. More worrying still for ordinary Germans was that the purchasing power of the mark fell even as prices continued to rise. Between 1914 and 1920 the cost of living rose 12 times (compared to three times in the USA, four in Britain and seven in France). A family of four could be fed on 60 marks a week in April 1919, but this went up to 144 marks in December 1920 and had risen to 249 marks a year later. Staple items such as tea and eggs were roughly 30–40 times more expensive than they had been before the war. By 1922, with Germany already suffering from 'galloping inflation', consumers were really beginning to feel the pinch. In July alone food prices rose by 50 per cent and a bank clerk's annual salary would provide only enough to feed his family for a single month.

This only served to heighten social and political tensions, providing 'a constant stimulus to labour militancy and anger at the market-place.'[10] As the purchasing power of the mark continued to fall there were outbreaks of strikes, protests and riots in German cities. State employees on fixed incomes were particularly badly hit as their wages did not keep pace with price rises, and in February 1922 there occurred the 'first (and last) major civil servant strike in German history.'[11] There was very little understanding amongst the general public as to what was happening, which only increased people's sense of helplessness and fuelled social tension. Many looked around for someone to blame and came up with a variety of scapegoats – foreigners, the trade unions, big business, war profiteers and in particular Jews. In Bavaria banknotes became known as *Judenfetzen* (Jewish confetti)[12], and as the slide into hyperinflation gathered pace there was an upsurge of anti-Semitic attacks on Jewish shops and

Weekly cost in marks of subsistence for a family of four in Berlin, 1920–23

Period	Food	Accomm-odation	Heating/Lighting	Clothing	Miscell-aneous
Aug. 1913–July 1914	9.8	5.5	1.9	5.9	5.8
Jan. 1920	86	8	12	70	44
June 1920	128	9	22	84	61
Dec. 1920	144	9	22	70	82
Jan. 1921	139	9	22	70	80
June 1921	142	9	25	63	72
Dec. 1921	249	10	41	128	129
Jan. 1922	257	11	43	128	109
June 1922	466	14	96	350	269
Dec. 1922	8,154	193	2,084	8,361	6,202
Jan. 1923	13,098	300	3,467	11,725	8,577
June 1923	98,579	1,045	22,287	73,889	56,782
Aug. 1923	6,307,538	9,800	1,755,761	4,783,333	4,120,458
Sept. 1923	162.2m	360,000m	49.2m	110.7m	104.8m
Oct. 1923	51,561.3m	24.6m	9,838.4m	49,605.6m	33,309m
Nov 1923	9,354.3bn	38.3bn	1,650.9bn	5016.7bn	4015bn

Source: Carl-Ludwig Holtfrerich, *The German Inflation 1914–1923* (New York, 1986), pp. 40–41

businesses. To some extent the government encouraged this tendency by denying that the amount of money in circulation was anything to do with the problem and continuing to peddle the line that inflation and rising prices were a consequence of the unreasonable demands place on the German economy by reparations.

By the beginning of 1923 the stage was set for the complete collapse of the German currency. German policy had always vacillated between evasion and compliance with Allied demands for reparations. The first instalment was paid punctually in August 1921, but by December Germany announced that it would not be able to pay the next instalment and asked for a moratorium. This was an ominous foretaste of things to come. In July 1922 the Germans announced that they would again not be able to make the necessary reparations payment. Under pressure from the USA to repay their wartime debts, Britain called in its outstanding loans to France. Already in financial difficulties, and with a post-war economy heavily reliant on German coal and coke, the French government cast around desperately for a way to compel Germany to make good on its debts. Having already occupied Düsseldorf and Darmstadt in January 1921 when Germany rejected provisional proposals for the final reparations figure, the French knew that Germany was capable of paying when placed under pressure. In November 1922 it was decided to revive a scheme first drafted during the Kapp Putsch: to invade and occupy the industrially important Ruhr district if Germany could not be convinced to pay. When renewed negotiations over reparations stalled the following January, secret orders were sent to French forces in the Rhineland telling them to prepare for the invasion of the Ruhr.

In the early morning of 11 January 1923, French and Belgian troops marched into the Ruhr, seizing Essen and Gladbeck, and within four days the whole of the region had been occupied. In response, the German Chancellor Wilhelm Cuno appealed to the population of the region to meet the invaders with 'passive resistance', asking them to down tools and not cooperate with the occupation forces. Germans of all parties and classes rallied to the call, and for a time the nation was united in an upsurge of 'republican-style patriotism' similar to that which had gripped the nation in August 1914, but this time the people were engaged in 'a peaceful campaign to defend Germany against foreign invasion, which stood in complete contrast to Imperial Germany's military campaign for foreign conquest.'[13] The only problem was that passive resistance had to be paid for, and was not cheap. The tactic was always regarded as a temporary one, to be pursued while the government sought a negotiated settlement to the crisis. But as the months passed and this settlement proved elusive, the government, unable to collect taxes from the Ruhr or obtain supplies coal confiscated by the French, was forced to fritter away its last remaining gold reserves on importing food and fuel.

At the same time, in order to cover the extra costs entailed by effectively paying unemployment benefits to almost the entire population of the Ruhr region, the government stepped up the printing of paper currency. During February 1923 the number of notes in circulation rose by 450 billion a week, and in early March the 'floating debt' rose by 800 billion in one day. At the height of the inflation 30 paper mills, 150 printing firms and 2,000 printing presses worked round the clock to produce the never-ending stream of paper money. In a speech on 17 August 1923, Rudolf Havenstein proudly declared that under his auspices the Reichsbank was issuing 20 billion marks of new money each day, of which five billion was in large denominations. The consequence was a reckless descent into hyperinflation.

Until the spring of 1923 the fall of the mark had been dramatic but steady, and therefore to some extent manageable; but as hyperinflation gathered pace over the summer the value of the mark fell

Exchange rates during the Great Inflation

Date	German Marks to the Pound Sterling	German Marks to the US Dollar
January 1920	233	64.8
July 1920	152	39.5
January 1921	243	64.9
July 1921	278	76.7
January 1922	811	191.8
July 1922	2,200	493.2
January 1923	83,190	17,972
July 1923	1,594,760	353,412
August 1923	21,040,000	4,620,455
September 1923	449,375,000	98,860,000
October 1923	112,503,000,000	25,260,208,000
November 1923	9,604,000,000,000	4,200,000,000,000

Sources: Edgar, Viscount D'Abernon, *An Ambassador of Peace*, vol. 2 (London, 1929), pp. 298–300; Matthew Stibbe, *Germany 1914–1933* (Harlow, 2010), p. 99

and prices rose not on a monthly or even a daily, but on an hourly basis. Between May and June 1923 the price of an egg rose from 800 to 2,400 marks and a litre of milk from 1,800 to 3,800 marks. In the Ruhr wages doubled, but prices trebled. The 1,000 mark note (the highest denomination note in circulation since 1876) was withdrawn because it cost more to produce than it was worth, and new 10-, 20- and 50-million mark notes were issued. The rate of currency depreciation became so great that a 5,000 mark cup of coffee was worth 8,000 marks by the time it had been drunk and 'the only thing to do with cash . . . was to turn it into something else as quickly as possible.'[14] Barter took over as the main form of commerce: a cinema seat cost a lump of coal, a bottle of paraffin could buy a shirt and one man paid the rent on his mistress's flat with a pound of butter a month.

The result was human misery on a massive scale. Particularly badly hit were those who relied on fixed incomes such as state employees (senior civil servants, but also clerks, railwaymen and postal workers), students, those on benefits and pensioners. These groups were particularly exposed to the deprivations of the inflation because increases in their grants or pensions failed to keep pace with the rate of inflation. Similarly, 'those of independent means who were living largely or exclusively from interest' – savers, landlords, mortgagees or people who had invested in war bonds – were badly hit because the principle of *Mark gleich Mark* (a mark is a mark) meant that almost overnight they found that their savings or

Inflation era prices (in German marks)

Item	1913	Summer 1923	November 1923
1 kg of bread	0.29	1,200	428,000,000,000
1 egg	0.08	5,000	80,000,000,000
1 kg of butter	2.70	26,000	6,000,000,000,000
1 kg of beef	1.75	18,800	5,600,000,000,000
1 pair of shoes	12	1,000,000	32,000,000,000,000

Source: Geoff Layton, *Democracy and Dictatorship in Germany 1919–63* (Harlow, 2009), p. 51

At the height of the inflation money became essentially worthless. Here 1 million mark notes are used as a notepad (Bundesarchiv, Bild 102-00193 / CC-BY-SA).

investments were worthless.[15] Although those in work were generally more insulated from the worst effects of the inflation, during the chaos of 1923, working class living standards declined because the trade unions were no longer able to negotiate wage increases that kept pace with price rises. At the same time, the economic upheaval caused by the hyperinflation and the Ruhr Crisis provided employers with an excuse to unilaterally revise important aspects of the Stinnes–Legien Agreement (see page 33) such as the eight-hour working day.[16]

However, the effects of the inflation were not felt evenly across German society. People in the countryside were better off than those in towns and cities because they had ready access to essential goods (foodstuffs and timber for fuel) and were therefore less reliant on money to secure the necessities of life. At the same time, some farmers and landowners were able to 'use hyperinflation to wipe out debts or purchase new machinery and household items on cheap credit (or in exchange for food).'[17] In addition, the old idea of 'the destruction of the middle class' needs to be unpicked. As Geoff Layton has suggested, 'the key to understanding who gained and who lost from the inflation lies in the nature of an individual's income and degree of indebtedness.'[18] Those in debt had the potential to pay off their loans or mortgages with depreciated marks, while those with good business sense could make use of cheap credit and inflated profits to acquire land, businesses, art collections and real estate from the desperate and naive. Many of Germany's leading industrialists took the opportunity to engage in a rash of mergers and takeovers, creating in the process a series of large industrial *Konzerne* (corporations) that later proved to be financially weak and vulnerable. Professionals such as doctors and lawyers suffered from a slackening off of business but were better suited to weather the storm than some because they could adjust their charges to an extent. Likewise, while some small businessmen went under (especially when currency stabilization led to a rash of bankruptcies in 1924), shopkeepers often managed to survive either by resorting to a sort of barter system or by taking advantage of the thriving black market. Furthermore, the inflation era and subsequent currency stabilization led to a 'levelling tendency' not only in the salaries of civil servants (provoking the resentment of senior officials who felt that their economic and social status was being undermined), but also between young and old, male and female and skilled and unskilled workers.[19]

But material hardship was only one side of the story. As important, maybe more so, was the cultural and psychological legacy of the inflation era on the German population. Whether or not they actually lost out, there was a general perception amongst some sections of the middle classes that the inflation and the measures introduced to restore economic stability from late 1923 onwards represented an assault on their social and economic standing that would lead to their 'proletarianization'. This was not merely a matter of wealth and prosperity. As they saw it, the social and political upheavals of the revolution and the economic chaos of the inflation era had wiped away respect for *Bildung* (self-cultivation), the traditional preserve of the educated professional classes, leaving a much more materialistic culture in which wealth and power, not education and culture, were king. In this way, professors, doctors, lawyers and senior civil servants felt as though they had not only lost their former prosperity, but also the social pre-eminence and respect that they felt was their due.

At the same time, the material pressures placed on people caused them to dramatically revise their moral outlooks. The fact that many Germans were forced into bending or breaking the law simply in order to survive during the worst of the hyperinflation created a new moral landscape in which the borders between legitimate and illegal business transactions became blurred. While the working classes engaged in prostitution and petty crime as a way to make ends meet, those with the means and the know-how engaged in more lucrative white-collar crime. Tax evasion became widespread, as did fraud, embezzlement and currency speculation. The once incorruptible

Criminal Convictions in Germany, 1910–1926

Year	Total tried	Total convicted	Of whom	
			Women	Adolescents
1910	685,751	538,225	86,926	51,315
1911	693,346	544,861	89,192	50,874
1912	722,745	573,976	91,653	55,949
1913	690,403	555,527	88,462	54,155
1914	560,024	454,064	77,870	46,940
1915	349,308	287,535	75,400	63,126
1916	350,400	287,500	86,400	80,399
1917	357,146	294,584	102,806	95,651
1918	408,147	341,526	127,923	99,498
1919	418,064	348,247	85,454	64,619
1920	733,458	608,563	118,749	91,171
1921	797,552	651,148	130,550	76,932
1922	760,706	636,817	113,884	71,124
1923	968,883	823,902	134,943	86,040
1924	827,021	696,668	114,488	43,276
1925	682,092	575,745	93,367	24,771
1926	700,201	589,611	89,344	24,066

Source: Richard Bessel, *Germany After the First World War* (Oxford, 1993), p. 242

Prussian civil service was well and truly corrupted as salaries no longer provided a subsistence income, and bribery became commonplace. Law and order virtually broke down, and the German prison population rose by on average 100,000 prisoners a day. This was part of a general post-war rise in criminality, but the statistics show a marked increase in trials and convictions during 1923. The 'pervasive, soul-destroying influence of the constant erosion of capital or earnings and uncertainty about the future'[20] led to a decline in ethical standards and an atmosphere where the old virtues of thrift, hard work and honesty became, if not vices, then mere foolish sentimentality.

CURRENCY STABILIZATION AND THE DAWES PLAN

As hyperinflation grew worse and worse, strikes and demonstrations demanding the daily payment of wages (so that they could be spent before they became worthless) were held in Leipzig, Dresden and Potsdam. On 20 July riots broke out in Breslau, leading to 1,000 arrests and a ban on open-air meetings in Berlin. In Saxony, the Social Democratic minister-president brought the KPD into the ruling coalition and raised 30,000 auxiliaries to supplement the police, a move that raised fears of a left-wing coup and ultimately led the central government and army to depose the Saxon government. At the beginning of August, the centre-right government of Wilhelm Cuno finally gave up the ghost and made way for a grand coalition of the SPD, DDP, Centre and DVP led by the leader of the DVP, Gustav Stresemann.

The new administration acted quickly to try and deal with the crisis: on 26 September President Ebert declared a state of emergency, suspending seven articles of the constitution and handing executive powers to Minister of Defence Gessler and Head of Army Command Hans von Seeckt. Less than a month later, on 13 October, an *Ermächtigungsgesetz* (Enabling Act) was passed in accordance with Article 76 of the constitution, granting Stresemann the power to introduce whatever means were necessary to bring matters under control. Two days later Finance Minister Hans Luther presented the cabinet with legislation designed to halt the collapse of the German economy by the introduction of a temporary currency, the

Rentenmark, backed not by gold but by industrial and agricultural assets.

However, these measures initially did little to halt either the government's fiscal problems or outbreaks of civil unrest. On 26 September Gustav von Kahr seized power in Bavaria and instituted a right-wing, semi-dictatorial regime, while members of the 'black Reichswehr' (former Freikorps fighters recruited by von Seeckt to bolster Germany's armed forces) staged an attempted coup at the Kürstin barracks near Berlin on 1 October. By November expenditure was 1,000 times higher than revenue, officials from the Finance Ministry were being partly paid in potatoes and the government was running out of cash to pay the army and police. On 6 November Berlin was struck by another wave of food riots and shops were looted by desperate consumers, and two days later Hitler staged his infamous Beer Hall Putsch in Munich.

On 13 November the financier Hjalmar Schacht was appointed Commissioner for National Currency, two days before the introduction of the new Rentenmark. Inflation was allowed to continue until the exchange rate reached 18,000 billion marks to the pound (4.2 trillion to the dollar), so that a paper mark was worth one-trillionth of a gold mark. This allowed Schacht and Luther to re-establish the gold mark at its 1913 exchange rate (4.2 to the dollar), thus allowing for a simple conversion of the old currency into the new Rentenmark – 1 trillion to one. While this new currency was in circulation the assets by which it was guaranteed (valued at 3.2 billion gold marks) were to be administered by the Rentenbank, a body of financial experts, politicians and bankers under the presidency of DNVP member and former Prussian finance minister, August Lenze. On the same day as the new exchange rate was set (20 November) one of the chief architects of Germany's inflationary strategy, Rudolf Havenstein, died. He was replaced as Reichsbank President by Schacht, who brought about stability 'in less than a week'[21] by declaring that emergency money (Notgeld) would no longer be accepted as legal tender and refusing credit.

Over the next two months further stringent economies were imposed on the public services: postal charges were put on a gold basis, ten per cent of personnel employed by the state railways were dismissed and official salaries were reduced to pre-war levels. Furthermore, three emergency revenue decrees placed taxes on a gold basis and imposed a heavy duty on inflation profits, leading to a dramatic revival of state income (the deficit between income and expenditure had been 99 per cent, but fell almost immediately to 92 per cent and was only 44 per cent by December 1923) and enabling the government to balance the budget in March 1924. However, the knock-on effects of these measures caused yet more hardship for some: interest rates of 100 per cent and a shortage of credit led to high prices and bankruptcies, while unemployment soared. By Christmas there were 1.5 million people out of work, double the number of early November. This meant that, even as prices began to fall, some families could still not afford to feed and clothe themselves, while the middle classes and pensioners were once again hardest hit because they were unlikely to be eligible for unemployment benefit. Many had to rely on municipal soup kitchens or charitable institutions, themselves badly hit by the inflation. This all served to undermine public confidence in the administration and make Stresemann's coalition partners nervous, leading to an unlikely combination of the SPD, KPD, Nationalists and 'proto-Fascists' bringing down Stresemann's second cabinet through a vote of no confidence on 23 November 1923.[22]

Meanwhile, negotiations with the Allies had been ongoing in an effort to bring an end to both the occupation of the Ruhr and the additional strain placed on the German economy by reparations. Whatever the Allies thought about Germany's previous assertions of its inability to pay, the collapse of the mark clearly confirmed them as fact rather than rhetoric. Even the French were persuaded that a bankrupt and destitute Germany was not in their interests, and, on 30 November, the Reparations Commission recommended that two committees of experts be established to review the payment procedures laid down by the London Schedule of Payments of 1921. The committee, under the American financier Charles G. Dawes, reported back in April 1924, proposing an economic and political compromise that would ease the financial strain placed on the Weimar Republic while going some way to satisfy French demands for a secure and durable payment schedule. The so-called Dawes Plan, which was approved by the London Conference of July–August 1924, provided Germany with an 800-million-mark loan designed to kick-start its economic recovery and a moratorium on reparations payments until 1925. After this the republic was liable for an annual annuity of 1 billion marks, rising to 2.5 billion by 1928–29. No schedule of payments – or even a total figure – was specified, but as a guarantee of future payments the Allies insisted that Germany hand over control of the railways and accept the appointment of an Allied currency commissioner.

Although the plan was roundly attacked by the parties of the Right, it was passed by the Reichstag on 29 August and almost immediately provided some relief to Germans suffering under the inflation and stabilization measures. Interest rates fell to 30 per cent, halving unemployment, while a series of international loans (Germany received £200 million in loans from the United States alone between 1924 and 1926, and by 1929 had been in receipt of a total of around £1 billion[23]) and investments helped to bring the official unemployment figure down to 436,000. Nevertheless, by 1928 it had become clear that Germany would be unable to meet its obligations as specified by the Dawes Plan, and the League of Nations called a conference, chaired by American financier Owen D. Young, to review the question. Negotiations were tense and long-winded, but the result was a new schedule of repayments, the Young Plan, announced on 7 June 1929. This provided a total figure of 112 billion marks to be paid over 59 years, and abolished Allied controls on German banking and railways. Although it reduced the annuities demanded by the Dawes Plan by 20 per cent, the Young Plan faced concerted opposition from the DNVP and the National Socialists, only being ratified by the Reichstag in March 1930. However, the plan was rapidly overtaken by the onset of the Great Depression and US President Herbert Hoover offered a moratorium in 1931. The following year the Lausanne Conference scrapped the plan, effectively bringing an end to reparations.

THE GREAT INFLATION IN CONTEXT

Most accounts of Weimar Germany tend to agree that its economic difficulties played a large role in undermining commitment to the new democracy and paving the way for the Nazi takeover of power in 1933. Yet Germany was not alone in facing economic dislocation in the interwar period. The other defeated Central Powers encountered similar economic, social and political difficulties to those faced by Germany in the aftermath of the First World War, but it is often forgotten that many of the victorious powers also emerged from the war with severe economic problems. Like Germany, France had gambled on securing reparations as a means of financing the war, and a continued reluctance to raise taxation ensured that government spending exceeded income by as much a 12 million francs a year, while the value of the French currency depreciated from 90 francs to the pound in December 1924 to 240 to the pound by July 1926. Italy, too, had resorted to borrowing and printing money as a method of financing its war effort, leading to ruinous inflation that saw the purchasing power of the lira fall by 25 per cent between 1915 and 1918. This, together with rising unemployment (2 million people out of work in 1919) and labour militancy, was an important contributing factor in bringing Mussolini's Fascists to power in October 1922. Even Britain, which had on the whole managed its war finances well, experienced a short period of inflation after the war.

Germany's hyperinflation was much more severe than anything experienced in Western Europe, but it was comparable with the economic upheavals felt by its wartime allies Austria and Hungary. The collapse of the multi-ethnic Habsburg Empire left Austria an impoverished rump state cut off by new national boundaries from its chief sources of fuel and food (coal from Czechoslovakia and grain from Hungary), while Hungary lost a third of its pre-war territory and with it supplies of natural resources it badly needed to keep its industry going. Industrial production stood at 30 per cent of pre-war levels in 1920, while agricultural yields were half what they had been in 1913. One third of the Hungarian population were out of work, and living standards were 40 per cent lower than they had been before the war. This, together with a record of war finance similar to that of Germany, led to severe food shortages and rampant inflation. In Austria the krone depreciated even more rapidly than the German mark, leading to panic buying, food hoarding and political unrest. By August 1922 the pound sterling was worth 350,000

Austrian kronen (compared to roughly 22 kronen to the pound in 1914), and only intervention from the League of Nations was able to stave off the collapse of the economy and with it the Austrian Republic. It was a similar story in Hungary, where by 1919 the currency was worth only ten per cent of its pre-war value, falling to 0.3 per cent by 1923. As with Austria, only an international bailout combined with stringent austerity measures enabled the government to stabilize the currency and bring a measure of economic normality back to Central Europe.

Germany was thus not alone in experiencing a dramatic hyper-inflation followed by a traumatic period of stabilization that bequeathed a legacy of long-term structural weakness to the economy. Germany's hyperinflation neither caused widespread cases of starvation as it did in Austria, nor led to a fascist takeover of power as in Italy. Why then has it become a byword for economic instability? Firstly, it was perhaps because those hardest hit by the inflation and stabilization were the best educated and most articulate sections of society who found the experience particularly traumatic because they had previously enjoyed nearly 50 years of prosperity and growth. Secondly, the collapse of the economy struck a further blow to national pride already dented by the humiliation of unexpected defeat. Coming on top of war, revolution and virtual civil war, hyperinflation reinforced the feeling that old certainties and values had been destroyed and replaced by chaos and disorder.

'THE GOLDEN TWENTIES': STABILITY AND PROSPERITY?

With the introduction of the Dawes Plan, Germany was able to return to some measure of normality after the trauma of war, defeat, revolution and economic crisis. The period between the stabilization of the currency in 1924 and the onset of the Great Depression in 1929 is often called *die goldenen zwanziger Jahre* (the Golden Twenties). This was a period of apparent political stability for the republic, during which Germany enjoyed a cultural and economic boom. Yet the consequences of the revolution and the inflation cast a long shadow, and bequeathed serious structural flaws that left the economy particularly exposed to any new economic crisis that might come along. Moreover, a closer examination of the evidence suggests that, economically at least, the lustre of Germany's golden twenties was little more than fool's gold.

Part of the problem was deep-seated 'structural' weaknesses in the Weimar economy that were partly a legacy of the revolution and ideological attempts to impose greater regulation and social mobility on Germany, and partly a consequence of the dramatic expansion and intrusion of the state into economic life that had taken place during the Great War. 'Modernization' and 'rationalization' were the buzz words of the day, and the state worked hard to promote these in the face of opposition from the unions who feared that the result of the implementation of 'modern' business models borrowed from America would be job losses. The creation of the *Reichswirtschaftsrat* (Reich Economic Council), in August 1919 was symptomatic of the widespread tendency towards 'organizationalism' in the Weimar economy. It was made up of 326 members representing both employers and workers, and was supposed to foster dialogue that would be beneficial to both. However, it ultimately proved ineffectual in bridging the gap between labour and capital and, although it continued to exist until 1934, it played a negligible role in economic life after 1923 as the post-war compact between employers and unions increasingly broke down.

Accompanying, and related to, this trend was the increased power of economic interest groups who had been brought in to assist with labour shortages and economic mobilization during the war and remained in a privileged position after it had ended. Business in particular resumed the pre-war habit of forming cartels (there were 2,500 in 1925, rising to over 3,000 in 1930) in order to set prices and standardize products. In the wake of the inflation there was a widespread belief that concentration and amalgamation was the key to economic growth, and a number of businesses merged in the mid-1920s (for example, I.G. Farben in 1925 and Vereinigte Stahlwerke and Daimler-Benz in 1926) which has been seen as a symptom of a risk-averse, overcapitalized and stagnating industrial sector.[24] These *Konzerne* joined the numerous new economic institutions and pressure groups that had been established after 1918, such as the *Reichsverband der deutschen Industrie* (National Association of

German Industry) who, together with traditional institutions such as the Reichsbank, jostled for influence over economic policy. This welter of complex competing and interconnected interest groups and institutions ultimately led to confusion and lack of coherence, and hampered the government in responding effectively to the challenges posed by the Great Depression.[25]

After 1924 real wages rose gradually, but so did housing costs and prices for staple goods. Likewise, employment figures were erratic in the period of stability and recovery. Seven per cent of Germans were out of work in 1925, a figure that rose to 18 per cent in 1926. It fell again to between 8 and 9 per cent in 1927, only to begin to climb again in 1928, a trend which continued until 1933. Similarly, economic performance in the so-called golden twenties was not all it have should been. In contrast to the dynamic, research-driven economy of the Wilhelmine period, Weimar's industrial output looked practically moribund: technological advances were limited and restricted to a few well-established industries (chemicals, mining, automobiles), while productivity and growth remained sluggish over the whole period, to the extent that one recent study has concluded that there was no growth in total factor productivity between 1913 and 1929.[26] Furthermore, Germany's reliance on exports meant that it was badly hit by the post-war contraction in world trade which saw a 31 per cent fall between 1913 and 1929, with German exports at 87 per cent of their pre-war value in 1925. By 1929, exports to Britain and the USA were three-fifths lower than they had been in 1913 and German exports were contributing only 14.9 per cent of total GNP between 1925 and 1929, compared to 17.5 per cent before the war. All this meant that Germany's economic recovery after the inflation was limited, a fact that was not lost on contemporaries who spoke of a weak or sick economy.[27]

At the same time, in some important respects the inflation sowed the seeds of Germany's unique vulnerability to global economic instability. After the stabilization of the currency in 1924, Germany became enmeshed in a global 'cycle of debt' and thus especially vulnerable in the event of a worldwide economic downturn. German reparations payments to Britain and France were used by those counties to help pay off their own war debts to the United States, who

Average annual growth rates of industrial output (per cent)

	1913–38	1913–25	1925–29	1929–32
Metal production	0.8	-2.9	5.1	-28.1
Metal working	4.2	2.3	6.7	-20.9
Mining	0.8	0.6	5.9	-31.3
Chemicals	5.0	2.4	8.8	-9.4
Textiles	0.1	-1.7	-0.4	-6.8
Gas, water, electricity	5.8	5.8	7.7	-7.8
Building	0.2	—	—	-29.9

Source: Harold James, *The German Slump* (Oxford, 1986), p. 115

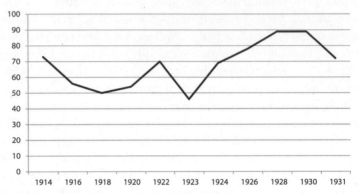

Growth of industrial production, 1914–31.

Source: Carl-Ludwig Holtfrerich, *The German Inflation 1914–1923* (New York, 1986), p. 183

in turn provided most of the foreign capital that was intended to kick-start the German economic recovery. Moreover, the government and the banks had not learnt the lessons of the early 1920s and continued to borrow at high interest rates while refusing to raise taxes. This enabled them to invest heavily in public works and pay reparations, but at the same time left the state finances dangerously exposed to fluctuations in world markets.

Thus, when the American economy went into a dramatic free fall in the wake of the Wall Street Crash, not only did the foreign investment upon which the German economy had come to rely dry up, but Germany also found itself under increased pressure, from both American investors who demanded repayment of earlier loans and from Britain and France who required reparations to help meet their own obligations to the United States. Under such pressures, German businesses went under, forcing millions into unemployment. Equally, already deeply in debt, the German government could see no way out of its economic predicament other than to reduce services, welfare costs and public sector wages, and increase taxes. These austerity measures were not only hugely unpopular, they also decreased demand (which only made matters worse) and had a dramatic impact on the financial and banking system.

THE GREAT DEPRESSION

German share prices had already experienced their own dramatic collapse on 13 May 1927 (two years before the Wall Street Crash) and German stocks had remained sluggish even as the American market boomed.[28] The first signs of recession were seen in 1928, but it was only once the effects of the wider global economic downturn came to be felt that the German slump became an economic

German foreign debts, 1931

Country	Cumulative debt (in millions of marks)
USA	5,265
Netherlands	1,174
UK	1,100
Sweden	797
Switzerland	512
France	475
Belgium	51
Italy	46

Source: R. Overy, *The Penguin Historical Atlas of the Third Reich* (London, 1996), p. 16

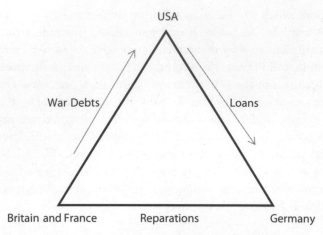

The Reparations triangle of the 1920s.

catastrophe. As American businesses retrenched in the wake of the stock market crash of October 1929, the steady stream of short-term investment in the German economy that had been forthcoming after 1924 all but dried up. Heavily reliant on injections of foreign cash, many German businesses responded by attempting to cut costs, usually by laying off staff. World trade slumped, cutting German exports by half and putting even more pressure on manufacturers. As belts were tightened and demand slackened in both home and international markets further cuts were made resulting in yet more unemployment, while without foreign investment many businesses could no longer compete and went under completely, leaving more people out of work. Unemployment rose to 2 million in the winter of 1929–30, reached 3 million in 1931 and was at 5.1 million by September 1932. The peak came in early 1933 when over 6.1 million Germans were out of work. Yet even these figures fail to give a true impression of the level of unemployment in the early 1930s, as 'working-class wives and teenagers living at home' were 'often . . . purged from the jobless rolls by officials who felt that each family deserved only one job.'[29] Few Germans escaped the effects of the Depression. Both skilled and unskilled workers found themselves facing long-term unemployment with all the feelings of helplessness and loss of status that this entailed. At the same time, their wives and families were forced to try to get by on the limited resources provided by unemployment benefit. But it was not only the working classes that were affected, 'the Depression also dragged down the middle class. From the small-scale shopkeepers to the graduate professionals in law and medicine, people struggled to survive in a world where their goods and services were decreasingly in demand. For such casualties the decline in their economic position was further accentuated by the loss of pride and respectability which accompanied poverty and unemployment.'[30]

At the same time, the Weimar Republic was in the grip of a banking crisis which bore distinct similarities to that of 2007–9. To a very great extent, economics is all about confidence. While people believe that the money in their pockets is worth a certain amount, or that the money in their bank accounts is secure, all is well. But once that faith is shaken, panic often turns fears into reality. This was what happened in the case of the British bank Northern Rock in September 2007 when investors rushed to withdraw their savings amidst fears that the bank was about to go into receivership. A similar panic occurred in Germany in April–May 1929 amidst fears that the Paris reparations negotiations would break down, and again in September 1930, when unexpectedly large electoral gains by the NSDAP led many Germans, fearing a right-wing coup, to withdraw their savings. But the most serious run on the banks came in the summer of 1931 when the collapse of the Austrian Credit-Anstalt aroused fears that German banks would fail. Matters were made worse when the Reichsbank announced in June that its gold reserves were running dangerously low, thus evoking memories of the inflation and fears of a widespread collapse. In early July it was rumoured that several institutions previously regarded as 'too big to fail' such as the Danatbank (*Darmstädter-und-Nationalbank*) and the Dresdener Bank were insolvent, thus intensifying the panic and leading to the close of all banks between 13 July and early August. The government responded with a massive bailout that effectively nationalized both banks, the appointment of a Reich Commissar for Banking and the establishment of special courts to try those accused of financial crimes.

Colin Storer

The 1931 banking crisis: Depositors rush to withdraw their savings after learning of the collapse of the *Darmstädter-und-Nationalbank* (Bundesarchiv, Bild 102-12023 / Georg Pahl / CC-BY-SA).

As bankruptcies soared and production fell by 31 per cent, the German government found themselves caught between falling tax revenue and rising expenditure on unemployment benefit. Social welfare provision amounted to 40.3 per cent of government expenditure in 1929–30, and it was assumed that this figure would go on rising as long as the Depression lasted. In August 1930, 15.7 per cent of those registered as unemployed were dependent on welfare support and this figure rose to 26.8 per cent in 1931 and 38.9 per cent in 1932. This was an intolerable situation, and the parties of the centre-right demanded that the government take matters in hand to balance the budget and provide some relief for business. The SPD, on the other hand, were chiefly concerned with insulating their working-class constituents from the worst ravages of the slump and wanted to see unemployment benefit increased, not cut. The political crisis engendered by the Depression will be described in greater detail in Chapter 6, here it is sufficient to say that it was the issue of public spending that ultimately brought down Hermann Müller's

Grand Coalition (1928–30) when the SPD and the DVP failed to agree on how to tackle the large deficit in the social insurance system caused by mass unemployment. The initiative therefore shifted to the president, who appointed Heinrich Brüning chancellor in March 1930. Believing that the key to Germany's economic misfortunes was its indebtedness to the Allies, he announced that his primary goal as chancellor would be to free the economy from the burden imposed on it by reparations payments. Although he was ultimately successful in the sense that he was able to secure an end to reparations payments in July 1932, it was at the price of deepening the economic and political crisis in Germany. Unable to borrow, the government saw no other option but to reduce services, cut benefits and public sector salaries and impose tax rises. On 8 December 1931 Brüning issued the (fourth) emergency decree, which cut wages by 10 per cent, salaries by 9 per cent, rents by 7.5 per cent and raised the transactions tax (*Umsatzsteuer*) from 0.85 to 2 per cent. This to some extent eased the state's fiscal situation, but it also had the effect of further decreasing demand.

Adolf Hitler is often credited with rescuing Germany from the Depression with policies aimed at stimulating the economy through a scheme of public works. A detailed examination of Nazi economic policy is beyond the scope of this book, but it is safe to say that there has been considerable debate over the issue of whether or not Germany's recovery was down to Hitler's policies, or merely an upturn in the international economic cycle.[31] There is certainly evidence that the German economy (like those of Japan, the United States and Britain) had begun to show signs of recovery in the summer of 1932. Nevertheless, it was only after the Nazi seizure of power that Germany's leaders felt able to shift their fiscal and monetary stance from deflation to reflation. Yet this should not mislead us into thinking that this was the result of ignorance or an innate economic conservatism at the very top of German politics. A committee of experts recommended such measures as early as 1931, while Brüning's fall in May 1932 was at least in part due to a scheme to resettle unemployed workers on the big east-Elbean estates. His successor as chancellor, Franz von Papen, attempted to address the crisis by raising public spending in late 1932, while one of the key features of Kurt von Schleicher's short-lived chancellorship was the announcement of an 'Emergency Programme' in December 1932 promising work-creation schemes. Rather, the failure to introduce radical and innovative measures to deal with the Depression was more a consequence of the fact that Weimar's politicians, as much as its populace, had been so demoralized by the inflation that they lacked both the means and the will to try untested measures to solve the crisis. The inflation had destroyed the state's ability to borrow in order to finance ambitious public works projects, making a Keynesian solution to Germany's economic ills unviable. At the same time, there was a very real fear that a return to deficit financing would result in another inflationary episode, and memories of the panic and upheaval of 1923 were still fresh enough to making risking this unthinkable. Add to this the widespread fear that such measures would lead to an electoral backlash that would deliver Germany into the hands of either the extreme Left or the far Right, and we can see the reasons for this timorousness.

Historians and economists have advanced a variety of complex theories to explain the Weimar Republic's descent into hyperinflation[32], although all agree that the basic cause was simply too much paper currency in circulation. Essentially, though, the blame for the collapse of Germany's finances in 1922–23 can be laid on a toxic brew of financial mismanagement, external pressure to pay reparations and internal social and economic cleavages. These were the long-term legacies of Germany's rapid industrial and economic growth between 1870 and 1914, and of the imperial regime's gamble on victory and the imposition of a huge indemnity on its enemies to finance its war effort. As a result, after 1918 Germany suffered from a deeply unstable and dislocated economy that was already prone to inflation. Political considerations prevented Weimar's politicians from taking steps to deal with this poisonous legacy, preferring instead to rely on deficit financing as a means of staving off domestic unrest and facilitating a pain-free transition to a peacetime economy. This might not have been too much of a problem if Germany had not also had to deal with the additional demands placed on its economy by the victorious Allies in the shape of reparations. Whatever the truth of

Germany's repeated assertions that it was fundamentally unable to meet the demands of the Allies, there is no doubt that the Ruhr Crisis precipitated a dramatic economic collapse. And although there was no accompanying political catastrophe, hyperinflation did leave a legacy of bitterness and instability that was to return to haunt Weimar's politicians when economic crisis struck once more at the end of the decade.

Thus the 'Great Inflation' was perhaps the single most traumatic event of the crisis-ridden life of the Weimar Republic, and it coloured the way in which many Germans looked at money and economics for decades to come. It brought incredible hardship to many, especially those who had been used to a relatively high standard of living and were perhaps least prepared to cope with such a dramatic change in their financial circumstances. But its effects went much deeper and broader than mere material concerns. It has long been suggested that a direct causal link exists between the two economic crises that bookended Weimar's golden years and the rise of Hitler. While it is true that political and economic considerations were never very far apart under the republic, to see the collapse of German democracy in the early 1930s as merely the consequence of the traumas of inflation and mass unemployment is somewhat simplistic. Other nations in Europe and elsewhere suffered similar economic upheavals in the mid-1920s and early 1930s with differing political consequences to those seen in Germany. Thus, while the impact of the Depression and the legacies of hyperinflation can been seen as contributing factors or important catalysts for the collapse of Weimar democracy, they are only convincing as explanations for the victory of Nazism when viewed in conjunction with other factors.

4

REVISIONISM AND THE SEARCH FOR STABILITY: WEIMAR FOREIGN POLICY

The issue of 'continuities in German history' has been the subject of much, often heated, debate. This has been particularly the case in the arena of foreign policy, where historians have long drawn parallels between the expansionism of imperial *Weltpolitik* and the Nazi drive for *Weltmacht* (world power). But where does the foreign policy of the first German democracy fit into this? There is no denying that after the First World War Germany was far from being 'a satiated power', and the desire to revise the post-war peace settlement was the guiding principle of Weimar foreign policy throughout its lifetime. It has been suggested that perhaps the chief difference between the foreign policy of the Weimar Republic and that of the Third Reich was one of methodology rather than ultimate aims. Shorn of not only its overseas colonies but also of Alsace-Lorraine and large chunks of territory to the east, forced to pay a huge indemnity to the Allies and denied the means to defend itself by the terms of the Treaty of Versailles, Germany felt humiliated and aggrieved after 1918 and many of its people hungered for a return to pre-war greatness. Although the democratic statesmen of the republic intended that revision of the treaty was to be brought about through peaceful means, and be limited in scope to retrieval of pre-war territory and status, Hitler was not only determined to overturn the post-war peace settlement through violence, but also dreamt of more than merely returning to the territorial *status quo ante* 1914. Indeed, some have seen Nazi foreign policy as 'the logical result' of the frustration felt during the republican period 'over not achieving its ends (revision in the east) by incongruous means (peaceful revision), without being able to give up the fatal juxtaposition of conflicting ends and means.'[1]

THE TREATY OF VERSAILLES

If the foreign policy of the German Empire was dominated by the issue of security and the fear of a war on two fronts, then the foreign policy of the Weimar Republic was similarly overshadowed by the Treaty of Versailles. The treaty was almost the only issue in German politics on which there was practically universal agreement during the Weimar period. Germans of all political persuasions saw it as unreasonable and unacceptable and were untiring in their efforts to revise or overturn this hated document. Part of the reason for this was the way in which the terms of the treaty were presented to the Germans. One of the chief reasons why the military leadership had been willing to hand over power to civilian authorities in the autumn of 1918 was the belief that a broad-based civilian administration would be better suited to negotiate a peace treaty with the Allies. But in the event there was no negotiation. The German delegation to the Paris peace conference was presented with the draft terms of a peace treaty on 7 May 1919 and given a mere two weeks to consider them and submit written comments. When they became known back home, the terms were considered so harsh that the government resigned rather than put their signatures to such a treaty. Attempts to negotiate concessions – calling for immediate membership of the League of Nations and the establishment of a commission to investigate the question of war guilt – proved futile, and the Germans were given the stark choice of signing the treaty as it was presented to them or facing an Allied invasion. In these circumstances the delegation had no choice but to sign the document, which they did – under protest – on 28 June.

By the terms of the treaty, Germany lost the territories of Alsace and Lorraine which had been taken from France after the Franco–

The German delegation to the Paris Peace Conference (Bundesarchiv, Bild 183-R01213 / CC-BY-SA).

Prussian War of 1870–71 (Article 51); West Prussia and Posen were transferred to Poland, thus forming the infamous Polish Corridor and leaving East Prussia isolated from the rest of the Reich, an island surrounded by new and potentially hostile states (Articles 27–28 and 87–88); the 'German-speaking industrial area' of Eupen–Malmedy was given to Belgium 'after a questionable plebiscite'[2] (Article 34); while North Schleswig, the most economically important part of Upper Silesia and Memel (Niemen) were all later lost after plebiscites (held in 1920, 1921 and 1923 respectively) returned majorities in favour of union with Denmark, Poland and Lithuania. Germany was forced to surrender all of its overseas colonies to the Allies (Article 119), while the Saar basin was placed under the administration of the League of Nations for 15 years and France given exclusive rights over the exploitation of its coal mines (Article 45). Despite the new Austrian Republic's desire for a union with its larger neighbour to the north-west, any such realization of nineteenth- century dreams of a *Grossdeutschland* were quashed by the forbidding of any such *Anschluss* (Article 80). The German Army was ordered to demobilize and, from the end of March 1920, it was forbidden to exceed seven infantry and three cavalry divisions in strength – a total of 100,000 men, of which no more than 4,000 could be officers (Articles 159–63). The General Staff (regarded by the Allies as the wellspring of German militarism since the days of Bismarck) was ordered to disband, and severe limitations were placed on the armaments that Germany was permitted to develop and store.[3] Conscription was banned and volunteers had to enlist for a minimum of 12 years (25 years for officers) so that Germany could not use a high turnover of recruits to train more men than were allowed. Restrictions were also placed on the training and manpower of police, coastguard and customs officers lest these organizations be used for covert military training. The Navy was to be reduced to little more than a coastguard of 15,000 men and 36 ships, and was forbidden the use of dreadnaughts and submarines (Article 181), while other modern military material such as aircraft (Article 198) and tanks were prohibited. On top of this, the Germans were to compensate the Allies for their losses during the war through the payment of reparations in cash and in kind (Articles 233–35). All this was justified by Article 231, the infamous War Guilt Clause, which stated that 'The Allied and Associated Governments affirm and Germany accepts the responsibility of Germany and its allies for causing all the loss and damage to which the Allied and Associated Governments and their nationals have been subjected to as a consequence of the war imposed upon them by the aggression of Germany and its allies.'[4] Finally, in order to ensure that the terms of the treaty were met, a strip of territory to the west of the Rhine was to be occupied by the Allies for a total of 15 years, the whole of the Rhineland was declared a demilitarized zone and Germany was not permitted to build any fortifications or station any military material or personnel in the region (Articles 428 and 42–43).

For the Germans – and not just for those in the political class, but for the population as a whole – these terms were wholly unacceptable. They were considered to be not only unfair, but also insulting: an affront to national honour. There were several reasons for this. Part of the problem was that many Germans, particularly those on the political Right, had trouble in accepting that Germany had lost the war at all. No less a figure than former Field Marshal Paul von Hindenburg declared publically that the collapse of the army on the Western Front had come not as a result of defeat on the field of battle, but rather as a consequence of the 'intentional mutilation of the fleet and the army' by left-wing forces[5], a view only underlined by the unfortunate wording of Friedrich Ebert's speech to returning troops on 10 December 1918 in which he told them that 'no enemy has vanquished you.'[6] Such statements led to the widespread belief that the German army had not been beaten by the Allies but had been 'stabbed in the back' by the forces of sedition and revolution, thus giving birth to the *Dolchstosslegende* (stab-in-the-back myth). In the minds of those who refused to accept that Germany had been defeated, the humiliating Treaty of Versailles therefore became inextricably linked with the November Revolution and the republic that was born out of it.

Furthermore, the fact that Germany had been denied the right and opportunity to negotiate the terms of the treaty only intensified the feeling that the settlement was vindictive and unjust. To be fair to the Allies, this had not been their original intention. To begin with they had envisaged a comprehensive and wide-ranging peace conference, in which all the interested parties – losers as well as winners – would get their say in the reordering of Europe. But such grandiose plans were overtaken by events: revolution in Russia and the collapse of the Habsburg and Ottoman Empires meant that several of the key players were no longer in existence and thus unable to put forward their views. It also became clear, as preliminary deliberations between the Allied and associated powers went on, that any negotiation with the defeated Central Powers was likely to expose the fragility of the facade of Allied unity. There was very little consensus as to what form the peace settlement should take. President Woodrow Wilson of the USA wanted to create a 'new world order' which stressed the principles of national self-determination and the 'new diplomacy'. He considered the creation of new democratic states and the establishment of the League of Nations to be the keys to creating a peaceful post-war world. The French on the other hand had no such grand designs – they were primarily concerned with their own security and wanted to weaken Germany as much as possible. In contrast, Britain had already achieved its aim of heading off Germany's challenge to British naval and economic superiority, and its main aim at the Paris Peace Conference was to ensure the survival of a stable and united Germany that could act as a barrier to the westward spread of bolshevism and as a counter-balance to French power on the Continent. Thus plans for a comprehensive peace conference were dropped because it was feared that, if the Germans were allowed to negotiate, the deep divisions and disagreements between the 'Big Three' would be exposed and they would be able to play the Allies off against one another in order to achieve a more lenient peace settlement, much as the French foreign minister Talleyrand had done in 1814–15.

On top of this there was outrage in Germany that the final peace terms seemed so different from President Wilson's Fourteen Points.[7] Even after the military leadership had thrown in the towel in October 1918, there was a widespread view among politicians and public alike that a negotiated peace would be based on these principles. Thus, when they were presented with what they saw as the *diktat* of Versailles, the Germans felt that they had been 'grossly deceived'.[8] As far as the Germans were concerned the victors were guilty of a monumental breach of faith. In their eyes the peace treaty as it was presented made a mockery of Wilson's desire for 'covenants of peace, openly arrived at', and the confiscation of their overseas territories did not seem to be a 'free, open-minded and impartial adjustment of . . . colonial claims'.[9] Furthermore, the prohibition of an *Anschluss* with Austria and the existence of sizable ethnic German populations in Czecho-slovakia, Poland and Romania seemed to expose the fact that 'national self-determination' applied only where it suited the Allies.

When it came to the actual clauses of the treaty, these too were regarded as unnecessarily vindictive and disproportionate. The loss of territory was a definite blow and, while some were prepared to swallow the bitter pill that was the loss of overseas colonies and Alsace-Lorraine (which had been German for only half a century), there were few who could accept the creation of the Polish Corridor and the loss of ancestral lands in the east. Silesia, Posen and West Prussia had enormous psychological significance, having been parts of the Kingdom of Prussia since the eighteenth century, won from its enemies by Friedrich the Great. In the nineteenth century they had been subjected to repeated attempts at 'Germanization' which included deportation of Poles and Jews, the compulsory purchase of the estates of Polish landowners, resettlement schemes and prohibitions on the use of the Polish language in schools and public services. At the same time there emerged the idea of a German *Drang nach Osten* (drive to the east) which saw Eastern Europe as Germany's 'frontier zone', analogous to the American West. After the First World War, racist pan-German notions of the inferiority of Slavic peoples combined with wartime accounts of 'the alien nature of the East [with] its primitive conditions, emptiness, dirt, disease, and omnipresent lice'[10] to create a sense of the Poles as a backward people unable to govern themselves. That territories which were considered to be both inherent parts of the German nation and the heartland of Junkerdom should be handed over to such people was regarded as a particular affront.

Equally, the demand for reparations was considered to be unreasonable, a deliberate attempt to kick Germany while it was down and prevent it from recovering its former economic strength. The problem was not so much the demand for reparations, as the scale of the indemnity imposed on Germany. It had always been expected that whoever lost the war would have to make some sort of reparations payment. This was normal practice: France had paid an indemnity of 700 million francs after the Napoleonic wars and, more recently, Germany itself had demanded reparations payments of 5 billion francs from France by the Treaty of Frankfurt (1871) and 3 billion gold roubles from Russia in the Treaty of Brest–Litovsk (1918). What most Germans objected to was what they regarded as the unrealistic scale of the reparations demanded by the Allies. In 1919 Germany was presented with a demand for a one-off payment of 20 billion gold marks, a down payment on the final figure to be decided upon by a committee and presented to the German government in May 1921. In effect Germany was compelled to sign a blank cheque when they signed the Treaty of Versailles. This in itself was bad enough, but when the Reparations Commission presented Germany with a provisional figure of 226,000 billion gold marks to be paid over 42 years, the Germans were appalled. They suggested their own figure a month later: a modest one-off payment of 30 billion gold marks. This was unacceptable to Britain and France, and French troops occupied Düsseldorf and Darmstadt. At the end of April 1921 the Reparations Commission fixed a global total of 152 billion gold marks, and at the beginning of May Britain and France issued an ultimatum to Berlin giving the Germans a month to agree to the bill or the Ruhr would be occupied. The Germans had no choice but to agree. The first instalment of reparations was paid punctually in August, but with inflation rampant it became increasingly clear that Germany would not be able to raise enough hard cash to cover the next payment.

However, perhaps what hurt the most was the enforced admission for responsibility for the war. 'War guilt' was a new concept in international relations. Prior to the First World War it had generally been the case that the causes of a conflict were kept out of the process of peacemaking, with the result that as a rule it was the loser who paid. This principle was applied in 1919, but the victors sought to put a gloss of legal legitimacy on the business of hard-headed politics by forcing Germany to sign a document in which they admitted sole responsibility for the death and destruction of four years of conflict. British Prime Minister David Lloyd George admitted as much when he declared at the London Conference in 1921 that 'German responsibility for the war . . . is the basis upon which the structure of the treaty has been erected, and if that acknowledgment is repudiated or abandoned, the treaty is destroyed'[11]. Article 231 was the lynchpin of the treaty, the clause by which all the other clauses – and especially the allied claim for reparations of sufficient magnitude that they would cover the costs of war pensions – were justified.

As such it was at this clause that Germany aimed its most vociferous denunciations. In response to accusations of war guilt, the German Foreign Office, the *Auswärtiges Amt*, rushed to publish 'carefully chosen, edited and – if necessary – falsified' official documents to prove that Germany had not been responsible for the war.[12] Such was the desire to refute the accusation of war guilt that a special section of the Foreign Ministry was established to encourage and subsidize the publication of attacks on the Versailles settlement.

Thus Germany became a major revisionist power, and the dominant theme in its foreign policy after 1919 was overturning the Treaty of Versailles. In this ambition it was not alone. There were plenty of European states who saw in the post-war peace settlement the frustration of their ambitions or the choking-off of their hopes. Even amongst the victorious powers there were nations who were profoundly dissatisfied with the settlement that emerged from the Paris Peace Conference. The Italian delegation had walked out of the negotiations when the Allies failed to deliver on the promises made in the Treaty of London (1915), while many of the new states of Central and Eastern Europe were dissatisfied with their borders as decided by the peacemakers. Even France can be seen as a revisionist power in the sense that it believed that the treaty in its final form failed to guarantee its security, and it would have preferred much more stringent controls on Germany. But it was amongst the ranks of the defeated nations that the drive for a revision of the treaties was felt most strongly. Austria, once the heart and head of a huge multi-national empire, was reduced to a rump state that left nearly 3 million Austrians living outside its borders. It was forced to recognize the independence of the successor states of Czechoslovakia, Hungary, Poland and Yugoslavia, cede South Tyrol, Trieste and Istria to Italy and reduce its armed forces to 30,000 men. Similarly, by the Treaty of Trianon (1920), Hungary lost two-thirds of its territory and nearly 60 per cent of its population (the territory that was handed over to Romania alone was bigger than that which remained Hungarian), 3 million ethnic Magyars remained outside Hungary and it lost most of its natural resources and industry. Both Austria and Hungary were to pay reparations, but the amount remained undecided at the time of their economic collapse in 1921–22 and in the event the Allies did not press their claims, thus placing even more pressure on Germany.

GERMAN REVISIONISM: CIRCUMVENTION

That the Treaty of Versailles should be revised was about the only issue in German politics on which there was almost universal agreement during the Weimar period. Yet there was no corresponding consensus as to how this should be brought about. On the one hand there were those who advocated openly flouting the terms of the treaty, whatever the consequences. These hardliners argued that any concession to the Allies was a betrayal of the Fatherland, and that reparations should not be paid, the disarmament clauses ignored and the territorial clauses rejected and overturned. Yet such a position was hardly realistic given Germany's domestic instability and international isolation. Perhaps this is why such populist sentiments were most commonly espoused by the DNVP and the parties of the extreme Right, who had the luxury of sounding off about Germany's problems from the comfort of the opposition benches without having to get involved with the practicalities of governing a major industrial nation. On the other hand, the republican parties took a more realistic view and accepted the peace for the time being, while working to overturn it at some unspecified date in the future. Weimar Germany was therefore faced with two alternative strategies for achieving a revision of the treaty: attempt to circumvent the constraints placed upon them by the Treaty of Versailles in order to rebuild military strength and secure alliances in preparation for a revision of the peace settlement by force, or seek to secure German interests and achieve a return to Great Power status through negotiation and conciliation with the Western Powers. Both strategies were tried, with varying degrees of success, by successive governments, but initially the focus was on circumvention.

Almost from the moment the treaty was ratified, Germany tried to avoid fulfilling its obligations. The government's successful refusal to hand over war criminals was bolstered by Holland's failure to hand over the former Kaiser to the Allies, and led to a stand-off in February 1920. Ultimately, a compromise was agreed in which Germany promised to establish a specially constituted Reich court in Leipzig in order to investigate accusations of war crimes. However, this resulted in little besides a few desultory attempts at trials and a handful of convictions. This early success in avoiding compliance with the terms of the treaty encouraged the Nationalists in thinking that the other clauses might be shrugged off just as quickly and easily, but this was not to be. Although the new Reichswehr did go some way to circumventing the prohibition of the General Staff by dividing its functions between various ministries, their attempts to persuade the Allies to allow them an army of 200,000 men were rejected. Furthermore, the Kapp Putsch and a breach of the demilitarized zone during operations against left-wing insurgents in the Rhineland led to French troops occupying Frankfurt – a clear signal that breaches of the treaty would not be tolerated under any circumstances.

Nevertheless, even as the civilian government shifted towards a more conciliatory policy, it also sought to make common cause with Russia in an attempt to escape from the economic and diplomatic straightjacket imposed on it by the Treaty of Versailles. From the beginning there had been those who saw the best hope for a revision of the treaty not in cooperation and negotiation with the west but in closer relations with Europe's other pariah state, the Soviet Union. Ironically enough, considering that Soviet Russia was the world's first communist state, this was a view most often endorsed by right-wingers. Prussian aristocrats such as Baron Adolf Georg Otto (Ago) von Maltzan, the head of the Russian department of the Foreign Office, and the head of the Reichswehr, Hans von Seeckt, as well as some prominent businessmen, argued that Germany should seek to cultivate closer economic and military relations with Russia at the earliest opportunity. Yet this was not as strange as the obvious ideological differences between the Bolsheviks and the German political and military elite may make it seem. Common antagonism towards Poland provided a bond between Berlin and Moscow, and there was a widespread feeling in the Foreign Office that the Bolshevik regime would not last and would sooner or later be replaced by something more in keeping with western political and economic norms. The policy of pursuing closer ties with the Soviet Union was therefore regarded as paving the way for relations with a post-Soviet regime, while in some quarters it was seen as simply a revival of the traditional eastward alignment that had dominated Prussian foreign policy in the nineteenth century. Even those who argued that the best chance for revision lay in negotiation rather than confrontation with the Allies saw no harm in seeking to normalise relations in the east, if only as a means of aiding economic recovery and forestalling Russian claims for reparations (an option theoretically left open to them by Article 116 of the Treaty of Versailles). But Russia also offered opportunities for economic and military renewal and development. Continuing discriminatory tariffs on German goods in the west meant that Germany sought new markets for its exports (always a key part of its economy), while the Soviet state was in dire need of capital investment from abroad. Moreover, there were those in the Reichswehr who saw in the Russian steppes the hope of circumventing Allied prohibitions on developing modern weapons and training a new army away from the prying eyes of the Allied Control Commission, something that the Russians were only too keen to acquiesce to in the hope of sharing in the military technology that was developed.

In the wake of the peace, the issue of the repatriation of 1.2 million Russian prisoners of war still in Germany (and 100,000 Germans in Russia) was used as a means to resume contact. An agreement to this effect was signed on 19 April 1920, to be followed a year later by a Russo–German trade treaty and the opening of official diplomatic missions incorporating trade legations in autumn 1921. At the same time, 'preliminary contacts with a view to military collaboration' had been authorized as early as January 1920, and in September 1921 secret meetings between senior German and Russian officers were held in the Berlin apartment of General Kurt von Schleicher, while a front company was set up to channel 75 million marks into the establishment of aircraft, munitions and poison gas factories on Russian soil.[13]

This cooperation paved the way for the signature of the Rapallo Treaty on 16 April 1922. This was not an alliance as such, but rather a treaty of friendship that established full diplomatic relations between the two states, saw them agree to renounce all claims for war damage and reparations and grant one another most-favoured-nation status. It was followed on 11 August by a secret Military Convention between the Reichswehr and the Red Army that extended existing military cooperation and led to the development of a tank base at Kazan and an aviation school at Lipetsk. The Allies were horrified by this 'unholy alliance' and saw it as a part of a German-led conspiracy to overturn the Treaty of Versailles. It also caused consternation at home. President Ebert strongly opposed the agreement, believing (with some justification) that it antagonised the Western Powers without delivering much of benefit to Germany, while the Social Democrats feared that better relations with Russia would increase the influence of the KPD. Even so, Rapallo 'did not mark . . . a fundamental turn to the east'[14], but was seen rather as a complement to the policy of conciliation in the west. By bringing an end to post-war isolation, the agreement with Russia secured Germany's eastern flank and opened the way for economic reconstruction through trade links in the east. At the same time it provided a means of placing joint pressure on Poland while avoiding the old nightmare of encirclement, while for some hardliners it opened up the possibility of joint military action against Poland which would ultimately lead to the collapse of the Versailles settlement.

GERMAN REVISIONISM: *ERFÜLLUNGSPOLITIK*

After the French occupation of Frankfurt in April 1920, the civilian government saw that it had little choice but to bow to Allied demands for reparations and to hope that through attempted compliance it could prove that these demands were unrealistic and thereby achieve peaceful revision of the treaty. This came to be called *Erfüllungspolitik* (the policy of fulfilment) a dual policy of economic development at home and reconciliation and appeasement abroad. This was most closely associated with Chancellor Josef Wirth and his foreign minister, Walther Rathenau. Along with Erzberger, Wirth had been regarded as one of the foremost progressives within the Centre Party and had served as finance minister under Hermann Müller and Konstantin Fehrenbach, during which time he had supported a progressive tax regime as a means of stabilizing Germany's precarious financial position. Appointed as chancellor at the age of 42 (making him the youngest chancellor in German history) when Fehrenbach's administration collapsed after the DVP withdrew in May 1921, Wirth believed that nothing could be gained from continuing attempts to circumvent the reparations clauses of the Treaty of Versailles and that the only way to convince the Allies of Germany's inability to pay was to make every effort to do so.

In the short term the policy of fulfilment seemed doomed to failure. Deeply unpopular at home, it seemed to confirm the nationalist

Right's arguments that the republic and its supporters were unpatriotic and un-German. At the same time, despite the failure of both sides to get to grips with the problem of reparations (a total of 12 international conferences held between 1919 and 1922 failed to break the impasse and find a formula, ultimately only serving to frustrate the French while increasing British suspicion of the ambitions of their ostensible ally), the international situation was not favourable towards such a policy. In particular, France was neither willing nor able to agree to any reduction in reparations. Like Germany, France had emerged from the war 'economically exhausted and a net debtor', beset by inflation and a shortage of manpower. Increasingly anxious about their own economic situation, the French became fixated on the reparations issue, looking to injections of German cash to both help solve their own fiscal problems and provide economic security by hamstringing German heavy industry and its latent military potential. Failure to secure reparations only intensified French fears for their security, while the Rapallo Treaty was perceived as 'a clandestine military alliance that posed a grave if indirect threat to French security' and a further indication that the Weimar Republic was little more than a facade designed to mask Germany's old aggressive nationalism.[15]

When Germany defaulted in July 1922, the French decided that enough was enough and determined to take action to seize what they regarded as rightfully theirs. French and Belgian troops marched into the Ruhr on 11 January 1923 with the intention to force the German government to make good on their obligations under the Treaty of Versailles, and if that failed then to extract reparations themselves in the form of confiscated coal, coke, timber and rolling stock. In response, the German government called on the people of the Ruhr to meet the invasion with 'passive resistance' while they appealed to Britain and the United States to help bring about a negotiated settlement. However, the intolerable strain placed on already overburdened government finances by nine months of passive resistance precipitated the slide into hyperinflation and with it yet more human misery. By September Germany was on the brink of collapse, and Gustav Stresemann, the new chancellor, had no choice but to call an end to passive resistance. Many Germans saw this as a humiliating surrender to the French, but Stresemann recognized that he had little choice – Germany was too weak to wage war against France, so its only hope was to adopt a conciliatory position and hope that Britain and America would intervene to force a compromise solution on the issue of reparations. This policy was vindicated by the unfolding of events. The occupation of the Ruhr had almost destroyed the German economy, but it had also placed a huge strain on French finances and seriously weakened the franc on the international markets. Britain had refused to back France either financially or militarily and, by January 1924, the French had no choice but to cooperate with an American initiative to establish a commission, under the financier Charles Dawes, which would investigate the whole issue of how Germany could pay reparations. The result was a plan designed not only to provide a workable schedule for German reparations payments, but also to facilitate the revitalization of the German economy (see Chapter 3).

FOREIGN POLICY UNDER STRESEMANN

Gustav Stresemann's period as chancellor was brief but, both during his short spell as head of government and in his subsequent role as foreign minister (a post that he held in every administration until his untimely death at the age of only 51 in October 1929), he proved that he had the political and moral courage to take the difficult and unpopular decisions that were necessary for the preservation of the republic. Born in Berlin in 1878, Stresemann had enjoyed a successful career in business before entering the Reichstag in 1907 as a representative of the National Liberal party. An ardent nationalist and annexationist during the war, the experience of defeat and revolution shook him profoundly and threatened to derail his political career. One of the main obstacles to the formation of a united liberal party in 1918 was the Progressives' distrust of Stresemann, who was widely regarded as an unprincipled nationalist. Yet as time went on, Stresemann came to see the new republican system as the best way to preserve Germany from either a right-wing dictatorship or a communist revolution. Often thought of as an archetypal 'rational republican', Stresemann's accommodation with the new regime was in fact more deep-rooted than a mere recognition that the republic was the least-worst option, and was based on a genuine belief in the need for consensus.[16] At the same time the war convinced him that the key to German prosperity was not economic rivalry and territorial expansion, but the common interests of the European states in the face of the economic challenge from the USA. This being the case, Germany's priority should be to become once more a 'credible ally' (*bündnisfähig*) for the west. It was an argument based on economic self-interest but it also assumed that such self-interest could lead to greater cooperation and understanding between nations. The Ruhr Crisis further convinced him that interdependence had another strand: that German security depended on French security. For as long as France felt threatened by the prospect of a resurgent Germany, it would do all it could to keep its neighbour down.

As the German economy began to recover, the Dawes Plan seemed to have, for the time being at least, resolved the conundrum of reparations, vindicating those like Stresemann and Wirth who had long argued that the best way to treaty revision was conciliation and negotiation rather than confrontation. Yet Germany still faced international hurdles in its path. The reparations issue might have been settled on a reasonably acceptable basis for all but the most hard-line nationalists, but the other clauses of the Treaty of Versailles remained unaltered and Germany was still far from being fully reintegrated into the community of nations.

Almost as soon as the Dawes Plan was settled a new crisis threatened to erupt. In December 1924, following a report by the Military Control Commission demonstrating extensive violations of the disarmament clauses of the treaty, the Allies decided that the area of the occupied Rhineland around Cologne would not be evacuated in January 1925 as scheduled. This apparent evidence of Anglo-French rapprochement so soon after the dramatic falling out during the Ruhr Crisis rang alarm bells in the German Foreign Office. It feared that the mutual defence pact with France favoured by the new British Foreign Secretary Austin Chamberlain would leave them permanently isolated and stiffen French intransigence, just when the prospect of increased mutual understanding seemed in the offing. At the same time, Stresemann was acutely aware of the effect that the failure to

Gustav Stresemann (left) at Locarno with British Foreign Secretary Austin Chamberlain (centre) and French Foreign Minister Aristide Briand (Bundesarchiv, Bild 183-R03618 / CC-BY-SA).

evacuate the Cologne zone on schedule would have on his right-wing critics at home.

Thus, in an effort to 'balance French claims for security with German demands for treaty revision'[17], Stresemann launched what he later called 'a peace offensive on a grand scale'[18] by reviving the idea of a tripartite Rhineland Pact that had first been proposed by the Cuno administration in 1922. Early in 1925, the German Foreign Office made an offer of an agreement that would include a guarantee of the Franco–German border together with a revised schedule for the withdrawal of allied troops for the Rhineland. The French were hesitant at first, particularly after 26 April when Germany's wartime 'dictator' Field Marshal Paul von Hindenburg was elected as president. This stimulated French suspicions that the Weimar Republic was little more than a front for the aggressive, nationalist Germany of old, but with the encouragement of Britain and the USA the proposal was treated seriously. The main sticking point was the lack of any guarantee of Germany's eastern frontiers – the most Stresemann was prepared to offer was mutual arbitration treaties with Poland and Czechoslovakia – which the French feared would leave their eastern allies dangerously exposed. After protracted negotiations and exchanges of notes (during which time Stresemann faced down pressure both from the Soviets – who threatened to reveal the extent of their military links with the Reichswehr – and the DNVP) it was agreed to hold a foreign minister's conference at Locarno, Switzerland, in order to discuss the proposal. The conference opened on 5 October 1925 and agreement was reached 11 days later. The resulting Locarno Treaties were signed in London on 1 December. These were designed to allay the security fears of all the participating nations and put an end to territorial disputes. The Treaty of Mutual Guarantee, saw the five European powers (Germany, France, Britain, Belgium and Italy) guarantee Germany's existing frontiers with France and Belgium while agreeing to uphold the demilitarization of the Rhineland. Germany undertook not to wage war against France and/or Belgium, and all three powers agreed to offer any disputes to the League of Nations for arbitration. Britain and Italy acted as guarantors of the treaties and were pledged to assist the victims of aggression, while all the signatories pledged themselves to renounce military action except in self-defence.

Locarno marked a turning point in Weimar Germany's relations with the outside world. Although it faced concerted opposition from the DNVP and the extreme Right, the ratification of the agreement ushered in a period of détente in Europe that, in spite of the strains later placed upon it, lasted at least until Stresemann's death in 1929. Locarno dramatically improved Germany's international standing and made it much harder for the Allies to justify the continuation of the occupation of the Rhineland, while at the same time it improved the republic's financial position as it opened the way for more foreign investment and trade treaties with the USA, Britain, France, Italy and Poland. Thereafter Germany was treated more like an equal than a former enemy, and the way was smoothed for Germany to be readmitted into the community of nations through membership of the League of Nations.

This possibility had first been raised in September 1924 by the newly elected British Prime Minister Ramsey MacDonald, but it soon ran into problems. Although the initiative was welcomed by Stresemann as a step towards Germany's rehabilitation as a Great Power, it also presented a problem as it was unclear how compatible this would be with Weimar's commitments to the Soviet Union. A staunch anti-communist who was sceptical as to the value of military cooperation with the Red Army (as chancellor he had tried to bring an end to this, only for the Reichswehr to carry on regardless[19]), Stresemann never saw close relations with Russia as being as important as an accommodation with the Western Powers, but he did see their value as a means of balancing Germany's commitments. This was partly because he viewed close relations with the Soviet Union as a way of maintaining pressure on Poland, but also because he was aware of the entrenched domestic opposition from Hindenburg, Seeckt and the nationalist Right to abandoning Germany's eastern option in favour of closer ties with the west.[20] He therefore argued for German entry to the League only on terms that would not drive a wedge between Germany and Russia. This proved unacceptable to the Allies and the matter was dropped. Negotiations were resumed in the wake of Locarno, only to stall again in March 1926 when Germany insisted that it be given a permanent seat on the League Council while vehemently opposing France's suggestion that this should be balanced by the extension of the same privilege to Poland. Nevertheless, over the summer Germany's path to membership of the League was smoothed, and on 10 September it was formally admitted, although it had to consent to Poland becoming a non-permanent member of the council.

Meanwhile, the Germans had been engaged in protracted negotiations with the Soviet Union which had been going on since before the signature of the Locarno Treaties. Alarmed at Stresemann's policy of *détente* with the west, which threatened to undermine their tactic of exploiting divisions between the capitalist states and raise the prospect of a future capitalist crusade against communism, in December 1924 the Soviets proposed an extension the political and military agreement made at Rapallo. The Germans, preferring to prioritize negotiations with the west which promised more immediate and important gains, prevaricated and ultimately were willing to commit themselves to nothing more than a trade treaty. Thus, on 24 April 1926, Germany concluded a commercial treaty with Russia. This was largely designed to counter domestic criticism that the policy of rapprochement with the west was one-sided and gave away too much. However, it also had great symbolic importance as a show of Germany's independence and right to act in ways that it thought appropriate to its political and economic interests, geographical position and status as a Great Power.[21]

After securing the Weimar Republic's entry into the League, Stresemann had high hopes of a wide-ranging agreement with France designed to allay French security concerns once and for all while finally ridding Germany of foreign occupation. However, such a final settlement remained elusive. Hopes of a general Franco–German agreement foundered when faced with French reluctance to commit and the realization that no progress could be made on reparations until after the US presidential election of 1928. Nevertheless, with the establishment of better relations after Locarno, British and German politicians increasingly regarded the occupation of the Rhineland as an anachronism, and in January 1926 the British withdrew their troops from Cologne, leaving only a token force at Weisbaden. Further negotiations followed, and in August 1927 Stresemann managed to secure a reduction of the occupying force in the Rhineland to 60,000 men and the signature of a comprehensive trade treaty with France.

Shortly afterwards, the French made an attempt to elicit a 'solemn declaration' of friendship from the Americans. Determined not to be drawn into the European security system, the US Secretary of State Frank Kellogg countered in December 1927 with a proposal for a multilateral peace pact. The International Treaty for the Renunciation of War as an Instrument of National Policy, or Kellogg–Braind Pact as it became known, 'directed that its signatories renounce war, but provided no means of enforcement' while 'in its final form, the draft was diluted to exclude wars of self-defence and for the fulfilment of existing treaty obligations.'[22] Nevertheless, it caught the public mood and seemed to offer an opportunity to breathe new life into the flagging Locarno spirit. Furthermore, it was consistent with Germany's policy of seeking to persuade the Allies that they had turned over a new leaf, and thereby pave the way to a revision of Versailles and the restoration of equality with other nations. This being the case, Stresemann seized eagerly on the opportunity and Germany was the first nation to accept Kellogg's proposals.

Nevertheless, a final settlement on the Rhineland and reparations remained an important goal that could not be overlooked. By the beginning of 1929 the government was acutely aware that Germany would not be able to meet its obligations under the Dawes Plan and that, unless some agreement was reached, foreign investors would lose confidence in the German economy. American bankers were to some extent open to proposals to revise the Dawes Plan, as it was clear that once it was obliged to pay the full annual instalments of reparations stipulated by the 1924 agreement Germany would lack sufficient funds to meet interest payments on US loans. On their side the French were also willing to agree to a revision, as long as it also took into account war debts. To this end, the League of Nations established a commission to review the question under the chairmanship of the American banker Owen D. Young. The resultant Young Plan (see Chapter 3), together with the question of the evacuation of the Rhineland, was the cause of tense negotiations at the Hague Conference of August 1929. The British and French clashed over their share of reparations and the French sought to extract concessions from Germany in return for agreeing to withdraw their troops from the Rhineland. However, Stresemann was aware that the French needed an agreement on reparations and war debts as badly as the Germans did, and managed to force their acquiescence to the evacuation of French occupying forces by 30 June 1930 by threatening not to sign the Young Plan.

FOREIGN POLICY AFTER STRESEMANN

Securing the liberation of the occupied Rhineland was Stresemann's last success, and he did not live to see it accomplished. In early October 1929 Stresemann suffered a stroke which left him paralysed and unable to speak, and he died a few days later. Stresemann's supporters regarded him as 'having restored Germany to the ranks of the Great Powers from the nadir of the Ruhr occupation and as

having provided a vital link between Right and Left which had stabilized the republic.'[23] In London, *The Times* called him an 'intelligent and practical patriot' who 'did inestimable service to the German Republic' and whose 'work for Europe as a whole was almost as great'[24], while in Paris public grief was 'so general and sincere' that it was 'almost as if an outstanding French statesman had died.'[25] But to his domestic opponents on the Right he was little more than a traitor who had sold out Germany to the west. At the time of his death Stresemann had been preparing to fight a referendum on the Young Plan orchestrated by the DNVP and the Nazis. While it was true that, by 1929, Germany no longer laboured under the same international constraints imposed upon it in 1919, the policy of peaceful revision had failed to deliver the more substantive results demanded by the Nationalists. A scheme by which Eupen–Malmedy would be returned to Germany in exchange for financial compensation was scotched by the French in August 1926, while efforts to induce Poland to acquiesce to a revision of the frontier through financial pressure were defeated by an international bailout of the Polish economy. Thus, despite Stresemann's achievements of the previous five years, Germany's chief aims – an end to reparations, the retrieval of territory in the east and equality in armaments – remained unfulfilled.

After Stresemann's death the Foreign Ministry was placed in the hands of his party colleague Julius Curtius. A staunch nationalist who had won two Iron Crosses as an artillery officer during the war, Curtius had long sought to modify the pro-western policy pursued by his predecessor, but almost his first act as foreign minister was to steer the Young Plan through the Reichstag. This earned him the hatred of the far Right, and he became the target of vociferous attacks by the DNVP, the *Stahlhelm* and the Nazis. Curtius remained as foreign minister under Heinrich Brüning, but almost from the start there was a change in gear in German foreign policy. When he came to power Brüning was politically committed to neither a conciliatory nor a confrontational programme and, as a result, his policy often seemed to fall between two stools, being 'either too uncompromising or not "national" enough' for his domestic critics.[26] Yet keenly aware that only success abroad could strengthen his position at home, the

President Hindenburg (centre) and Minister-President of Prussia Otto
Braun (right) arriving at the celebrations to mark the end of the
occupation of the Rhineland in Koblenz, 22 July 1930 (Bundesarchiv,
Bild 102-10168 / Unknown / CC BY SA).

new chancellor was determined to pursue a more assertive foreign
policy in the hope that rapid gains would shore up Germany's precarious economic and political situation. Essentially, the polarization of
domestic politics and the renewed economic crisis after 1929 meant
that Brüning could not afford to wait for his policy to bear fruit as
Stresemann had done: he needed results and he needed them quickly.

Brüning is often accused of pursuing a ruinous economic policy
in the hope of persuading the Allies to cancel reparations which he
regarded as the true cause of Germany's economic crisis. However,
'he had never intended for Germany to have the highest unemployment rate in Europe' or the hardships that this entailed.[27] Indeed,
this would have been completely against his paternalist attitude
towards the less fortunate in society. Instead, the Chancellor's original
intention had been to put pressure on Britain and France to revise
the Young Plan by allowing a trade surplus to build, thereby creating
jobs in export industries while undermining the international case

for reparations. But it soon became clear that, while the trade surplus did grow from 1.6 million in 1930 to 2.9 million in 1932, exports were not growing, merely shrinking more slowly than imports. This realization, together with growing pressure from the extreme Right, pushed the government into a new course and they embarked upon a more active and assertive foreign policy. In January 1931 the Council of the League of Nations tacitly approved Germany's view that Polish minority policy was discriminatory and the source of friction along the frontier between the two countries. Shortly afterwards, Germany succeeded in pressuring the British into abandoning plans to incorporate what had, until 1918, been German East Africa into its neighbouring colonial possessions. At the same time, the German government managed to win Russian and Italian (and to some extent British) support for its claim to equality in armaments with the other European powers.

In the meantime, Curtius and Bernhard von Bülow – nephew to the architect of *Weltpolitik* in the 1890s, and the state secretary of the Foreign Office from June 1930 – pushed for the conclusion of a *Zollunion* (customs union) with Austria. At first Brüning was unenthusiastic, thinking, like his predecessor, that any such preliminary moves towards *Anschluss* could only be considered once reparations had been cancelled. However, in February 1931, he dropped his objections after increasingly desperate appeals from Austrian business for closer economic ties to Germany. A draft treaty was prepared in secret and approved by the cabinet on 18 March before being announced to the world three days later. This created a diplomatic storm, with France and Britain (who feared that it would herald political union between the two states, much as the nineteenth-century *Zollverein* had presaged German unification) demanding that the matter be referred to the League of Nations. However, the plan was soon overtaken by events. On 11 May, the bankruptcy of Austria's biggest bank, the Credit-Anstalt, and the subsequent Austro–German banking crisis killed the projected customs union, as the Austrian government withdrew from the project in order to seek financial assistance from the Western Powers.

The customs union fiasco cost Curtius his job, as he had only secured Brüning's support for the idea on the condition that he take full responsibility for its success or failure, and the Chancellor took on the Foreign Ministry himself. Never afraid to use his economic policy – and the outcry from the opposition which often resulted – as a means of putting pressure on the Allies, at the Chequers Conference of June 1931 Brüning pointed to the uproar caused by his second emergency decree as evidence that a moratorium on reparations was necessary in order to stave off the threat of revolution as well as economic collapse. This approach had considerable success and, on 20 June, US President Herbert Hoover announced a one-year freeze on reparations. However, Brüning did not remain in office long enough to see his goal realized as, in May 1932, he was ousted by the conservative clique surrounding Hindenburg.

The change of government brought with it a new, more aggressively revisionist, foreign policy. While Brüning had showed a willingness to negotiate and cooperate with the British, despite his refusal to make concessions to France, international antipathy to the new government meant that his successor was forced to pursue a more dramatic and unilateral course, withdrawing from the moribund International Disarmament Commission in July 1932. At the same time, the new chancellor, Franz von Papen, managed to secure an end to reparations, but only by agreeing to a scheme by which Germany would be given three years to recover its credit-worthiness before paying a final settlement of 3 billion marks, a plan that was so unpopular that the German delegation that signed it was pelted with rotten eggs on their return home. However, the Lausanne Agreement, and Papen's 'new course' in foreign policy as a whole, was overtaken by events and no more reparations were forthcoming. The rapid fall of Papen and his successor Kurt von Schleicher, and the appointment of Adolf Hitler as chancellor in January 1933, meant that the agreement was never ratified and Germany never made another payment.

The First World War cast a long shadow over Weimar Germany, and nowhere was this more evident than in attitudes towards the Treaty of Versailles. The terms of the treaty, coming on top of the unexpected loss of the war, were regarded as a humiliation and an affront that could not be borne. While it might be thought that the almost universal opposition to the Versailles Treaty would have provided one of the few areas of consensus in the fractious politics of the Weimar Republic, it did in fact become one of the chief areas of contention between Left and Right, moderates and radicals, republicans and Nationalists. From the very beginning, the necessary but unwilling signature of the peace treaty by the left-of-centre 'Weimar Coalition' led to them being branded as traitors and helped to undermine the republic itself in the eyes of its critics. Subsequently, although there was widespread agreement on the need to revise the peace settlement, the means by which this goal could be achieved was a deeply divisive issue and fiercely contested. Thus, German foreign policy in the Weimar period veered between confrontation and conciliation with the Western Powers and evasion and compliance with the terms of the treaty. As a result it all too often appeared unfocused or deliberately mendacious to foreign observers, as successive chancellors and foreign ministers sought to balance the considerations of domestic politics with the demands of geopolitics.

By 1923, attempts at evasion had achieved nothing except economic collapse and the occupation of the Ruhr. This exposed Germany's fundamental weakness in international affairs to all except the most blinkered of reactionaries, and it convinced all responsible and moderate politicians that only through negotiation could Germany regain its former status and go some way to solving some of its internal difficulties. Above all, Stresemann and those who supported him saw the economy as the key to German recovery, and recognized that closer integration into the community of nations, not isolation and opposition, were the way to escape the 'shackles of Versailles'. Yet although Stresemann's policy of *détente* did much to bring Germany back into the mainstream of European politics, the goals of a final settlement on reparations, equality of armaments, union with Austria and the recovery of lost territory in the east all remained beyond his grasp. Ultimately, it was only through the aggressive and bellicose policy of Adolf Hitler that Germany made any headway in achieving these aims.

After Stresemann's death his policy of conciliation and compromise was abandoned. As the Great Depression gripped Europe and aggressively nationalist regimes in Italy and Japan began to embark on imperialist adventures, governments of all nations were less open to compromise and sought to protect their own economic and political interests. At the same time, renewed internal pressure from the extremist parties impelled the Brüning and Papen governments to embark upon a more assertive policy in the hope of allaying domestic difficulties through foreign policy successes. Although this did achieve some success – an effective end to reparations in July 1932 – it also ultimately played into the hands of the radical Right. Rather than detaching support from the Nazis, these small victories only seemed to vindicate the Nationalist claim that revision could only be achieved through confrontation. Such ideas were further encouraged by the apparent success of Hitler's brinkmanship over the remilitarization of the Rhineland in 1936 and *Anschluss* with Austria in 1938, and they ultimately paved the way for war with Britain and France when he tried to recover the eastern provinces lost in 1918 by invading Poland in September 1939.

5

WEIMAR SOCIETY AND CULTURE

After the political and economic upheavals of the period between 1918 and 1923 the Weimar Republic experienced a brief period of relative peace and prosperity between 1924 and 1929. During this period, Germany returned to some semblance of economic and political normality and appeared to be entering a period of consolidation that would eventually see it resume its place among the modern industrialized nations of the world. Yet the deep divisions that had existed within German society during the imperial era persisted and, in some cases, became more pronounced. The attempts made by the parties of the 'Weimar Coalition' to foster a sense of commitment to democracy and improve material conditions through progressive social policy made some progress towards improving the lot of the least fortunate in society, but huge disparities of wealth and status remained and state welfare spending continued to be a contentious issue, especially after 1928. Such established social divisions were only exacerbated by the demographic changes wrought by the Great War, which focused new attention on potential areas of social discord such as female emancipation and generational conflict. These issues had existed before 1914 but gained a new significance in the 1920s

At the same time Weimar Germany became, in the words of one historian, a 'laboratory of the apocalypse where modern Europeans tested the limits of their social and cultural traditions'[1]. The social changes wrought by modernity, together with the political and economic upheavals of the early years of the republic, combined to create a heightened sense of anxiety which was widely reflected in the culture of the period. German painters, architects and scientists were at the forefront of the European avant-garde, and Germany achieved a reputation as the fountainhead of new ideas and new technologies. Yet many Germans remained profoundly alienated from this culture of urban modernity, attacking everything from the 'Americanization' of the German workplace to jazz music, and viewing avant-garde art as degenerate, decadent and un-German.

THE OLD ELITES: ARISTOCRACY AND OFFICER CORPS

The news of the military collapse and formation of the republic was greeted with a mixture of shock and horror by the Prussian aristocracy. For many *Junker* (see page 9) the German state was inextricably linked with the Hohenzollern monarchy, and they felt that the one could not exist without the other. Many saw in the transition from monarchy to republic the collapse of everything they believed in and had been brought up to trust and admire. This engendered a profound sense of dislocation and anxiety which was only intensified by one of the few measures of social engineering embodied in the Weimar constitution, the abolition of aristocratic ranks and titles. Furthermore, although the old social and business elites still had a political voice via the DVP and the DNVP, their influence was much diminished from the days of Bismarck and Wilhelm II, at least until the last days of the Hindenburg presidency.

However, big business and the large landowners continued to exert considerable political as well as economic influence. In the wake of the revolution the Weimar Coalition had no appetite for land reform, not least because it was feared that this would lead to further civil unrest and put the food supply to the towns under threat. Thus, the Prussian system of large estates owned by aristocrats remained in place and was even subsidized by the public purse. Forty-one per cent of land was owned by these estates, many of which had been held by the same family for centuries. These large landowners continued to exercise political control of local affairs, and even in 1927, 24 per cent of Prussian local officials (*Landräte*) were noblemen. In East Prussia, of the 32 members of the *Landschaft* only six were *Junker*, but most of the remaining members owned estates of over 200 hectares each.[2] Yet the way in which the Prussian *Junker* gained most political influence was through the aging President Hindenburg. Already predisposed to be sympathetic towards the landed and military interest, the old field marshal was further enmeshed into this circle when he was given the estate of Neudeck as a gift on his eightieth birthday in 1927. Thereafter, Hindenburg spent as much time as he could in the country, where he rubbed shoulders with his aristocratic neighbours and himself became a large landowner with a personal interest in agricultural prices. In this way, the *Junker* were able to maintain a disproportionate influence on the political and economic life of the republic and, to some extent, maintain the elite position they had enjoyed under the empire.

The old aristocracy also exerted considerable influence in public life through their domination of the upper echelons of the Reichswehr. In order to reduce the wartime army of over 3.8 million men (or even the pre-war standing army of 700,000 men) to the 100,000 demanded by the Treaty of Versailles, three out of every four officers were dismissed; around 20,000 men in all. Those who were retained were mainly senior officers who had commanded regiments before and/or during the war, younger regular officers who had held appointments to the General Staff and a few junior officers or senior non-commissioned officers (NCOs) who had commanded companies in the field. This preference for regular and/or staff officers meant that many of the middle-class reservists – who had made up eleven-twelfths of the wartime officer corps – were returned to civilian life, and the post-war army continued to be dominated by the old imperial elite. Although many noblemen refused to let their sons serve in the new republican army after the revolution, by 1922 such objections had largely been overcome and the military was once again seen as a respectable career for young aristocratic men. Nevertheless, the primary aim of the Army Command was to create a professional and highly efficient fighting force that could form the core of an expanded army. Promotions were thus never made based on class or social background alone. Noble applicants to the officer corps still had to prove their intelligence and ability by meeting the minimum educational requirements and passing the four-and-a-half-year training programme before they could be commissioned. Even so, this still favoured men from upper- and middle-class backgrounds who could boast a better standard of education than men from the lower classes. In 1925, of the 38 general officers 21 were nobles, while 40 of the Reichswehr's 90 colonels were also from aristocratic backgrounds. In 1931, 19 of the 41 generals were noblemen as were 38 of the 104 colonels. In the army as a whole the nobility were disproportionately represented, making up 21.7 per cent of its strength in 1920, falling to 20.5 per cent in 1926 but rising again to 23.8 per cent in 1932. This should be compared to the population as a whole where the aristocracy made up only about 0.14 per cent. Weimar's politicians were not unaware of this disparity, and the SPD repeatedly attempted to change the system so that experienced NCOs would automatically be eligible for promotion to officer rank – as happened in the French army – even adopting this as a key plank of their defence policy at their 1929 party conference. However, such attempts to change the social composition (and with it the political reliability) of the Reichswehr floundered in the face of the intransigence of the officer corps and opposition from within the ranks.[3]

THE COUNTRYSIDE

Another area where the aristocracy retained a measure of their former social, economic and political power was in the countryside, especially in the grain-producing regions east of the river Elbe. This was partly because traditional ways of life and loyalties persisted longer in the countryside and partly down to a growing feeling of embattled solidarity in the face of metropolitan capitalism, which to some extent transcended class barriers. As elsewhere in Europe, the trend towards urbanization had been a feature of German society since the middle of the nineteenth century but, with the collapse of the monarchy and the establishment of the new republic, this trend seemed to be intensified and highlighted. As far as many in rural Germany were concerned the advent of the republic 'meant socialism, increased state control of agricultural prices and the victory of the urban consumer as the dominant voice in parliamentary politics'[4] , and their fears were not allayed by a more assertive workforce, loss of status and the continued drift to the towns in search of higher wages and shorter hours. Prussian agriculture suffered from the perennial problems of poor soil quality, poor infrastructure leading to difficulty in reaching markets, high production costs and low yields, while low food prices, increased competition from abroad and high interest rates combined to create a difficult economic climate for the agricultural sector. Even those who had managed to pay off their debts during the inflation quickly accrued new ones after 1924, and by 1927 many farmers were struggling to keep their heads above water.

The government responded with various schemes to try and alleviate rural indebtedness. In 1924 the Marx government introduced protective tariffs for agriculture, and in 1926 a programme of cheap credit and tax breaks for the large landowners of East Prussia was introduced – essentially a return to the pre-war system of subsidies. These measures were bolstered by a concerted programme of economic assistance for East Prussia in 1928–29 which saw billions of marks being channelled to the large estates in an effort to place them on a more secure financial footing. But with the onset of the world economic crisis such measures became woefully inadequate. As international prices collapsed, farmers could not find buyers for their produce and bankruptcies threatened. In an effort to stop the rot the government issued a Law on Help for the East (*Osthilfe*) in July 1930, which aimed to provide 650 million marks for the rescheduling of debts and a further 225 million marks to resettle unemployed workers on vacant land. A year later these sums were increased to 950 million marks and 250 million marks respectively. However, even these vast amounts proved insufficient, and, at the end of 1931, far-reaching land reforms – which would see large estates that were incapable of making a profit broken up and parcelled out to unemployed workers – were proposed in cabinet. Although they were rejected, these proposals provoked a storm of protest from the *Junker* who managed to prevail upon the aging president to reject the draft bill and ultimately withdraw his support from the Brüning government.

THE MIDDLE CLASSES

More than any other section of Weimar's social strata, the middle classes have been the focus of historical research. Initially supporting the Weimar coalition in large numbers, the *Mittelstand* gradually turned first to the DNVP, then to special interest and splinter parties such as the *Wirtschaftspartei* (Business Party) and finally to the Nazis in search of protection from the perceived threat of the loss of their political, economic and cultural status. This fear of 'proletarianization' – a loss of social position leading to being subsumed into the working classes – haunted the lower middle classes throughout the Weimar period and was only exacerbated by the economic upheavals of hyperinflation and the Great Depression. Many blamed big business and the corporate rich for their perceived woes, but it was the Left and the unions that filled them with horror and left them feeling that if market forces did not rob them of their wealth and position, radical social legislation and/or violent revolution would.

Like middle-class voters in all countries throughout history, the Weimar *Mittelstand* complained about their hard-earned taxes being misspent on expensive welfare projects for 'lazy' and feckless workers and 'benefit scroungers'. However, it was the fallout from the inflation period that caused perhaps the most resentment, so much so that 'the agitation for redress of the wrongs of the inflation served to undermine the political stability of the Weimar Republic.'[5] The introduction of the *Rentenmark* had serious implications for those who had either borrowed or lent money under the old system. Either these debts would become worthless along with the old currency – effectively wiping out the debt, freeing the debtor from his or her obligations and leaving the lender out of pocket – or some way of transferring debts into the new currency had to be devised. Public pressure led to the introduction of the Revaluation Law of 16 July 1925, which was designed to redistribute wealth from those who had gained from the inflation to those who had lost out, but the complexities of the issues – and the vastness of some of the sums involved – quickly led to a moratorium on revaluation payments. This did not stop people challenging the principle of revaluation in the courts, and between 1925 and 1933 there were around 2 million such legal cases, resulting in hundreds of thousands of people feeling that they had been inadequately compensated for their losses during the inflation, while (to their eyes) workers and those on benefits had been able to take advantage of the economic chaos to negotiate higher wages.

However, like all other social groups, the middle classes were far from being homogéneous. Historians have often divided them into upper (academics, doctors, lawyers, etc.) and lower (shopkeepers, tradesmen, etc.), but they might also be differentiated as old and new. While the upper middle classes to some extent were better able to maintain their place in society, this did not insulate them from the sense of anxiety that infected their less fortunate fellow citizens. In particular, they were deeply concerned about the perceived loss of respect for, and the value of, education and *Bildung*, while the hardships wrought by the inflation and depression created fears of 'an academic proletariat' and drove the professional classes into the arms of the DNVP and the Nazis.[6] The so-called old lower middle classes were those whose livelihoods and values 'were rooted in an idealized vision of a pre-industrial past' like craftsmen, artisans and shopkeepers.[7] This gave them a strong sense of social identity, but in the post-war era they faced ever more competition from mass production and large-scale retailers (trends that had existed before the war but intensified after 1918) which only heightened their rejection and fear of industrial modernity. The new lower middle classes were made up of those in the service industry, such as shop workers, and other white-collar workers such as clerks and junior civil servants; what the cultural critic Siegfried Kracauer termed 'the salaried masses' (*Die Angestellen*)[8]. Between 1907 and 1925 the number of such employees rose from 1.3 million to 5.3 million, but this expansion brought with it a lack of job security. At the same time, women coming into the labour market drove down wages (female white-collar workers earned on average 33 per cent less than their male colleagues) and increased competition for jobs.

THE WORKING CLASSES

In contrast to what the German middle classes, in particular self-employed tradesmen and retailers, believed, in many ways it was the urban poor who suffered most from Germany's post-war economic upheavals, as they always had done. Despite the efforts of the Social

Democrats in government at both national and regional levels, life for working people remained difficult and there were still extremes of wealth and poverty in Weimar Germany, even if living standards did begin to slowly improve after 1924. The Stinnes–Legien Agreement that gave full legal recognition to the unions and established an eight-hour working day – both long-standing demands of organized labour – was a step forward, but it did not benefit all workers evenly and remained a source of contention not only between workers and employers, but also between different sections of the working class. In the immediate aftermath of the war and during the inflation period, working-class city-dwellers faced severe shortages of affordable food, fuel and housing, making them particularly susceptible to infectious diseases such as tuberculosis. Even as late as 1929, one official study suggested that consumption of meat, bread, dairy products, fruit and vegetables was much lower than it had been before the war. War widows, orphans and disabled ex-servicemen were particularly badly hit by the inflation and subsequent government cut-backs, and, as with white-collar employees, there was little job security for unskilled workers even in the 'golden twenties'.

The authorities did make some attempt to alleviate these problems, but often in a patchy and unfocused way. The Social Democrats tended to focus their attention on their core constituency of skilled workers, championing their rights and presenting themselves as the party of the working class, while to some extent ignoring the unskilled, homeless and otherwise disenfranchised sections of the urban proletariat. The KPD, too, 'tended to have a rather scornful view of the urban poor' and this may help to explain why many young unskilled workers embraced Nazism instead of Communism after 1930. At the same time a new breed of middle-class social workers, midwives and welfare reformers attempted to apply new enlightened and scientific methods to deal with the problems of the urban poor, only to face obstruction and small acts of defiance from those who they were trying to help but who resented the intrusive and patronizing attitude of the social services. Similarly, the authorities struggled to control the gangs of young boys (or, after 1929, unemployed youths) who roamed the working-class districts looking for distraction, and who only seemed to confirm fears that the war had caused a complete and irrevocable collapse of parental authority and an unprecedented outbreak of criminality.

Nevertheless, the Social Democratic authorities in Prussia in particular took pains to do all they could to improve the lives of working people, raising social insurance and pensions and investing in new, affordable housing that allowed some of the better-off workers to move out of the old, overcrowded tenements into clean, modern apartment buildings with amenities such as electric lighting and indoor toilets. There were also more opportunities for education and training opened up to workers by the extension of adult education. Evening classes specifically designed for working men were offered by a number of philanthropic and educational institutions. Even so, the curriculum was designed to 'raise the consciousness of workers and make them a force for political and social change'[10], rather than to provide retraining or better employment prospects, so both the effectiveness and the usefulness of such classes are debateable. Building on the educational reforms of the imperial era, which had seen *Realgymnasien* and *Oberrealschulen* open up secondary education to the masses and provide a more modern curriculum focusing on the sciences and technical subjects, instead of the classical education provided by the *Gymnasien*, Article 146 of the constitution called for 'organically developed' public schools in which a good education providing the best life chances would be available to all regardless of wealth and background. Furthermore, it was hoped that these schools would instil a sense of civic responsibility in young Germans, along with the critical faculties necessary for a well-functioning democracy.

However, the ability of the Reich government to achieve these aims was somewhat limited. This was in part due to the provisions of the constitution itself – while central government had responsibility over higher education, the individual states retained control over secondary and primary education. Nevertheless, the SPD authorities in Prussia were assiduous in trying to make the education system more equitable and bring it into line with the principles expressed in the constitution. They raised the age at which pupils were examined to determine in which of the three streams of the

German schools system they would be placed, introduced a system that would allow more movement between streams and attempted to narrow the gap between opportunities available for boys and girls in an effort to get more women into university. All these measures were designed to improve the life chances of less wealthy pupils and to encourage more social mobility, as only those attending the *Gymnasien* would go on to university and professions such as the civil service, law and medicine. However, the reformers faced opposition from the Centre Party who were dismayed at the secularizing trend in social democratic educational policy, and from within the educational establishment itself. Many teachers remained opposed to the republic on principle, while old educational methods such as learning by rote remained standard.

GENDER AND SEXUALITY

The 1920s witnessed a sexual revolution that was in many ways more radical than that of the 1960s, although often overlooked because it was less strident and overt. Not just in Germany but throughout the western world, traditional gender roles and conceptions of sex and sexuality were challenged with varying degrees of success. This was made possible by the profound demographic impact of the First World War. Directly or indirectly, the conflict changed the way that women worked, behaved and even looked. For the first time, women entered the workplace en masse to fill the vacuum left by men conscripted and sent away to fight. Middle-class women took responsibility for wartime welfare activities while their working-class sisters were able to move into better paid, skilled occupations previously reserved for men; changes that granted them unprecedented independence and recognition from the state and society for the important role they played in keeping the nation going in wartime. This emancipatory aspect of women's wartime experience was more than offset by the anxiety caused by waiting for news of loved ones at the front, but both the shift into the public sphere and the hardships suffered during the war raised the consciousness of German women, making them keenly aware of social rights and duties.[11]

The role in the war effort played by women helped to break down some of the resistance to female suffrage, but there still remained ingrained resistance to changes in gender roles and deep anxiety about gender imbalance. The death of millions of men in combat, and the inability of hundreds of thousands more to carry out their normal function as husband, father and provider due to the effects of physical or mental injury, led to a 'crisis of masculinity' which left nearly 2 million young women without the prospect of marriage.

The new republic to some extent adopted a somewhat ambivalent attitude towards these issues. One of the first acts of the Council of People's Representatives was the extension of equal voting rights to all men and women over the age of 20 on 12 November 1918, a move which was subsequently incorporated into the new constitution. However, the state was also anxious for a return to pre-war norms in employment and social relations, and many women were displaced from their wartime jobs by the post-war demobilization decrees. At the same time, Article 109 of the Weimar constitution only granted men and women equal rights as citizens 'in principle', thus leaving open 'the possibility that local, provincial, or state laws might choose to interpret the law differently'.[12] Similarly, while the constitution envisioned family life based on equality between husband and wife, the Civil Code of 1900, which gave men dominance over women in matters of property, employment and child rearing, was kept unchanged. Thus, the citizenship rights afforded to women in 1920 sought to reaffirm their roles as wives and mothers and paper over the disruptions to family life and relations between the sexes caused by the war.

However, the changes wrought by war and by industrialization were too profound to be undone by the framers of the Weimar constitution, or even Hitler's National Socialist regime 13 years later. The extension of voting rights to women created a whole new set of constituents for whose votes the political parties competed vigorously in 1919–20, but on the whole both female activists and women voters tended to adhere to the parties that best reflected their social, religious or cultural values, with Catholic women generally supporting the Centre Party or working-class women the SPD and so on. Once they had won the vote, many politically active middle-class women turned away from parliamentary politics and interested themselves in social welfare and reform, a trend which has often been seen as evidence of a 'willing return to traditional gender roles.'[13] Yet for many women the two spheres were seen as complementary rather than mutually exclusive and, although German women tended to vote in lower numbers than their male compatriots, the Weimar Republic still had a better record of female participation in politics than many other European nations: in 1927 there were 35 women parliamentarians in the Reichstag and 40 in the Prussian Diet, compared to only four female MPs elected to the British House of Commons in 1924.

At the same time, women increasingly 'breached the confines of the home to enter the spectacle-world of consumption.'[14] As businesses woke up to the existence of untapped potential revenue from an increasingly well-educated, independent and solvent section of society, women increasingly became the focus for the advertising of household goods and fashion items. Furthermore, despite the mass expulsion of women from the workplace at the end of the First World War, they re-entered the labour force in unprecedented numbers during the 1920s. After 1925, the trend towards economic rationalization led to more and more women entering the labour market as cheap, unskilled workers. The number of female white-collar workers grew by 200 per cent between 1907 and 1925, meaning that two-thirds of those employed in the service sector were women. This created a whole generation of young, unmarried women who were to some extent freed from the constraints of home and family by their disposable income. This they often chose to spend on fashion, cosmetics, glossy magazines, going to the cinema, sporting activities and other entertainments in an effort to display their individuality and forge a distinct identity for themselves through their recreations and behaviour. Gone were the long hair, corsets and flowing dresses of the pre-war period, to be replaced by bobbed hair (the so-called *Bubikopf* or page boy hairstyle), shorter skirts and 'tubular' styles of dress. The image of the flapper and the vamp, as exemplified by celebrities such as Josephine Baker, Louise Brooks and Marlene Dietrich, became commonplace and was much imitated by fashion-conscious young women who were usually also keen

The fashionably modern look of the 'New Woman' (including bobbed hair and 'short' skirts) was exemplified by female celebrities such as the American actress Louise Brooks.

cinema-goers. The absence of men, both during and after the war, meant that many women had to abandon hope of ever taking on the traditional roles of wife and mother and focus their energies on their careers, while the gender imbalance in society meant that the rules of the dating game changed. With so many more women than men, competition for partners was fierce and women became more assertive and adopted more liberal attitudes towards sex and sexuality.

Nevertheless, although more women entered the workforce during the Weimar period than ever before, their status remained low and they were the first to lose their jobs when times were tough. As pervasive as the image of the 'new woman' was in literature, advertising and popular culture, it has often been pointed out that it bore little resemblance to the lives of most German women. The 'new woman' phenomenon was a product of urban consumer culture that was mainly restricted to the larger cities and there were few 'new women' in rural areas. Furthermore, in the 1925 census, 4.2 million women (a third of Germany's female adult population) described themselves as wage earners, half of whom were in poorly paid manual jobs.[15] New white-collar positions in the service industry or secretarial sector offered some degree of social mobility for young, working-class women, but the vast majority of them found themselves working long hours for little pay in dead-end jobs. Beyond this there were still two-thirds of German women who were not in work, and not all of them were unemployed because they were wealthy enough to be able to afford a life of leisure: more young single women received welfare support than men in the years before the Great Depression, in part because employers usually gave preferential treatment to male job applicants. Matters became even worse after 1929, when competition for employment became ever more cut-throat. One of the ways in which the government sought to respond to the growing crisis was by prohibiting married women from working in the civil service, thus giving the move back towards more traditional gender roles official sanction. At the same time, working women were often the focus of anxiety and contempt from the male-dominated labour establishment: unions attacked the 'feminization' of the factory workplace, which they saw as part-and-parcel of the trend towards rationalization, while young women were often dismissed – not only by politicians of all parties but also by some older feminists – as 'frivolous' and 'flighty', more concerned with fashion and having a good time than with serious social and political issues.[16]

There was little that was unique in the changes and challenges faced by German women in the Weimar period. All of the combatant nations had made use of female labour during wartime and emerged from the Great War with significant gender imbalances, factors which, together with the ongoing processes of industrialization and modernization, brought about significant changes in gender roles and attitudes, not just in Europe but across the globe. Similarly, the 1920s and 1930s also saw a period of heightened interest and discussion of issues relating to sex and sexuality throughout Europe.[17]

Yet gender and sexuality were also the focus of a profound sense of anxiety that underpinned the fragility of the Weimar economy and politics. The death of so many men in the First World War together with the continuing downward trend in the birth rate which had begun before 1914 (Germany's was the lowest in Europe by 1933) 'fanned anxieties about "gender disorder" and "immorality".'[18] During the war the eugenic ideas which had begun to dominate discussions of declining national health and efficiency, not just in Germany but throughout Europe, were stimulated by the desire to breed more and better soldiers and helped to engender an obsessive anxiety about the health of the German race in the post-war period.[19] In the immediate aftermath of military defeat, these anxieties focused on the perceived increase in the spread of sexually transmitted diseases which was thought to pose a tripartite threat to public health, population growth and public morals. But as the Weimar period went on, these concerns were increasingly focused on the supposed lax sexual morals of the young (and young women in particular) who were shirking their national duty by pursuing careers rather than having children.

Such feelings were not merely the preserve of the Nationalists or religious Right, but were often espoused by liberals, republicans and members of the women's movement as well. While acknowledging the existence of female sexuality, middle-class sex reformers clearly viewed it in terms of procreation and ultimately underpinned both traditional views of the 'proper' role of women as wife and mother and emerging concerns about 'racial health' and recouping wartime losses. The state was prepared to back the declaration in Article 119 of the constitution, which said that marriage and motherhood should enjoy the support and protection of the government, with practical action and funds made available to welfare and public health programmes that stressed 'family values'. Even surprisingly liberal measures such as the 1927 Law for Combating Venereal Diseases (*Reichsgesetz zur Bekämpfung der Geschlechtskrankheiten*) – which borrowed from similar legislation enacted in Scandinavia and decriminalized prostitution in towns with populations of above 15,000 people, outlawed brothels and made it easier for individual prostitutes to rent rooms – were enacted at least in part in the hope of halting Germany's demographic decline. This apparent contradiction can be seen as an expression of what Laurie Marhofer has called the Weimar state's desire to introduce 'a new system of management' of society 'in which welfare paved the way to ethical behaviour' and better personal and national health.[20]

Even so, under the republic there was a growing perception – which has persisted among historians to this day – that Germany was a haven of sexual tolerance. The burgeoning Sex Reform movement offered advice to couples on achieving a healthy, pleasurable and productive sex life; while liberal feminists joined forces with Socialists and Communists to campaign for the decriminalization of abortion and against restrictions on birth control. Germany had 26 magazines aimed at a gay or lesbian audience during the 1920s (although most had only limited print runs and even more limited life spans) and it has been estimated that by 1929 there were between 65 and 80 bars (or *Dielen*) catering for an exclusively homosexual clientele, as well as 50 clubs catering for lesbians, in the Reich capital alone. The Berlin police commissioner estimated that there were around 100,000 homosexuals in the capital in 1922 (not including 25,000 rent boys), a figure which had risen to 350,000 by 1930.[21] This subculture achieved an international reputation that made Berlin a destination for sex tourists from across Europe (and from the UK in particular) and saw establishments such as the notorious Eldorado transvestite bar appear in mainstream guidebooks.[22] At the same time, Dr Magnus Hirschfeld, whose *Institut für Sexual-Wissenschaft* (Institute for Sexual Science) had been established in 1919 with the help of a grant from the Social Democratic government of Prussia and was handed over to the state in 1924, spearheaded an effective gay rights movement which campaigned tirelessly for greater understanding and tolerance of homosexuality. The 1929 vote to abolish paragraph 175 of the German penal code – which prohibited male prostitution and sexual acts between men – and replace it with a new law imposing an age of consent (21 years and over), is often seen as evidence of growing toleration of what had previously been regarded as 'deviant' sexuality, but more recently this interpretation has been called into question. The proposed change in the law was extremely controversial amongst the homosexual emancipation movement, many of whose members argued that it was a mere 'illusion of liberation', while those who proposed the reform did so from the perspective of merely changing a 'failed' and unenforceable law while still arguing that homosexuality went 'against nature.'[23] It has therefore been suggested that, to some extent, the apparent sexual tolerance of Weimar Germany may have been more a product of the imagination than a reality.

THE URBAN REPUBLIC

In the wake of the First World War, the trend towards urbanization which had begun in the late nineteenth century continued apace. Towns and cities throughout Germany continued to grow as millions of young Germans flocked to them in search of work, and the split between the agrarian east and industrial west became ever wider. The city became the focal point of Weimar political, social, economic and cultural life, and municipal authorities became the primary point at which citizen and government interacted in the new democratic state. The large-scale public building and social welfare projects undertaken by the large metropolitan centres became 'barometers of the success or failure of the Weimar experiment and . . . encouraged a close identification of the republic with municipalities that remains to this day.'[24] But it was 'Red' Berlin that came to be most identified with the Weimar Republic and its culture. Although it is perhaps going too far to say that 'Weimar was Berlin, Berlin Weimar'[25], it is certainly true that during the 1920s the Reich capital for the first time became more than simply *primus inter pares* with the other great German cities, overtaking Munich and Dresden as Germany's pre-eminent political, cultural and social centre.

Under the auspices of the Social Democratic city authorities, who felt that modernization and rationalization could bring social harmony, Berlin enjoyed an unprecedented period of expansion: by 1925 it had a population of 4 million people, and this continued to grow by 80,000–100,000 people a year. This was both a consequence of, and a driving force behind, Weimar's increasingly rationalized, technologized, consumer economy and society, and by 1928 Berlin was the third largest city in the world after London and New York. In order to accommodate this rising population, town

Berlin by night: the modernist traffic tower in Berlin's Potsdamer Platz, December 1924 (Bundesarchiv, Bild 102-00892 / CC-BY-SA).

planners adopted modern ideas in an attempt to transform the urban environment, rationalizing the city so that 'work, living, leisure, and commerce were . . . assigned to different zones.'[26] In Berlin and other cities throughout the Reich, old slum areas were cleared, to be replaced by new suburban housing estates mostly comprising around 500 to 1,000 dwellings equipped with modern conveniences such as electricity, indoor plumbing and central heating. Fashionable young architects such as Bruno Taut were commissioned to design these new estates, while the city's transport system was overhauled and the latest technology applied to the overhead and underground railway (S-Bahn and U-Bahn) networks in order to bring suburban dwellers to work and shop in the heart of the city.

At the same time, the visual landscape of the city was transformed. Pedestrians vied with greater levels of traffic as a growing population and new technology brought more and more means of transportation into the cities. One 1928 survey recorded that each hour 2,753 vehicles passed through the Potsdamer Platz in central Berlin, where in 1924 the authorities erected a huge and iconic modernist traffic light which was visible a kilometre away.[27] In keeping with the youthful spirit of the age, the city received a facelift: gone were the neo-classical facades and neo-gothic buildings of the nineteenth century, replaced by tall, sleek, functional office blocks and department stores in concrete, glass and steel, exemplified by Erich Mendelsohn's Columbus House. Advertising reached hitherto unseen levels of 'volume and sophistication'[28] during the 1920s, and as the decade progressed the hand bills and paper posters that were splashed across walls and billboards were joined by increasing numbers of illuminated neon signs hawking the wares of the new consumer culture.

The city was no less busy by night, when it became a veritable *smorgasbord* of mass entertainment. In 1926 the Funkturm radio tower was erected, putting Berlin at the centre of Germany's modern broadcasting and communications industries, while the Haus Vaterland on the Potsdamer Platz allowed Berliners to frequent a 1,000-seat cinema, the largest cafe in the world and a series of themed bars all under one roof. The German film industry had benefitted greatly from the halting of foreign imports from the USA, France and Denmark during the war, as well as greater organization and state funding as the government sought to harness the new medium for propaganda purposes. In particular, the forced merger of all the main German production companies in 1917 to form Universum Film A. G. (Ufa) created Germany's largest and most well-known production company of the Weimar period. Filmgoing remained one of the popular leisure activities in interwar Germany, and there were 3,878 cinemas in Germany in 1925, rising to 5,000 five years later. Although the vast majority of films produced during the Weimar period (and those most popular with audiences) were escapist comedies or sensationalist melodramas, the period also saw the acceptance of cinema as a serious art form, and the artistic vision of German directors and technological innovations that they developed gained a world reputation. Ufa's Neubabelsberg studios in Berlin became a Mecca for critics and professionals who wanted to watch the masters at work, and several Anglo-American directors openly acknowledged their debt to German cinema of the 1920s.

Mass spectator sports also became popular and sportsmen like Max Schmeling, who became world heavyweight champion in 1930, became national heroes. There was a distinctly modern feel to this sport mania: six-day bicycle races and motor racing at the Avus racing track were hugely popular, and drivers such as Manfred von Brauchitsch and Fritz von Opel became household names. At the same time, the gaudy bars and nightclubs of the Kurfürstendamm in central Berlin achieved an international reputation as the places to go for a good time. The abolition of censorship in 1918 led to a proliferation of saucy cabarets and risqué floor shows in which young women in various states of undress featured heavily. Even during the worst days of political and economic crisis there were plenty of Germans who were prepared to escape from their problems in the dives and dance halls of Berlin, while the bitter experience of the inflation discouraged thrift and persuaded many people that it was a much better idea to spend their earnings on a good time while they had the chance.

Yet behind this glitzy exterior, the Weimar cityscape had a darker side. Poverty, deprivation, fear and alienation haunted the less affluent sections of Germany's big cities, and Nazi propaganda 'infamously juxtaposed the hard living conditions, anonymity, and moral corruption of the big city with rural and traditional ways of life.'[29] Faced with the daily struggle to survive, many working-class Germans were prepared to do anything to make ends meet, especially in the chaotic economic and political conditions of the early and late phases of the republic. The 1920s have been called 'the golden age of Berlin crime'[30], and certainly there was a widespread public perception of lawlessness and disorder during the Weimar period. By 1929 it was estimated that there were around 15,000 missing-persons cases reported annually and that the Berlin police were handling over 50,000 complaints a year, ranging from burglaries to murders. Convictions for theft in the capital alone were 81 per cent higher in the three years from 1919 to 1923 than they had been for the three years before the war, while those for receiving stolen goods were 245 per cent higher. Nationwide, annual criminal convictions soared from 538,225 in 1910 to 823,902 in 1923. Yet even when crime rates began to fall after the inflation period, until they were lower than pre-war levels, there was still a perception of widespread criminality, focusing on the three areas of juvenile delinquency, prostitution and murder.[31]

Between 1913 and 1918 the number of adolescents convicted for criminal offences doubled, and youth crime rates continued to rise throughout the early 1920s. It was only after the Juvenile Justice Act of 1923 lowered the age of criminal responsibility and allowed judges greater leeway in sentencing that rates began to drop. This only seemed to confirm claims that Weimar's cosmopolitan consumer culture was riddled with moral turpitude, and it was widely thought that the growth of the number of women and children brought into the workforce during the war, together with the death of so many male authority figures, had fundamentally weakened the traditional patriarchal German social structure, opening the way to widespread criminality and sexual licence.

If youth criminality seemed to confirm conservative accusations of Weimar immorality, the highly visible sex trade only reinforced such claims. Industrialization and urbanization had transformed prostitution from something that professionals did behind closed doors to an occupation undertaken by amateurs who plied their trade in busy urban spaces. For many women, prostitution was 'a way of managing economic crisis', and 'the only certain way of making ends meet' when faced with low wages, unemployment or separation from a male breadwinner.[32] In contrast to what both contemporary and later feminist writers would have us believe, Germany's prostitutes of the Weimar era were perhaps surprisingly assertive and independent, facing up to the authorities, forming their own trade union and supported by a wide range of individuals and services in the wider community.

Nevertheless, prostitution was a risky business and those who participated in the trade lived under the threat of potential violence. The fact that the victims of all three of the most celebrated serial killers of the Weimar period included several people (both male and female) who were engaged in the sex trade speaks volumes for the risks that prostitutes took daily in the course of their activities. Fritz Haarmann, the so-called Butcher of Hanover, murdered 24 tramps and male prostitutes between 1919 and 1924; Karl Grossmann is thought to have murdered around 50 women before he was caught in 1921; and, most famously of all, Peter Kürten, the Vampire of Düsseldorf, was convicted in April 1931 of nine murders and seven attempted murders, but he confessed to a total of 79 offences, including murder, rape and child molestation, committed over a 17-year period. There were even suggestions of cannibalism in both the Haarmann and Grossmann cases, as it was rumoured that the murderers had sold the flesh of their victims during the years of hardship after the war. The public took a salacious fascination in the crimes of all three of these men, which were related in lurid detail in the press and only served to reinforce the 'myth of the anonymous killer' which 'was a powerful one for expressing anxieties about urban anonymity and the threat of danger from the margins.'[33]

Yet we should not be misled into thinking that Weimar Germany was in fact the sink of iniquity that many of its citizens believed it to be. 'Berlin was by no means the most violent city in Germany'[34], and by international standards German crime rates were not exceptionally high.[35] Weimar Germany had one of the largest and most modern police forces in Europe, and the homicide division of the Berlin detective force or *Kriminalpolizei* was used as a model by similar forces in Germany and across the Continent. Under the energetic leadership of Ernst Gennat, who invented the term 'serial killer' (*Serienmörder*), the homicide division of the Berlin '*Kripo*' pioneered techniques such as fingerprinting, ballistic tests and psychological profiling, reflecting the Weimar tendency towards rationalism and functionalism evident in other areas of economic and social policy.

Nevertheless, Weimar Germany continued to be perceived as being particularly lawless. In part this was a consequence of mass literacy. There were over 4,000 newspapers, magazines and illustrated papers published in Germany by the mid-1920s, and Berlin alone had 50 daily newspapers and produced over 30 per cent of all German periodicals by the end of the decade. These communicated stories of violent crime and sexual offences in lurid detail to an avid readership. As Todd Herzog has noted, Weimar Germany was 'fascinated by criminals and their crimes' and 'seemed to take pleasure in the spectacle of crime, in imagining itself as a criminal space.'[36]

WEIMAR CULTURE

If the new urban republic was the home of mass consumer culture and alienation, crime and uncertainty, the cities – primarily Berlin, but also other major urban centres such as Munich and Dresden – also became the home of a new spirit of inquiry and experimentation in the arts and sciences. Weimar Germany produced 'a distinctive culture, both brilliant and singular'[37], perhaps one of the few genuinely unique features of the republic and certainly one of its foremost and enduring achievements. Germany, and Berlin in particular, became a Mecca for writers, artists and other intellectuals who desired to drink in the heady atmosphere of intellectual ferment. These were mostly German-speakers from the former Austro–Hungarian Empire – Arnold Zweig, Robert Musil and Franz Kafka among them – but also included Russian refugees such as Vladimir Nabokov and British writers such as W. H. Auden, Virginia Woolf and Graham Greene.

Despite the fact that Austrian and German scientists were ostracized by the international scientific community for much of the 1920s 'by 1933 Germans had won more Nobel Prizes than anyone else' (one a year between 1918 and 1932, two in 1918, 1925 and 1927 and three in 1931), 'more than the British and Americans put together.'[38] Albert Einstein was awarded the Nobel Prize for Physics in 1921 for his explanation of the photoelectric effect and Werner Heisenberg revolutionized the field of theoretical physics when he invented quantum mechanics in 1925 and the uncertainty principle in 1927. Arnold Schoenberg and Alban Berg effectively reinvented classical music with the invention of serialism and atonal music, while jazz, satirical songs, performance poetry and expressive dance all thrived in Germany's vibrant cabaret scene. Germany was the home of world-famous research centres such as the Berlin Psychoanalytic Institute (established 1920), the Institute for Social Research in Frankfurt-am-Main (established 1923) and the Warburg Institute for Art History in Hamburg (established 1926). The Frankfurt School in particular, via the work of the philosophers and sociologists Theodor Adorno, Max Horkheimer and Herbert Marcuse, went on to have a strong and lasting influence on western thought in the second half of the twentieth century. In philosophy Martin Heidegger both prefigured post-war existentialism and 'gave respectability to the German obsession with unreason'[39] with his examination of man's place in the universe in *Sein und Zeit* (*Being and Time*, 1927), while a 'golden generation' of German historians including Ludwig von Pastor, Percy Schramm and Ernst Kantorowicz helped to formulate ideas about the culture and politics of the Middle Ages that remain influential to this day.

In his seminal examination of Weimar culture, Peter Gay comments that 'the republic created little; it liberated what was already there.'[40] This is certainly true in the sense that many of the techniques and styles prevalent in the arts in the Weimar period originated before or during the war, but also in the sense that the work produced by German writers, artists, directors and architects was often deeply personal. Expressionism had begun in the early 1910s, but it continued to dominate German painting, literature and even cinema in the years immediately after the war. Expressionist architecture such as Mendelsohn's Einstein Tower in Potsdam and Höger's Chilehaus in Hamburg eschewed traditional views about the functionality of buildings and made use of steel skeletons overlaid with concrete to create sinuous lines in an effort to make the buildings look organic. Meanwhile, Expressionism brought a sense of what Lotte Eisner has described as 'Germanic gloom' to Weimar cinema.[41] Expressionist themes of alienation, madness and the evil of authority dominate films like *Das Cabinet des Dr. Caligari* (1919), which was hailed by some contemporaries as 'the first work of art on the screen'[42], and Friedrich Wilhelm Murnau's *Nosferatu* (1922) – the first ever cinema adaptation of Bram Stoker's *Dracula*. Similarly, Expressionist theatre was often combative and deliberately challenging for audiences, and plays like Ernst Toller's *Transformation* (1919) and George Kaiser's trilogy *The Coral* (1917), *Gas* (1918) and *Gas II* (1920) demonstrated both an Expressionist aesthetic and Expressionist themes such as a rejection of bourgeois values and spiritual awakening.

However, by 1922 there had been a move away from the raw emotion of Expressionism towards 'a more sober and practical approach to everyday reality.'[43] This manifested itself in a new naturalism in art, literature and cinema, which has become known as *Neue Sachlichkeit*, or New Objectivity. This was in many ways 'a style with no particular artistic programmes or manifestos'[44] rather than a clearly defined artistic movement such as Expressionism, and it encompassed socially critical 'Verists' such as George Grosz, Rudolf Schlichter and Christian Schad, as well 'Classicists' such as Georg Schrimpf. Politically engaged artists like Grosz, or writers like the left-wing physician and novelist Alfred Döblin, used this new artistic style to hold up a mirror to society and present a warts-and-all portrayal of Germany's social ills. Otto Dix's *Großstadt Triptych* (1927–28) illustrates the social conscience of the Verists well, with its contrast between the hedonism of the wealthy and the poverty of crippled war veterans at society's margins. Similarly, Dix's *Three Whores* (1926) does not romanticize or sentimentalize prostitution as nineteenth-century French artists such as Manet and Toulouse-Lautrec had done, but presents an unflattering depiction of Berlin sex workers. Likewise, George Grosz's *The Pillars of the Establishment* (1926) is even blunter in its critique of German society, lampooning the bourgeoisie for their innate conservatism and their traditional values and morality.

Like Expressionism, New Objectivity was not restricted to painting and visual art. It soon crossed into other art forms, producing novels such as Alfred Döblin's *Berlin Alexanderplatz* (1929), the story of criminal Franz Biberkopf's struggle for redemption amongst the seedy underworld of Berlin, and Ludwig Renn's anti-war novel *Krieg* (1929) and its sequel *Nachkrieg* (1930). Bertold Brecht mirrored the social criticism of the Verists in plays like *Die Dreigroschenoper* (*The Threepenny Opera*, 1928), and *The Rise and Fall of the City of Mahagonny* (1929), which viciously sati-rized the politics, mores and morals of Weimar Berlin. Films such as the documentary *Berlin: Die Sinfonie der Großstadt* (1927), which portrayed a day in the life of the German capital, and *Der Letze Mann* (1924), the story of a man who is chewed up by the system and cast on to the scrap heap once he has outlived his usefulness, also demonstrated a desire to strip away idealism and present modern life as it was lived in all its bleak normality, which was in keeping with the ideals of *Neue Sachlichkeit*.

Weimar Germany became the home to an unprecedented flowering of artistic experimentation. "Triad" by Rudolf Belling, exhibited at the Lehrter Bahnhof, Berlin, August 1929 (Bundesarchiv, Bild 102-08322 / CC-BY-SA).

In architecture, the movement most closely associated with New Objectivity was the Bauhaus. Inspired by medieval guilds, the English Arts and Crafts Movement and the *Deutsche Werkbund*, the architect Walter Gropius founded the Bauhaus in 1919 in an effort to bring together all the creative arts in one workshop. But far from being little more than a design school, the Bauhaus also became a style and a brand, one of the most enduring and well-known from the Weimar period, which stressed simple design and sought to make mass-produced items beautiful. Innovation was actively encouraged, and the most modern techniques and technologies were adopted by the Bauhaus' designers. The aim was to combine beauty and functionality and to produce buildings, furniture and sculpture that both looked good and served a specific purpose. In this way the objectives of the Bauhaus artists were very similar to those of the Social Democratic Prussian government: to improve everyday life by improving the surroundings in which it took place.

All this was not only disturbingly modern but also dangerously foreign as far as some commentators on the Right were concerned. The interwar period saw the beginnings of the cultural polarization between modern consumer capitalism (as exemplified by the United States) and Soviet-style communism (championed by the Soviet Union) which was to dominate Europe and the world for much of the remainder of the twentieth century. For many commentators there was little doubt which economic and social model held sway in Weimar Germany. In both political discourse and popular culture (particularly in advertising) there were explicit links drawn between economic modernization, republicanism and national stability in the post-inflation era. All of the parties of the Weimar Coalition, even the Marxist SPD, were in favour of the transformation of Germany into a mass-consumer society as embodied by the United States, which they saw as being a hallmark of economic modernity.[45]

Just as Fordist notions of 'rationalization' borrowed from the US-dominated economic thinking in the republic, American trends in entertainment and design – everything from fashions to advertising techniques to the 'industrialized merriment'[46] of the Weimar entertainment industry – were eagerly adopted by metropolitan Germans of the 1920s, until some complained that Berlin was 'more American than America.'[47]

Yet 'contrary to the widespread depiction of Weimar Germany as an era of pessimism or as a Janus-faced epoch drawn between an overly optimistic delusion of feasibility (*Machbarkeitswahn*) and cultural pessimism' commentators from across the political spectrum demonstrated 'a fundamentally optimistic belief in the malleability of the future and the possibility of achieving a "better" or a "new time."'[48] This was accompanied by an 'activist tendency' that saw many intellectuals and politicians argue that the foundations of this brave new world could be laid in the here and now through creative action. Thus there was a very real belief that Germans of the Weimar period were building Utopia. Yet radicals on both sides of the political divide were soon disappointed and although the parties of the Weimar Coalition continued to refer to the republic itself as a 'new time', few were convinced and many continued to confidently look forward to a new beginning. Intellectuals and politicians therefore persistently sought to identify the forces, groups and individuals who would be agents of change, the vanguard of the future in the present day and harbingers of the particular Utopia that they desired.

Although the First World War in many ways had a profound effect on German politics and society, there was, at least at first glance, no root and branch social transformation during the Weimar period. The old hierarchical class structure remained in place, and established elites – the nobility, big business and the officer corps – retained a certain amount of power and influence. Yet this apparent continuity with Imperial Germany masked more fundamental changes in social relations. The demographic catastrophe of the Great War helped to create circumstances in which pre-war social trends became fixtures of post-war society. The absence of men changed social and sexual attitudes and behaviours in the 1920s and 1930s and opened up educational and employment opportunities for women and the young, at the same time as causing widespread moral panics. The development of a 'new' middle class made up of 'the salaried masses' of young, well-educated men and women fuelled the growth of Weimar consumer culture, and urbanization continued apace, further eroding old values and transforming the working lives and leisure activities of the working and middle classes. As the cities expanded beyond recognition they became increasingly identified with the modern, cosmopolitan culture of the republic, exemplified by American imports such as jazz, department stores, mass advertising and the 'new woman'. New media such as cinema and radio became increasingly popular and sophisticated, while modern styles in art and literature came to dominate the cultural scene. But there were still many in Germany who failed to identify with these social and cultural developments and regarded them as evidence of the 'decadence' of the republic. Many on the Right feared that traditional German *Kultur* was under threat from the twin forces of Russian Bolshevism and 'Americanization', anxieties that often manifested themselves in moral panics focused on areas such as prostitution, youth crime and 'trashy and immoral' entertainments.

Yet there was little about all this that was unique to Weimar. Urbanization and industrialization had already brought about the

development of an urban consumer culture by the turn of the twentieth century, and the growth of the service sector of white-collar
workers had been going on since at least 1900. Generational conflict
and female emancipation had also been features of Wilhelmine
society (which had its own, earlier, version of the 'new woman' in
the 1890s), while anxieties over the effects of industrial modernity
on their social position had also haunted shopkeepers and artisans
in the imperial era. At the same time, Weimar Germany was not
particularly unique in its collective anxieties and neuroses. Moral
panics over juvenile delinquency, female emancipation and the health
of the nation have their parallels in modern hysteria over 'hoodies',
paedophiles and the effects of violent and sexual images in the
media on youthful minds. Across Europe and the world, other
nations were facing similar difficulties and expressing their concerns
in strikingly similar ways. Industrialized nations across the globe
struggled to come to terms with the demographic changes wrought
by modernity and conflict, while struggles between town and country,
labour and capital, raged everywhere. The 'new woman' of the
1920s was an international phenomenon, as was deep concern over
the moral and physical wellbeing of the young in the post-war
world.

Nevertheless, this should not distract us from the very real cultural
and social achievements of the Weimar period. The extension of the
welfare state helped to alleviate the suffering of millions, and there
was a greater degree of social mobility under the republic (even if
it did come at the expense of job security). Despite the limits on
female emancipation pointed out by historians such as Kathleen
Canning, the Weimar Republic extended equal voting rights to women
before Britain, the USA and France and had more women sitting in
parliament by the mid-1920s than any of the more established democracies. The social activism of the Weimar state, together with a
debatable degree of sexual tolerance, secured an end to the repressive and intrusive system of state-regulated prostitution and nearly
succeeded in having the law prohibiting homosexuality struck down
(almost 40 years before the Sexual Offences Act of 1967 achieved
the same result in Britain). At the same time, the Weimar Republic
left a scientific and artistic record second to none, providing new

theories in theoretical physics and philosophy that laid the foundations of our present understanding of the world and mankind's place in it, as well as deeply influential new styles of music, architecture and visual art. The cinema of the Weimar Republic rivalled that of Hollywood and provided technical and stylistic innovations that helped transform the medium into an art form, while the literature and theatre of Weimar Germany still have an audience today.

6

CRISIS AND COLLAPSE, 1929–33

The apparent calm and relative stability of Weimar's middle period was shattered by the onset of a new economic crisis in 1929. As unemployment rose, the social tensions and anxieties which had simmered beneath the surface throughout the 'golden twenties' came to the fore, while disagreements over how to cope with the Depression broke the fragile political consensus that had emerged since 1925 and once more exposed the deep divisions in German political culture. For those who desired a reconfiguration of German politics this new crisis presented opportunities to challenge the political order established in 1919, and democracy faced renewed assaults from the radical Right that further intensified the sense of uncertainty and fear that gripped the country. Faced by loss of livelihood and self-respect, many Germans turned to the political extremes in search of salvation, while traditional elites attempted to maintain their hold on power and reshape the republic into a political system more in keeping with their ideals by trying to harness this rising tide of right-wing radicalism. This proved to be a serious miscalculation on their part which ultimately led neither to a military dictatorship nor restoration of the monarchy, but instead delivered Germany into the hands of Adolf Hitler and his followers.

DEMOCRACY IN CRISIS

After the stabilization of the currency in 1924, Germany entered a period of relative political calm during which, as we have seen, progress was made towards consolidating the republican system while Gustav Stresemann secured a number of key foreign policy successes (although they were not always seen as such at the time). Having turned their backs on the opportunity to found a revolutionary socialist state in 1918–19, and having done so much to defend the liberal-democratic republic in its first tumultuous years, the SPD withdrew into opposition after 1923, thus ceding the political battlefield to the moderate parties of the centre. Thereafter, Germany was governed by the Centre, DDP and DVP who, without the left-wing SPD, were able to find enough ideological common ground to steer the republic on the path to economic recovery. It is a testament to the level of consensus that was achieved in Weimar's middle years that even the nationalist DNVP was twice briefly persuaded to put aside its opposition to the republican system and enter into government in 1925 and 1927–28.

However, even during this period of 'relative stabilization' there were disturbing signs that structural weaknesses within the political system and the fragmented nature of Weimar political culture had not been vanquished but merely temporarily put aside. Both the Communists on the Left and *völkische* Nationalist groups on the Right continued to snipe at the republic from the sidelines, while the rise of a host of single-issue bourgeois splinter parties such as the Business Party (*Wirtschaftspartei*) and German Peasant's Party (*Deutsche Bauernpartei*) in the mid-to-late 1920s increased competition for middle-class voters and put pressure on the DDP and DVP. Furthermore, with the largest single party in the Reichstag in opposition, the remaining parties were left with the options of either trying to bring the DNVP into government or forming minority governments dependent on the tolerance of either the left- or right-wing opposition in order to pass legislation. The governing coalition repeatedly broke up and reconfigured itself in an effort to establish working parliamentary majorities to deal with each successive issue in foreign and domestic affairs in this period, in the process of which it became clear just how much division there was between the parties.

The sudden death from appendicitis of Friedrich Ebert on 28 February 1925 highlighted these differences, as the parties all scrambled to field their own candidates for the presidency. No fewer than seven candidates were put forward in the first round of the election, so unsurprisingly none of them managed to secure the necessary outright majority. For the second round the 'people's bloc' made up of the Centre, SPD and DDP, all agreed to support the former Chancellor Wilhelm Marx, who seemed certain to win. However, alarmed by the prospect of another seven years of republican rule, the political Right rallied behind a latecomer to the contest, the 78-year-old wartime hero Field Marshal Paul von Hindenburg. Presented by his right-wing supporters as the saviour of the Fatherland, Hindenburg's carefully constructed mythic status as the 'victor of Tannenburg' enabled him to secure a narrow victory over Marx and his other opponent, the Communist Thälmann.[1]

Although the hopes of his supporters and fears of his detractors that the new president would bring about an immediate shift to the Right were not realized, Hindenburg's election did mark a turning point in Weimar politics and would prove to have fateful consequences for the republic. Although he had no great love for democracy, the field marshal had sworn an oath to discharge his office in

Results of the Presidential Elections, 1925

	First round (29 March 1925)		Second round (26 April 1925)	
Turnout	68.9%		77.6%	
Votes cast	27,016,760		30,567,874	
Braun (SPD)	7,802,497	(29%)	—	
Held (BVP)	1,007,450	(3.7%)	—	
Hellpach (DDP)	1,569,398	(5.8%)	—	
Hindenburg (Independent)	—		14,655,641	(48.3%)
Jarres (DVP, DNVP)	10,416,658	(38.8%)	—	
Ludendorff (DVFP)	285,793	(1.1%)	—	
Marx (Centre)	3,887,734	(14.5%)	13,751,605	(45.3%)
Thälmann (KPD)	1,871,815	(7%)	1,931,151	(6.4%)

Source: Anna von der Goltz, *Hindenburg: Power, Myth and the Rise of the Nazis* (Oxford, 2009), p. 96

accordance with the law. He therefore always kept within the letter of the constitution and greatly endeared himself to republicans by backing Stresemann's foreign policy and retaining Ebert's State Secretary Otto Meissner as presidential chief-of-staff. Nevertheless, there were clear indications of the new president's attitude towards the republic: he remained an honorary member of the anti-democratic *Stahlhelm*, publically endorsed the 'stab-in-the-back' myth and continued to 'lend his weight to numerous right-wing causes, especially those of symbolic importance.'[2] Under Hindenburg there was a gradual shift away from the primacy of parliament towards a more presidential style of government which was facilitated by the difficulties in securing workable parliamentary majorities. This enabled the President 'to bring his personal and political preferences to bear on the formation of governments' which effectively meant that 'if at all possible the DNVP should be included in government' and the SPD kept out of office as a matter of principle.[3] Thus, almost from the very beginning, Hindenburg made no secret of his desire for a more right-wing configuration of politics, while at the same time jealously guarding the powers and privileges granted to him by the constitution.

Whatever the feelings of the President and the coterie of aristocratic and military advisors that surrounded him, the SPD's success in the Reichstag elections of 20 May 1928 made it impossible to form a government without them. While the parties of the Right and centre suffered significant losses, both the SPD and KPD increased their representation in parliament, with the Social Democrats securing nearly one third of the total number of seats. As a result, after difficult negotiations the SPD chairman Hermann Müller formed a 'grand coalition' of the SPD, DDP, DVP, BVP and Centre. Almost from the beginning, though, the great diversity of interests between the government's constituent parts became apparent. In August, a storm broke out within the SPD when it became known that the Chancellor had approved the construction of a new battleship despite opposition to it within his own party, while disagreements over welfare payments and foreign policy only increased tensions between the coalition partners. The final straw was the Wall Street Crash of October 1929 and the subsequent economic depression. As unemployment rose and more and more German businesses and landowners faced bankruptcies and foreclosures, the stark ideological differences between the SPD and the DVP were exposed. The DVP, already under pressure from its middle-class constituents to take a more conservative stance, refused to countenance any increase in welfare spending, while the SPD, fearful of losing support to the Communists, pushed for an increase in unemployment benefits. This impasse led to the fall of the coalition, on 27 March 1930, when the President refused to grant Müller emergency powers to force through his budget. The Social Democrats withdrew from the government and returned to opposition, and Hindenburg asked the Centre Party politician Heinrich Brüning to form a 'presidential cabinet of experts'.

Brüning came to office declaring that his prime objective remained the same as that of the previous government, namely 'to secure parliamentary approval for a genuinely balanced budget . . . so that the Reich would not suffer a disastrous cash-flow crisis.'[4] In April a 'Five Year Plan' to 'bolster the economy through lower production costs and large-scale public works' was announced, and 1.5 billion marks were allocated for the construction of roads, canals and public housing, but these plans had to be shelved after negotiations between businesses and the unions broke down.[5] This left the government with no choice but to introduce tax rises and drastic cuts in government spending, which only increased the numbers of people out of work. At the same time, the failure to reach a broad-based solution to the economic crisis made a confrontation between the Chancellor and parliament inevitable when the Reichstag voted against the budget.

When Brüning attempted to force his austerity measures through by use of Article 48, the Reichstag voted to overturn the emergency decree, giving him no option but to ask Hindenburg to dissolve parliament and call new elections in the hope of securing a popular mandate for the cuts. However, this move seriously backfired when the electorate sent a clear message of their discontent and lack of faith in the ability of the existing system to deal with the economic crisis by rejecting the moderate parties and turning to the political extremes. Although the share of the vote of both the SPD and the government's chief supporters, the Centre Party, remained stable (the former losing ten seats while the latter gained six), both the DVP

President Paul von Hindenburg
(right) with Defence Minister
General Wilhelm Groener,
September 1930 (Bundesarchiv,
Bild 102-10425 / Unknown /
CC-BY-SA).

and DNVP saw their share of the vote halved, while the Communists gained 23 seats. The big winners, though, were the previously negligible NSDAP who saw their share of the vote rocket from 2.6 to 18.3 per cent, giving them 107 seats and making them the second largest party in the Reichstag after the Social Democrats.

Deeply alarmed by this development, the leadership of the SPD was prepared to tolerate the Brüning administration as the lesser of two evils and decided to enter into 'objective cooperation' (*Sachliche Zusammenarbeit*) with the government. Although this meant that the Chancellor was able to survive confidence votes in parliament, it simultaneously helped to undermine his position with Germany's true power brokers. Hindenburg and the powerful clique of advisors who surrounded him – his son Oskar, State Meissner, Defence Minister Wilhelm Groener and his wartime *protégé* Kurt von Schleicher, now head of the *Ministeramt* (political office) of the Reichswehr – anachronistically continued to regard the SPD as the main threat to Germany and were determined to neutralize them as

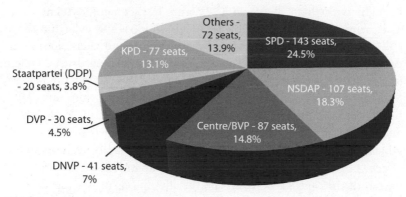

Reichstag Election Results, 14 September 1930s.

a political force and bring about an authoritarian reconfiguration of German politics. Initially it had been thought that Brüning, a former officer and staunch Catholic who had dedicated his life to public service, would be the man to bring this plan to fruition, but as time went on it became clear that he had a strong commitment to the rule of law and was determined to govern in accordance with the constitution as far as possible. Although he undoubtedly presided over a 'drift towards authoritarianism'[6] in which normal democratic procedure was increasingly sidelined – Article 48 was used five times in 1930, rising to 44 times in 1931 and 60 in 1932, while sittings of the Reichstag declined from 94 in 1930 to 41 in 1931 and a mere 13 in 1932 – Brüning's willingness to work with the SPD and resistance to calls to dissolve the Reichstag indefinitely and abandon constitutional government altogether, ultimately led Schleicher to conclude that while he made an excellent foreign minister he was not the 'strong man with the military spirit' that was required to lead Germany.[7]

THE RISE OF THE NAZIS

The advent of a new economic crisis further radicalized a population that had already lived through revolution, counter-revolution, hyperinflation, foreign occupation and all the uncertainties that these brought with them. Between 1929 and 1932 unemployment rocketed from just over 1 million to 6.1 million, while even for those still in work wages fell drastically and many had their hours cut. By 1933 half those registered as unemployed had used up all their unemployment insurance and were reduced to relying on means-tested local government benefits which provided a minimum level of subsistence. Production slumped to 58 per cent of 1928 levels, and a drop in agricultural prices caused a debt crisis in rural areas which led to widespread bankruptcies and foreclosures. As these effects began to be felt, many Germans abandoned the moderate parties of the centre who had been the champions of Weimar democracy in favour of groups that offered radical solutions. This led to an increase in electoral support for the Communists, who were particularly well placed to appeal to disillusioned workers at a time when it appeared that the very foundations of capitalism were crumbling. The KPD nearly doubled their representation in the Reichstag between 1928 and November 1932, their share of the overall vote rising from 10.6 to 19.9 per cent.

At the same time, the Depression turned the Nazis into a mass movement with a national profile for the first time. Often dismissed as a negligible force in German politics between the failed putsch of 1923 and the electoral breakthrough of 1930, the NSDAP had already emerged as the only radical nationalist party on a national scale. Even before the Wall Street Crash the party had a network of over 3,000 branches throughout Germany, and by 1928 it had more members than either the DDP or DVP and was able to capitalize on the increasing restiveness of the nationalist milieu. In many ways, the swing towards the Nazis in 1930 can be seen as the culmination of a trend in which the established middle-class parties had gradually seen 'their organizations disintegrate, their local authority collapse, and their voter base erode.'[8] Ever since the collapse of the DDP's share of the vote in 1920, middle-class voters had been migrating to the Right, and by 1930 even the conservative–nationalist DNVP was deemed too staid and mired in the existing political system to be an effective representative of their desires. This suggests that for many middle-class voters at least, turning to the extreme Right was not merely a response to the Great Depression but also a sign of a deeper-seated dissatisfaction with the democratic system.[9]

Nevertheless, the Nazi network of activists did not necessarily lead to electoral success. In 1928 the NSDAP polled only 2.6 per cent of the vote, less than either the BVP or the Business Party, and secured a mere 12 seats in parliament. Their profile was raised by their participation in the campaign against the Young Plan in 1929, during which they were able to make use of the media empire controlled by the DNVP leader Alfred Hugenburg to present themselves as a radical nationalist alternative, not only to the left-wing and republican parties but also the traditional Right. However it was the Depression that really transformed their fortunes. 'Crisis was Hitler's oxygen'[10], and the renewed descent into economic turmoil revitalized the NSDAP's fortunes. 'Vague appeals to economic justice' had always been part of the Nazi Party's programme[11], and in the hard times engendered by the Depression these found an increasingly receptive audience, especially when coupled with denunciations of Marxism, big business and the 'ineffectual' Weimar state. At the same time, the Nazis fanned the flames of the political crisis by taking their struggle against democracy and 'Marxism' to the streets. In Prussia 155 people were killed and 426 injured as a result of political violence between 1929 and 1931, the majority of them Communists and Nazis, indicating that the struggle for control of the streets was largely a two-way conflict between the forces of the political extremes. Yet, even as they helped to spread violence and uncertainty throughout Germany, the Nazis presented themselves as a 'reserve force for order', who fought to preserve private property from the unruly masses of the Communists.[12]

By the autumn of 1931 it looked increasingly as though Brüning's days were numbered. The banking crisis, and the embarrassing collapse of the scheme for a customs union with Austria over the summer, forced a cabinet reshuffle and left the Chancellor unable to rely on the continued support of the DVP and the Business Party. At the same time, Schleicher and the right-wing cabal surrounding the President were becoming increasingly impatient and were urging Brüning to shift his government even further to the Right. Feeling that their chance for power was imminent, the forces of the 'national opposition' (the DNVP, the Nazis and the *Stahlhelm*) met at the resort of Bad Harzburg on 11 October 1931 and proclaimed a united front against the government and the republic. However this show of right-wing unity was short lived. Amidst an atmosphere of mutual distrust and antagonism the 'Harzburg Front' rapidly evaporated after Brüning managed to survive a vote of no confidence on 13 October, and the 'national opposition' proved unable to agree on a common candidate to challenge Hindenburg for the presidency.[13]

The presidential elections of March 1932 took place in an atmosphere of rancour and unrest that recalled the dark days of 1918–19 and witnessed a dramatic reversal of the voter coalitions that had elected Hindenburg in 1925. With the forces of the political extremes each making their own bids for the presidency, all of the moderate parties, including the SPD, lined up behind the Chancellor to support the re-election of the ailing Hindenburg. With some irony, only the nationalist DNVP refused to support the incumbent and fielded their own candidate, the deputy leader of the *Stahlhelm*, Theodor Duesterberg. Amidst violence on the streets and ferocious rhetoric on the hustings, the first round of voting took place on 13 March. The initial vote knocked Duesterberg out of the race but was so close as to necessitate a run-off poll on 10 April, in which Hindenburg secured a majority of 19.4 million votes (53 per cent) to Hitler's

Results of the Presidential Elections, 1932

	First round (13 March 1932)		Second round (10 April 1932)	
Turnout	86.2%		83.5%	
Votes cast	37,648,317		36,490,761	
Duesterberg (DNVP)	2, 557,729	(6.8%)	—	
Hindenburg (Independent)	18,651,791	(49.6%)	19,359,983	(53%)
Hitler (NSDAP)	11,339,446	(30.1%)	13,418,547	(36.8%)
Thälmann (KPD)	4,983,341	(13.2%)	3,706,759	(10.2%)

Source: Anna von der Goltz, *Hindenburg: Power, Myth and the Rise of the Nazis* (Oxford, 2009), p. 145

Chancellor Heinrich Brüning campaigning on behalf of Hindenburg during the 1932 presidential elections (Bundesarchiv, Bild 102-13229 / CC-BY-SA).

13.4 million (36.8 per cent) and the Communist Thälmann's 3.8 million (10.2 per cent).[14] This was a big disappointment to Hitler, who had poured massive amounts of cash and energy into his campaign, and he now had no option but to set his sights on the chancellorship instead.

In the difficult times caused by the Depression, many people were more open to the racist, nationalist and anti-democratic ideas of the NSDAP than they would have been at other times, and 'there can be little doubt that Nazi ideology did successfully identify itself with certain populist fears and desires which had already found expression in the intellectual and cultural history of Germany over the previous century.'[15] But who actually voted for the Nazis? Despite the fact that the party originated and was based in Catholic Bavaria, support for the NSDAP tended to be highest in the protestant north and east of Germany. This indicated two key factors in support (or lack of it) for the National Socialists: religion and urbanization. Despite picking up votes from some blue-collar workers, the working-class vote still tended to be divided between the SPD and KPD. Similarly, while the party won an increasing percentage of the Catholic vote after 1928, 'the NSDAP was never able to undermine the solid foundation of Catholic support for the Zentrum [sic]. Backed by the Church, the Zentrum [sic], like the Marxist parties, offered its followers a well-defined belief system vigorously reinforced by an extensive network of political, social, and cultural organizations.'[16] The Nazi vote was therefore lowest in the big cities of western Germany, such as Cologne and Düsseldorf, and highest in rural Pomerania. At the same time, the party tended to elicit a higher proportion of support from farmers and peasants, the lower middle classes (shopkeepers, artisans, etc.) and white-collar workers who feared a catastrophic loss of status unless drastic action was taken to uphold their social position, than it did from the urban working class who on the whole continued to support the Social Democrats. All this led to the traditional view that the Nazis were supported by the middle classes, who turned to them when faced with economic hardship and the loss of their social position at the onset of the Great Depression.

However, more recent research has shown that patterns of support for the extreme Right were more complex than was once thought. It has been argued that 'the Nazi/white-collar relationship remained far weaker than traditionally assumed, even after the onset of the Depression', and, although they were denounced by the trade unions and the parties of the Left, the Nazis picked up support from a 'size-able body of workers in handicrafts and small-scale manufacturing.'[17] In particular there are interesting discrepancies between party membership and electoral support: while peasants tended to vote for the Nazis in higher numbers than other social groups, they were less likely to join the party. Similarly, while electoral support for the NSDAP tended to be lower among the urban workers, they still made up 31.5 per cent of party members, while 63 per cent of the SA was from a working-class background. In 1930, 13 per cent of all workers voted Nazi – a figure that rose to 27 and 28 per cent in the 1932 elections. By the summer of 1932, one in ten Nazi voters

had defected from the Social Democrats.[18] It was a similar story with the young: disillusioned by Weimar politics and with little prospect of getting a job during the Depression, young people joined the party and its organizations in large numbers. In 1933, 61 per cent of party members were aged between 20 and 30.

Social composition of the Nazi electorate, 1928–32

	May 1928 (%)	Sept 1930 (%)	July 1932 (%)	Nov 1932 (%)
Working class	40	40	39	39
New Mittelstand	22	21	19	19
Old Mittelstand	37	39	42	41

Source: Matthew Stibbe, *Germany 1914–1933* (Harlow, 2010), p. 182

Defections from other parties to the Nazis, May 1928–July 1932

Transfer of Votes	KPD to NSDAP (%)	SPD to NSDAP (%)	ZP/BVP to NSDAP (%)	DVP to NSDAP (%)
May 1928 to Sept. 1930	5	10	9	26
Sept. 1930 to July 1932	5	16	10	36

Transfer of Votes	DNPP to NSDAP (%)	Others (%)	NSDAP to NSDAP (%)	Non-Voters (%)
May 1928 to Sept. 1930	31	11	38	14
Sept. 1930 to July 1932	33	49	85	19

Source: Matthew Stibbe, *Germany 1914–1933* (Harlow, 2010), p. 181

Colin Storer

The figures cited above indicate that the traditional class-based explanation for the rise of German fascism is inadequate and begs the question: how were the National Socialists able to appeal to such a wide cross section of German society? Part of the answer is their skilful use of propaganda. Hitler had demonstrated an uncanny and cynical awareness of the power of propaganda from his earliest days in politics, and from April 1930 Josef Goebbels was placed in charge of the party's propaganda. Together they set up a highly efficient and sophisticated propaganda machine that allowed them to centrally control how the Nazi message was presented to the public, targeting money and efforts in key areas. Furthermore, feedback was encouraged from grass-roots level, so that the effectiveness of their efforts could be judged and successful campaigns and messages reproduced elsewhere. Goebbels practised mass politics on a grand scale, deluging the German people with leaflets, posters, etc., but at the same time producing specific material aimed directly at different social groups which played on their fears and concerns. In this way, the Nazis sought to be all things to all men and to some measure succeeded in convincing vastly different groups that they had their interests at heart. Furthermore, while the other parties continued to rely on tried and tested methods such as posters, leaflets and speeches to get their message across, the Nazis employed modern technology such as loud-speakers, film and radio, as well as publicity stunts such as Hitler's 'Flight over Germany' during the 1932 presidential election campaign, to get their message across to a mass audience.

Through these methods the Nazis managed to present themselves as anti-Marxist, while at the same time being untainted by association with big business (unlike the DVP and DNVP) or collaboration with the Social Democrats (unlike the Centre or DDP). The SPD's toleration of the Brüning administration meant that between October 1930 and May 1932 the NSDAP could present itself both as the only true opposition party aside from the KPD and as an anti-Marxist movement representing the 'national' interest. 'Moreover, because the NSDAP was not saddled with government responsibility before 1933, the party could make extravagant and often blatantly contradictory appeals to mutually hostile groups without having to reconcile those promises.'[19] At the same time, the Nazis 'mobilized unfulfilled reformist

expectations' and held out the prospect of radical change that both broke with older traditions tainted by association with 'the politics of failure'.[20] The Nazi party became a unique phenomenon in German politics: 'a catch-all party of social protest' that 'managed to project an image of dynamism, energy and youth that wholly eluded the propaganda efforts of the other parties.'[21] However, this meant that its appeal was wide but not deep, and by 1932 their support had already begun to fragment. Although by the beginning of 1933 they were the only party able to claim to be a broad-based *Volkspartei* whose appeal transcended traditional class and gender barriers, it seems unlikely that the Nazis would have been able to maintain their electoral appeal as economic conditions improved and it is therefore a tragic irony that Hitler was installed as chancellor just at the moment when their fortunes had begun to wane.

FROM BRÜNING TO HITLER

Hard on the heels of Hitler's failure to win the presidency came another blow to the Nazi leadership when the state finally decided to take action to curb the excesses of the SA. Political violence had been on the increase since 1929, but it rose exponentially during the election campaigns of 1932. The Nazis claimed that 10,000 of their rank-and-file members had been wounded in clashes with the Communists, while the KPD reported 75 deaths at the hands of the Nazis in the first six months of 1932 alone.[22] A ban on the wearing of uniforms had already been imposed in December 1931 but this had little effect as the Combat Leagues merely continued their marches and punch-ups in plain clothes. However, with the supposed threat of a Communist coup receding, and under heavy pressure from the SPD and the governments of the *Länder*, Brüning managed to overcome the opposition of the Reichswehr (as represented by Schleicher) and, on 13 April 1932, persuaded Hindenburg to sign an emergency decree prohibiting the SA. Nazi hostels were closed down, party offices raided by the police and arms, equipment and uniforms were confiscated.

However, although this to some extent curbed the violent excesses of the Nazis – or at least drove them off the streets and into pubs and meeting halls[23] – it could not save the administration. Despite all Brüning's efforts on his behalf during the recent election campaign, Hindenburg was deeply displeased that he had faced such concerted opposition in the polls and particularly that the Nationalists had run against him. Schleicher, who increasingly hoped to harness the mass appeal of the Nazis, capitalized on this displeasure and conspired to bring down both the Chancellor and his former mentor the Defence Minister Wilhelm Groener. Worn down by ill-health and a whispering campaign orchestrated by Schleicher, Groener was compelled to resign from the government on 10 May and, with the loss of his greatest champion in the President's inner circle, Brüning's days were numbered. Under increasing pressure to bring more right-wingers into the cabinet and form a Centre–NSDAP coalition in Prussia (where the SPD and State Party vote had collapsed in the recent *Landtag* elections and the Nazis had polled 36 per cent of the vote), Brüning's position became untenable and he was forced to resign on 30 May 1932.

After a weekend of confusion, during which both Schleicher's and Hindenburg's favoured candidates ruled themselves out of the running, the almost unknown Westphalian aristocrat Franz von Papen was named chancellor. A former cavalry officer and conservative Catholic, Papen had never held any office more senior than military attaché to Washington during the Great War and, although he had known Schleicher since they had been military cadets together, he had so far failed to distinguish himself as a Centre Party member of the Prussian *Landtag*. However, recent calls for Brüning to 'transform the "concealed dictatorship" through which he had governed for the past year and a half into a genuine national government, a dictatorship on a broad national foundation', had attracted the attention of Schleicher who apparently believed that Papen would be able to bring the Centre Party into the new cabinet.[24] However, this was a serious mistake. Offended by the intrigues which had ousted Brüning and anxious to avoid being linked to the forces of reaction, the Centre Party withdrew its support from the new government and Papen only managed to avoid being expelled from the party by resigning first. Papen was thus forced to lead a hastily cobbled together 'cabinet of barons' drawn largely from the ranks of the

DNVP, seven of whom were noblemen and most with little or no experience of practical politics. In return for the NSDAPs tolerance of the new government, Hitler was promised the repeal of the SA ban and new elections, and the Reichstag was dissolved on 4 June.

Never widely supported in either parliament or the country, the cabinet's popularity plummeted when it issued its first emergency decree on 14 June implementing swinging austerity measures that 'virtually abolished the system of unemployment insurance'.[25] The following day the ban on the SA was lifted, plunging Germany into a new orgy of paramilitary violence which culminated in a riot in the Hamburg suburb of Altona, on 17 July, that left 15 people dead and 50 injured. Of the 155 deaths in Prussia from political violence in 1932, 105 took place during the election campaign of June–July, while the police recorded 461 riots causing 82 deaths and 400 injuries during the first seven weeks of the campaign alone.[26] The public outcry that followed led to a new ban on political demonstrations but also provided the pretext for the unconstitutional dissolution of the SPD–Centre coalition in Prussia on 20 July and Papen's assumption of dictatorial powers in Germany's largest state. This *Preussenschlag* (Prussian coup) was designed to simultaneously weaken the SPD, 'placate Hitler . . . and advance the government's plan of centralizing political authority', but in actual fact all it achieved was to bring about a revival of popular support for the KPD and SPD and provide the Nazis with a precedent for their unconstitutional actions after 1933.[27]

Meanwhile, the National Socialists had reached the high water mark of their electoral success. The DDP, DVP and *Wirtschaftpartei*'s share of the vote collapsed, but while the Centre, SPD and DNVP all suffered losses, their support remained reasonably consistent. Even so, from July 1932 the two extremist parties – the KPD and NSDAP – together outnumbered all other parties in the Reichstag. The Nazis in particular had consolidated their gains in 1930, polling 37.3 per cent of the popular vote and securing 230 seats in the Reichstag, making them the largest single party. This removed any hope that Hitler would pursue a policy of 'objective cooperation' to Papen's government as the SPD had for Brüning. Hindenburg and Papen therefore attempted to harness the popularity of the

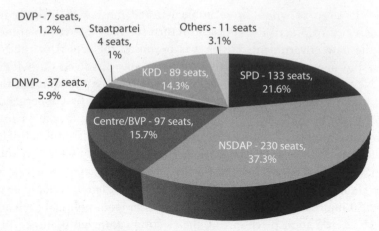

Reichstag election results, 31 July 1932.

Nazis by offering Hitler the post of vice-chancellor in a 'government of national concentration', but the Nazi leader refused anything other than the chancellorship. When the Reichstag reconvened on 12 September it was immediately prorogued when the Communists and Nazis joined together to defeat the government in a vote of no confidence, and new elections were called in the hope of weakening the position of the NSDAP and gaining a working majority for the government.

The results of the election of November 1932 clearly showed that the Nazis' popularity had peaked in July, as they lost 34 seats and their share of the vote declined by 4 per cent. What is more, the cost of fighting three election campaigns in one year had left the party virtually bankrupt. Yet the electorate also decisively rejected Papen's government, with nearly 90 per cent of voters backing the opposition parties.[28] When a second attempt to bring the Nazis into the government failed, Papen proposed dissolving parliament, declaring martial law and establishing a presidential dictatorship, but by this time the Chancellor had lost the support of his former backers in the President's inner circle. Annoyed at Papen's growing self-confidence and jealous of his close relationship with Hindenburg, Schliecher took this opportunity to withdraw the support of the army, declaring at a cabinet meeting on 2 December that the

Chancellor Franz von Papen
(right) with Presidential
Chief-of-Staff Otto Meissner,
11 August 1932 (Bild 102
13743 / CC-BY-SA).

Reichswehr was incapable of opposing the domestic anarchy and foreign invasion that would be the inevitable result of the Chancellor's proposals.[29] This led to Papen's fall and his replacement by the arch-intriguer Schleicher who now decided that it was time for him to emerge from the shadows and accomplish his aims himself.

Schleicher has often been dismissed as an arch reactionary who desired to destroy the republic and replace it with a restored monarchy or a military dictatorship. However, his outlook was more pragmatic than this. Rather than concentrating on divisive arguments about what form the state should take, he preferred to concentrate on dealing with political realities. When assessing the situation Germany found itself in after the Great War he took as his model Friedrich Wilhelm I of Prussia. His reading in German history convinced him that, as in the days of the 'Soldier King', the state

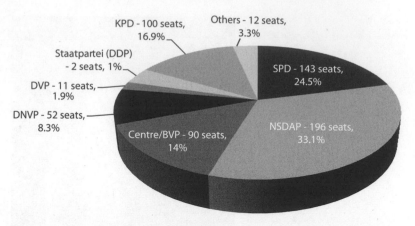

Reichstag election results, 6 November 1932.

needed to pursue a conciliatory foreign policy in order to concentrate on 'streamlining the economy', centralizing the power of the state and building up its military power.[30] At the same time, he believed that attempting to repress mass political movements (except those which openly espoused a violent transformation of the political and economic order) was counterproductive and that instead the political parties and Combat Leagues should be harnessed to the state. To this end, Schleicher made overtures to the Nazis in the hope of simultaneously 'taming' them and bringing their popularity behind his government. When these efforts failed he had no choice but to make the same appeal to Hindenburg to allow him to rule without parliament as his predecessor had done, an appeal that Hindenburg rejected using Schleicher's own arguments that such a move would lead to civil war.

Meanwhile, feeling betrayed, Papen had been intriguing against the new chancellor and entered into secret negotiations with the Nazis, which were designed to bring about his return to power with majority support in the Reichstag. Fearful that the ongoing economic crisis would bring about a communist revolution, and underwhelmed by Schliecher's performance as chancellor, the conservative elements within German society swung their support behind Papen who persuaded Hindenburg to dismiss Schleicher and appoint Hitler as chancellor in a coalition government that would contain only three Nazis, on the basis that as vice-chancellor Papen could control Hitler. Wearied by the constant political upheaval of the past two years, Hindenburg allowed himself to be convinced and duly appointed Hitler as chancellor on 30 January 1933.

THE END OF THE REPUBLIC

The massed ranks of the SA celebrated Hitler's appointment with a torchlit procession through the streets of Berlin, but their leader's power and position were by no means absolute and far from secure. Hitler was one of only three Nazis in a cabinet of 12 (Wilhelm Frick was Minister of the Interior and Hermann Göring was Minister without Portfolio); the NSDAP–DNVP coalition did not have an unassailable majority in the Reichstag so any legislation that it tried to introduce could easily be blocked if the other parties were prepared to work in concert; and finally the previous few years had shown that the Chancellor could only govern effectively if he retained the confidence of the President. This posed a problem for Hitler because it was well-known that Hindenburg had nothing but contempt for him. Nevertheless, Hitler had several advantages – firstly he was the leader of the largest single party in Germany and the ineffectual Papen and Schliecher governments had proven that the conservatives could not govern effectively without his support. Furthermore, there was a widespread fear amongst German conservatives that the only alternative to a Nazi government was civil war or a communist coup. More importantly, Hitler's appointment as chancellor gave the Nazi Party access to the full resources of the state. This came into its own during the Reichstag elections of March 1933.

Within 24 hours of his appointment Hitler had called new elections, hoping that this would provide him with the parliamentary majority necessary to alter the constitution. However, these were far from being free and fair. On 31 January 1933, Hitler used his position as head of government to issue an 'Appeal to the German

People' in which he blamed the prevailing conditions (including, ironically enough, the atmosphere of violence and intimidation in which the election campaign was taking place) on the democratic system and the terrorist activities of the Communists, while presenting his government as a 'national uprising' which would restore Germany's pride and unity. At the same time, as Prussian Minister of the Interior, Göring controlled the police force of the largest of the German *Länder* and was able to enrol 50,000 extra police officers, most of them recruited from the ranks of the SA. Socialist and communist rallies and meetings were routinely broken up by the police or Nazi thugs, and 69 people were killed during the five-week election campaign. Then, on 27 February, the Reichstag was burned down in an arson attack by an unemployed Dutch bricklayer, Marius van der Lubbe. Historians have long debated who was ultimately responsible for the fire, with many accusing the Nazis of having orchestrated the affair themselves as a pretext for a clampdown on their political opponents. Whatever the truth of the matter, the Nazi leadership were quick to present it as evidence of a wide-ranging communist conspiracy and persuaded the President to issue the Decree for the Protection of the People and the State which effectively suspended civil liberties in Germany and increased the power of central government over state authorities.

Despite all this, when Germany went to the polls on 5 March 1933 the Nazi gains were actually quite limited. Their share of the vote only increased by just over 10 per cent, giving them 288 seats in the Reichstag, meaning that they could only secure a majority with the aid of the 52 Nationalist deputies. This was a severe political blow to Hitler's plans because a clear two-thirds majority was necessary to introduce any changes to the constitution. Nevertheless, this was merely a setback and not a defeat. Without the majority necessary to alter the constitution, Hitler proposed the passage of an Enabling Bill that would 'effectively do away with parliamentary procedure and legislation and which would instead transfer full powers to the Chancellor and his government for the next four years. In this way the dictatorship would be grounded in legality'.[31] Correctly assuming that the Communists (or at least those not in prison) and the SPD would vote against such a measure, Hitler therefore had to

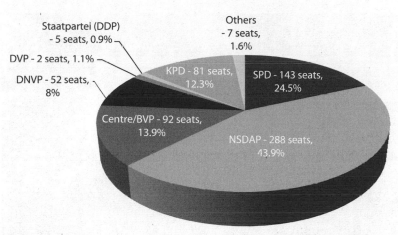

Reichstag election results, 5 March 1933.

reach out to the Centre Party in order to have any chance of securing the passage of the law.

But it was just at this moment that the delicate alliance between the Nazis and the forces of traditional conservatism threatened to be upset. The election campaign had built up a momentum within the lower ranks of the NSDAP that Hitler and the rest of the National Socialist leadership were finding difficult to contain. These elements scorned the legal route to power and pressed for the immediate creation of a Nazi dictatorship which would introduce radical measures, by violence if necessary. This threatened to destroy Hitler's image as a reasonable politician and alienate conservative elites and nationalist support in the Reichstag. Fearing that if this was to happen not only would he be unable to pass his Enabling Bill, but Hindenburg and his conservative advisors might also seek to use the army against him, Hitler organized a great ceremonial act of reassurance, the so-called Day of Potsdam, where, in the presence of Hindenburg, the former Crown Prince and many of the highest ranking officers in the Reichswehr, Hitler explicitly aligned National Socialism with the forces of traditional Prussian–German conservatism.

Two days later, on 23 March 1933, the Reichstag was opened in the new venue of the Kroll Opera House. In his speech to the

The Day of Potsdam, 21 March 1933. Hitler shakes hands with the aged President Hindenburg and symbolically aligns himself and his party with traditional Prussian militarism. (Bundesarchiv, Bild 183-S38324 / CC-BY-SA).

assembled Reichstag, Hitler announced that he would respect the rights of the Catholic Church and uphold religious and moral values; false promises that the Centre Party deputies chose to believe. When the vote on the Enabling Act was taken it was passed by 444 votes to 94. From that point on Hitler was able to enact legislation, including amendments to the constitution, without having to subject them to the approval of either parliament or the President. This freed him from the necessity of ruling by presidential decree as his predecessors had done and gave all the Nazis' subsequent actions a veneer of legality. Over the next 12 months they centralized political power in Germany, broke the power of the trade unions and dealt ruthlessly with opposition from both within and without their own party. By the end of 1934 Germany was a one-party state, the army had sworn an oath to serve not the state but Hitler himself, and the Nazi leader had assumed the powers of both chancellor and head of state.

WHY DID WEIMAR FAIL?

For much of the past 80 years, historians have been preoccupied with the question of how and why such a well-educated and cultured people as the Germans could have succumbed to Nazism and its message of hatred and violence. For a long time the answer was thought to be simple: flaws in the German character and the peculiar path of German history made the collapse of democracy and descent into totalitarian dictatorship inevitable. Yet as we have seen, there was nothing inevitable about Hitler's route to the chancellorship let alone his consolidation of power over the next year or so. Indeed, more recent scholarship has definitively exploded deterministic arguments about the Nazi seizure of power and demonstrated that even if normal democratic procedure had effectively been dispensed with after 1930 a Nazi dictatorship was far from inevitable.

No single explanation for the failure of German democracy is entirely satisfying. In many ways Weimar collapsed beneath the cumulative weight of successive crises and the forces ranged against it. Repeatedly buffeted by political and economic turbulence, the Weimar Republic became associated in the minds of many of its citizens with turmoil and uncertainty. This left a legacy of fear and anxiety that came to colour much of the political, social and cultural life of the republic. By 1933, after experiencing war, defeat, revolution, counter-revolution, hyperinflation, foreign occupation, unemployment, violence on the streets and three election campaigns (and three governments) in a single year, most Germans were exhausted and fearful. A political system that had – even during a period of apparent calm given them six governments in five years appeared completely unable to provide the stability they longed for, and so many of them seized eagerly on the exaggerated promises and radical solutions offered by the political extremes. Although it was far from being a 'republic without republicans', when push came to shove there were simply too few individuals and institutions prepared to stand in defence of the democratic system.

This was at least in part a consequence of the fragmented political culture of the republic. Although the old assertion that the

195

democratic roots of Germany's political institutions were shallow must be questioned (see Chapter 2), Weimar's political parties were unable to overcome their divergent ideological positions and reach compromise and consensus, especially after the onset of the Great Depression seemed to herald the terminal crisis of the capitalist system as predicted by Marx. This essentially guaranteed the breakdown of a democratic system that relied on consensus between parties in order to form functioning coalition governments and allowed extremist splinter parties to gain representation in parliament. At the same time, the legacy of bitterness left by the events of 1918–23 meant that the SPD and KPD – who shared a measure of ideological common ground and who together represented nearly half of the electorate – hated one another almost more than they despised the extreme Right and were ultimately unwilling to form a united anti-fascist front. This may not have saved the republic, but would have at least preserved Germany from the Nazis.

Furthermore, this political fragmentation was mirrored by a lack of social consensus. Although the Weimar state had done much to help those at the bottom of society, it had not managed to bridge the gulfs of social and economic inequality that divided the nation. When these gaps were widened further by the Depression, large sections of the population abandoned whatever faith they had had in democracy and turned to the political extremes. This was particularly true of the *Mittelstand*, who felt increasingly embittered as their unrealistic expectations of the republic were not being met and who, more than any other section of society, longed for stability and order.

But perhaps the key factor in bringing the Nazis to power was not so much popular support as the backing, or at least tolerance and ambivalence, of powerful established elites. As we have seen, despite all the socio-economic changes that took place during the Weimar period, the traditional arbiters of power in German society – the large landowners and aristocracy, the officer corps and big business – continued to exert a great deal of social, economic and political influence. This became even more apparent after 1929, when deadlock in the Reichstag meant that the President and his advisors became increasingly important figures in the day-to-day politics of the Weimar Republic. None of these had any great affection for democracy – indeed, 'Hindenburg had begun to dig Weimar's grave by hollowing out parliamentary democracy in the era of presidential cabinets' – but they had no love for the Nazis either. Their aim was an authoritarian 'government of national concentration', but the unprecedented growth and electoral success of the NSDAP after 1929 meant that they could not be ignored. Ultimately, both Papen and Schleicher made the fateful error of believing that they could 'tame' Hitler and harness the popularity of the Nazis to their own ends, and Hindenburg was persuaded to put aside his distaste for the 'Bohemian corporal' and appoint Hitler chancellor. Thus the Nazis were handed power as a result of political intrigues among the ruling elite just as their electoral support was on the wane.[32]

However, it is important to remember that the collapse of Weimar democracy did not happen in a vacuum. Germany was not the only country to experience economic depression and political uncertainty in the interwar period, and in many ways the failure of the republic can be seen as part of a wider European 'crisis of liberal democracy'. Faced with severe socio-economic problems, frustrated nationalism, ethnic conflict and a fear of communism, European democracy became increasingly embattled as the interwar period went on. By the middle of the 1930s the brief 'vogue for democracy' that had gripped Europe in the wake of the First World War had come to an end, and of the ten new states that had emerged from the Great War only Finland and Czechoslovakia remained democracies. Hungary had been dominated by the authoritarian regime of Admiral Miklós Horthy since the collapse of Belá Kun's short-lived Soviet Republic in 1920, Mussolini's Fascists had seized power in Italy in 1922 and Spain entered a period of military dictatorship after 1923. Portugal, Lithuania and Poland all saw democracy overthrown by military coups in 1926 and King Alexander of Yugoslavia established a royal dictatorship in 1929. The Weimar Republic was therefore not the first European democracy to collapse and nor would it be the last. Indeed, compared to some of its neighbours, Weimar democracy appears strikingly robust! Nevertheless, in the final analysis Weimar Germany followed the path of other, similar, democratic regimes as they struggled to cope with the economic, political and social challenges of the period, turning away from liberal democracy and embracing instead authoritarianism and fascism.

Conclusion

DID WEIMAR FAIL?

Generations of students have answered essay and exam questions that are variations on the theme: 'why did the Weimar Republic fail?', and, for a long time, seeking to understand how and why the Germans had succumbed to Nazism was the conundrum at the heart of scholarly interest in the republic. Yet as Weimar studies have taken a more 'cultural turn' in the past 30 years or so, historians have ceased to see the republic as little more than a prelude to the Third Reich and focused more and more attention on all aspects of German society and culture in the 1920s. This has led to an interdisciplinary reshaping of the debate on the history of Weimar Germany in which the lines that once delineated political, cultural and social history have been broken or at least blurred. This new interest in the 'culture of politics' and 'politics of culture' has moved away from the 'high politics' of elections, parliamentary debates and political speeches and increasingly focused on the importance of signs, symbols and myths in shaping Weimar politics and culture. It has also led historians to increasingly challenge the old narrative of the inevitable collapse of the Weimar Republic and shifted the question at the heart of the study of the Weimar Germany from 'why did democracy fail?' to ask in what ways and to what extent it failed.

Born out of military defeat and violent revolution, the Weimar Republic was in many ways an unwanted and unloved polity that inherited a bitter legacy of political and social division. Germany's long history of political disunity, coupled with the deep social and cultural cleavages created by the experience of industrial modernity,

made the republic a fractured commonwealth riven by ideological conflict and social anxiety. These divisions were widened and deepened by the early tumultuous years of democracy, when the new state faced violent challenges from both Left and Right at the same time as it struggled to deal with international and economic crises. The constitutional settlement that emerged in the summer of 1919 was a compromise between conflicting visions of the state that, although well-meaning, proved to be deeply flawed. In trying to strike a balance between the sovereignty of the Reichstag and a strong executive it betrayed a lack of faith in parliamentary democracy, while at the same time it created a political system that relied on consensus and compromise to function properly but ensured that the widest possible expressions of opinion could gain representation.

Against the odds, German democracy survived the upheavals of the early 1920s (unlike some of its western European neighbours) and entered into a period of relative stability after 1924. However, the old social divisions between rich and poor still existed and, although the state did much to help the less fortunate in society, the economic upheavals of the inflation era had left many impoverished and resentful. The stabilization of the currency left middle-class Germans feeling that they had been unfairly treated while the working classes and unemployed benefitted from wage increases and generous welfare payments. At the same time, although the economy stabilized between 1925 and 1929, there was no return to the pre-war boom years and productivity remained comparatively low while unemployment steadily increased. Reliance on foreign capital and the continuing burden of reparations payments left Germany dangerously exposed to fluctuations in the international economy, and when the American stock market crashed in October 1929 Germany was particularly badly hit by the subsequent global economic downturn.

With the onset of the Great Depression, German businesses began to go bust and unemployment rose rapidly. By 1932 one in three German workers was unemployed, and it appeared that capitalism had entered into a period of terminal decline. The effects of the Depression were all-pervasive and reawakened memories of the uncertainty and hardships of the 'years of crisis'. Yearning for stability

and security, German voters (many of whom had already begun to desert the moderate pro-republican parties of the political centre) abandoned the democratic parties in search of radical solutions to Germany's ills on the political extremes. At the same time, the Depression highlighted and exacerbated the ideological fissures between the political parties and made the formation of coalition governments almost impossible. Unable to command a majority in the Reichstag, from the summer of 1930 successive governments were forced to rely on presidential emergency powers to pass legislation, and parliamentary democracy effectively ceased to function. From this point onwards, the political initiative lay not so much with the people or the representatives of Weimar's political class as with the aging President Hindenburg and the coterie of aristocrats and army officers who made up his inner circle of advisors. Never particularly enamoured with democracy, these men had long desired an authoritarian reconfiguration of German politics, but they ultimately shied away from abandoning parliamentary politics altogether. In the final months of the republic, the desire to give 'presidential government' a sheen of legitimacy by harnessing the popularity of the Nazis and intrigues within the President's inner circle ultimately led to Hitler's appointment as chancellor at the end of January 1933.

However, the history of the Weimar Republic is more than a mere litany of failure and bad luck. Weimar democracy was in certain key respects deeply – some would say fatally – flawed, yet at no point was its demise inevitable. It may have come into being almost by accident and faced concerted opposition from both Left and Right throughout its lifetime, but the republic was still able to mobilize mass support at least until 1929. Elections in 1919 and 1920 returned a clear majority for the parties of the 'Weimar Coalition', thus demonstrating overwhelming popular support for the new democracy. Although the electorate moved to the Right throughout the 1920s, it was only after the onset of the Great Depression and the emasculation of the Reichstag in 1930 that the opponents of the Weimar state could claim a mass following. Under the republic 'Germans lived in the most democratic setting they had ever experienced, with a raucous free press and an intense, lively, streetscape of political theatre.'[1] Political participation remained consistently high and there was a greater degree of consensus amongst Weimar's political class (at least in the middle years of the republic) than some historians have suggested. The supposed flaws within the constitution – proportional representation, Article 48, etc. – were not flaws in themselves, but only became so when they combined with other factors, such as the pressures placed upon the system by economic and political crisis or a president determined to uphold the letter of the constitution but at best ambivalent towards the spirit that lay behind it. Finally, recent research has suggested that the republican state was much more adept at making use of political symbolism and harnessing popular enthusiasm than it has often been given credit for.

At the same time, Weimar Germany's legacy was more positive than is often realized. Alongside its failures there were also real and lasting achievements that, although submerged during the Nazi era, resurfaced in the 1950s and 1960s. Weimar 'established political liberties, opened up new avenues of representation' and 'enabled many people to live more freely chosen, more emancipated lives' than had been possible before 1918.[2] It led the world in social legislation, cultural experimentation and sexual tolerance and blazed a trail that many societies would later follow. Perhaps the greatest and most enduring legacy of Weimar Germany is the great flowering of art and literature, science and learning that it engendered. The republic 'produced an entire generation of probing, searching artists and intellectuals'[3] and 'one can barely count the bristling and bracing paintings, novels, poems, philosophical treatises, theatrical stagings and films' produced during the Weimar era 'that still, almost one hundred years later, move and engage us on every conceivable level – intellectually, aesthetically, emotionally, erotically.'[4] German scientists of the Weimar period laid the foundations of theoretical physics, German composers transformed music and German philosophers and sociologists profoundly changed the way people thought about themselves and the world around them. At the same time, the eight-hour working day and the welfare state improved the lives of millions of Germans and provided models of social intervention that would be widely imitated after the Second World War. Women gained not only the vote but also more options and greater freedom to decide for themselves how they would live, work and dress, in some ways preparing them for even greater moves towards equality and emancipation in the wake of the Second World War; while Weimar's open discussions of sex and sexuality and liberal attitudes towards homosexuality prefigured the 'sexual revolution' of the 1960s. These successes are often forgotten, or at least dismissed as temporary achievements invalidated by their rollback under the Third Reich, but it was these very accomplishments that made the republic so contested and mobilized such vociferous opposition from the forces of the radical Right.

Additionally, the circumstances of its birth meant that the fortunes of the republic were inextricably linked to developments on the international stage. To some extent the success or failure of the republic was, from the beginning, dependent on the actions of other nations and the vagaries of the global marketplace. The Treaty of Versailles, reparations and an economy reliant on foreign investment and export revenue meant that Weimar's political class could not remain aloof from international affairs even if they had wanted to; and the desire to wipe away the stain on their national honour left by defeat and the humiliating terms of the peace settlement meant that revisionism, either through peaceful negotiation or through confrontation, remained the abiding theme of German foreign policy throughout the interwar period. Although some of its key aims – recovery of the Polish Corridor, equality of armaments, etc. – remained out of reach, it is doubtless one of the great achievements of the republic that within seven years of the humiliating peace treaty Germany had recovered much of its pre-war international standing. Through the untiring efforts of Gustav Stresemann, Weimar Germany was able to overcome the suspicion of its former enemies and rejoin the community of nations as an equal in 1926. This was followed by the withdrawal of occupying troops ahead of schedule in 1930 and finally a moratorium on reparations payments in 1932. That these goals were achieved peacefully, although sometimes at the cost of domestic political harmony, is testament not only to the political skill of Stresemann, but also to the levels of consensus that could be achieved under the republic.

Moreover, when one begins to look at Weimar Germany from a comparative international perspective then its achievements become even more striking. One of the themes of this book has been an attempt to view the Weimar Republic in the context of the international situation of the 1920s and developments amongst its neighbours. The contention of those historians who espoused a *Sonderweg* view of German history was, simply put, that Weimar democracy failed because Germany was not Britain or France. But this is to 'assign Germany the part of the twentieth-century delinquent whose role is to certify the basic political virtue of France, Britain and the United States'.[5] It is true that Germany's democratic traditions and institutions were not as mature and deep-rooted as those of Britain or the United States, but then each of these had been a nation state for at least a century longer than Germany. And although it did ultimately succumb to dictatorship, the Weimar Republic held out against the forces ranged against it for longer and left a more lasting legacy than many of its near neighbours. Of the 'new democracies' that emerged from the First World War, Germany preserved its parliamentary democracy longer than any other save Austria and Czechoslovakia. Germany's experience of revolution and counter-revolution, political violence and economic dislocation in the first half of the 1920s was far from unique and is mirrored by developments throughout Central and Eastern Europe and even in the British Isles.

The Weimar Republic also had one of the most open and progressive societies in Europe. It extended the franchise to women on an equal basis to men before any of the more established democracies of Western Europe or the United States, and by the mid-1920s had more female parliamentarians (at both federal and state level) than the United Kingdom. Weimar Germany was widely regarded as a haven of sexual tolerance and progressive social ideas, and it was one of the first states in Europe to enact progressive legislation on prostitution and to consider the decriminalization of homosexuality. Finally, the shift to the Right at the end of the 1920s, and the ultimate abandonment of democracy when parliamentary politics seemed unable to adequately cope with renewed economic crisis at the onset of the Great Depression, was a Europe-wide phenomenon in which Germany was not the first, nor the last, state to abandon democracy in favour of a more authoritarian or fascist alternative.

Considering what came after it, the fact that Weimar democracy ultimately failed to survive was a tragedy not just for Germany, but also for Europe and the wider world. Yet this should not detract from the myriad achievements of the republic's 15 years of existence. In trying to understand how and why the Weimar Republic collapsed we should not lose sight of the positive features of its history. The story of the republic is one of creation as well as destruction, whether that be the formation of democratic institutions, the building of a modern urban consumer society or the manufacture of great works of art, and it deserves to be remembered as such. It was a remarkable period in German history that demonstrates both the best and worst features of democratic politics and what can happen to modern industrial societies when they face extreme conditions. Indeed, given the pressures placed upon it and the consistent opposition it faced from large sections of German society, that Weimar democracy endured as long as it did is a remarkable achievement in itself.

Appendices

Appendix 1: The Weimar Party System

Party	Abbreviation	Core Constituency	Notes
Bayerische Volkspartei (Bavarian People's Party)	BVP	Catholic Bavarians	A regional off-shoot of the Centre Party that seceded over the Centre's support for centralized government. It remained essentially the Bavarian wing of the Centre Party, but its refusal to work with the SPD in the Bavarian *Landtag* led to it making alliances with the anti-democratic parties of the Right.
Deutsche Demokratische Partei (German Democratic Party)	DDP	Supporters from a broad spectrum of German society, from trade unionists to bankers, but rooted in the middle classes.	The DDP emerged out of an attempt to create a single liberal party in 1918 and was made up of a merger of the former Progressive Party with the left-wing of the old National Liberals. Its leaders were largely liberal intellectuals (leading to it being dubbed the Professor's Party) and its members made an important contribution to drafting the Weimar constitution. Like the other centrist parties, it shifted to the Right in the late 1920s and was renamed the *Deutsche Staatspartei* (German State Party) in 1930.

Party	Abbreviation	Core Constituency	Notes
Deutsche Volkspartei (German People's Party)	DVP	The upper middle classes. In 1930 a third of its Reichstag deputies were leading businessmen.	Made up of those National Liberals who felt excluded from the DDP due to their annexationist views, it attempted to strike a balance between liberalism and nationalism. They favoured increased centralization and a strong presidency. If not actively anti-republican, it had strong reservations about the Weimar system.
Deutsche Zentrumspartei (Centre Party)	ZP	Roman Catholics. Encompassed all areas of German society from aristocrats to workers, but most were active church-goers.	Established in 1870 to represent the interests of German Catholics in the newly united Germany, attempts to rebrand itself as a non-denominational Christian People's Party in 1918 came to nothing. One of the most stable political forces during the Weimar period, it participated in almost every coalition government between 1919 and 1933. It shifted to the Right again in the late 1920s and voluntary disbanded after Hitler's rise to power.

Party	Abbreviation	Core Constituency	Notes
Deutschenationale Volkspartei (German National People's Party)	DNVP	Conservative aristocrats and industrialists, civil servants and the lower middle classes.	The political focal point of conservative anti-republicans, it was formed when the old German Conservative Party and the Free Conservatives merged with other right-wing interest groups in November 1918. An alliance of big business and the landed interest, it was conservative and monarchist but worked in coalition with the parties of the centre in the mid-1920s. Under pressure from the 'New Right' in the late 1920s it lurched to the Right and ended by supporting Hitler.
Kommunistische Partei Deutschlands (Communist Party of Germany)	KPD	The radical working class, the unemployed, young workers.	Formed by an alliance of radical left-wing forces (the Spartacists, the Left Radicals and the Revolutionary Shop Stewards) at the end of 1918, the KPD opposed western-style democracy and favored a revolutionary overthrow of the republic and the establishment of a worker's state modelled on the USSR. After 1920, it increasingly came under the direction of Moscow and participated in a number of armed uprisings against the state. Its support was bolstered by

Party	Abbreviation	Core Constituency	Notes
			the defection of USPD members in 1920 and by the economic crisis after 1929, but it never enjoyed mass support amongst the working class.
Nationalsozialistische Deutsche Arbeiterpartei (National Socialist German Workers' Party)	NSDAP	Core support came from the lower middle classes, peasants, the unemployed and female voters, but the NSDAP aspired to be a true *Volkspartei* attracting mass support from across German society.	Founded in 1919 as the German Worker's Party (DAP), the NSDAP was an anti-republican ultra-right-wing Nationalist party whose programme included 'socialist' economic and social elements but was mainly virulently nationalistic and anti-Semitic. Led from 1921 by Adolf Hitler, it attempted to seize power in an armed *coup d'état* in November 1923. Refounded in 1925 after Hitler's release from prison, from then on it pursued a policy of gaining power through legal means, even though it remained fundamentally opposed to the republic. Although its support was limited in the early years of the Weimar period, it became the largest single party in the Reichstag in 1932.

Party	Abbreviation	Core Constituency	Notes
Sozialdemokratische Partei Deutschlands (German Social Democratic Party)	SPD	The 'aristocracy of labour': the skilled working class and trade unionists. SPD voters tended to be older, in work and property owners. Four-fifths of their support came from the working class and the party did little to reach beyond this core support.	A moderate socialist party, the SPD strongly supported parliamentary democracy. As the mainstay of the Weimar Coalition it worked together with the moderate bourgeois parties to uphold the republic in the face of opposition from both Left and Right. Boasting a well-established membership (1 million in 1919) and social organizations, it was the largest single party in the Reichstag between 1912 and 1932.
Unabhängige Sozialdemokratische Partei Deutschlands (Independent German Social Democratic Party)	USPD	Radical elements of the German labour movement.	The USPD broke away from the SPD in 1917 over the issue of continuing support for the German war effort. It favoured radical social and economic change during the November Revolution and it split in 1920, the majority of its members joining the KPD. The remainder rejoined the SPD in 1922.

KPD USPD SPD | DDP ZP/BVP | DVP DNVP NSDAP

Left   Centre   Right

Appendix 2: Reichstag Election Results, 1919–33

	1919	1920	May 1924	Dec 1924	1928	1930	July 1932	Nov 1932	1933
Turnout (%)	82.7	79.1	77.4	78.8	75.6	81.9	84	80.6	88.5
BVP	–	1.238	0.946	1.134	0.945	1.005	1.192	1.095	1.074
		4.4%	3.2%	3.7%	3.1%	3.0%	3.2%	3.1%	2.7%
		21	16	19	16	19	22	20	18
DDP	5.641	2.333	1.655	1.920	1.505	1.322	0.371	0.336	0.334
	18.5%	8.3%	5.7%	6.3%	4.9%	3.8%	1%	1%	0.9%
	75	39	28	32	25	20	4	2	5
DNVP	3.121	4.249	5.696	6.206	4.381	2.458	2.177	2.959	3.136
	10.3%	15.1%	19.5%	20.5%	14.2%	7%	5.9%	8.3%	8%
	44	71	95	103	73	41	37	52	52
DVP	1.345	3.919	2.694	3.049	2.679	1.578	0.436	0.661	0.432
	4.4%	13.9%	9.2%	10.1%	8.7%	4.5%	1.2%	1.9%	1.1%
	19	65	45	69	45	30	7	11	2
KPD	–	0.589	3.693	2.709	3.264	4.592	5.283	5.980	4.848
		2.1%	12.6%	9%	10.6%	13.1%	14.3%	16.9%	12.3%
		4	62	45	54	77	89	100	81
NSDAP	–	–	1.918	0.907	0.810	6.409	13.745	11.737	17.277
			6.5%	3%	2.6%	18.3%	34.3%	33.1%	43.9%
			32*	14	12	107	230	196	288
SPD	11.509	6.104	6.009	7.881	9.453	8.577	7.959	7.248	7.181
	37.9%	21.7%	20.5%	26%	29.8%	24.5%	21.6%	20.4%	18.3%
	165	102	100	131	153	143	133	121	120
USPD	2.317	5.046	0.235	0.099	0.021	–	–	–	–
	7.6%	17.9%	0.8%	0.3%	0.1%				
	22	84	–	–	–				
Wirtschaftspartei	0.275	0.218	0.694	1.005	1.397	1.362	0.146	0.110	–
	0.9%	0.8%	2.4%	3.3%	4.5%	3.9%	0.4%	0.3%	
	4	4	10	17	23	23	2	1	
Zentrum	5.980	3.845	3.914	4.119	3.712	4.127	4.589	4.230	4.425
	19.7%	13.6%	13.4%	13.6%	12.1%	11.8%	12.5%	11.9%	11.2%
	91	64	65	69	62	68	75	70	74
Others	0.208	0.651	1.824	1.36	3.1	3.459	0.98	1.066	0.629
	0.7%	2.2%	6.2%	10.8%	4.5%	10%	2.7%	3%	1.6%
	3	–	19	12	31	49	9	11	7

The figures for each party indicate number of votes polled (in millions), percentage share of the vote and number of seats at the beginning of the session.

*As part of the *Völkisch-Nationaler Block*.

Source: Eberhard Kolb, *The Weimar Republic (2nd ed)* (Abingdon, 2005), pp.224–5.

Appendix 3: Chancellors of the Weimar Republic

Term in Office	Days in Office	Name	Party	Coalition
13 Feb. – 20 June 1919	130	Philipp Scheidemann	SPD	SPD-DDP-ZP
21 June 1919 – 26 March 1920	277	Gustav Bauer	SPD	SPD-DDP-ZP
27 March – 8 June 1920	72	Hermann Müller	SPD	SPD-DDP-ZP
21 June 1920 – 4 May 1921	317	Konstantin Fehrenbach	Centre	ZP-DDP-DVP
10 May 1921 – 22 Nov. 1922	553	Josef Wirth	Centre	1st & 2nd: ZP-SPD-DDP
22 Nov. 1922 – 12 Aug. 1923	263	Wilhelm Cuno	Independent	DVP-DDP-ZP-BVP
13 Aug. – 30 Nov. 1923	103	Gustav Stresemann	DVP	1st & 2nd: DVP-SPD-DDP-ZP
30 Nov. 1923 – 15 Jan. 1925	412	Wilhelm Marx	Centre	ZP-DVP-DDP
15 Jan. 1925 – 12 May 1926	482	Hans Luther	DDP	1st: DVP-DNVP-ZP-DDP-BVP 2nd: DVP-ZP-DDP-BVP
17 May 1926 – 12 June 1928	792	Wilhelm Marx	Centre	1st: ZP-DDP-DVP-BVP 2nd: ZP-DVP-DNVP-BVP
28 June 1928 – 27 March 1930	637	Hermann Müller	SPD	SPD-DDP-DVP-ZP-BVP
30 March 1930 – 30 May 1932	792	Heinrich Brüning	Centre	1st: ZP-BVP-DVP-DDP-Business-KVP 2nd: ZP-DDP-BVP-KVP
1 June – 17 Nov. 1932	170	Franz von Papen	Centre	DNVP
3 Dec. 1932 – 28 Jan. 1933	55	Kurt von Schleicher	Independent	DNVP
30 Jan. 1933 – 30 April 1945	4473	Adolf Hitler	NSDAP	NSDAP-DNVP

Source: Tim Kirk, *Cassell's Dictionary of Modern German History* (London, 2002)

Notes

Introduction

1 Published in English as *The Weimar Republic: The Crisis of Classical Modernity* (London, 1992).

2 For an exploration of the use of the term 'crisis' in the historiography of the Weimar Republic see Rüdiger Graf, 'Either–Or: The narrative of "crisis" in Weimar Germany and its historiography', *Central European History*, Vol. 43, No. 4 (2010), pp. 592–615.

3 The original remark, made in a letter to the British Prime Minister and Foreign Secretary Lord Palmerston, was 'L'Italie est un nom géographique' (Italy is only a geographical expression). But the same could be said of Germany prior to unification.

4 Frederick the Great, *Memoirs of the House of Brandenburg from the Earliest Accounts to the Death of Frederick I. King of Prussia . . . By the Present King of Prussia* (London, 1758), Vol. 1, p. 183.

5 Walter Oppenheim, *Habsburgs and Hohenzollerns 1713–1786* (London, 1993), pp. 32–33.

6 Quoted in David Blackbourn, *History of Germany 1780–1918: The Long Nineteenth Century (2nd ed)* (Oxford, 2003), p. 17.

Chapter One

1 Eric D. Weitz, *Weimar Germany: Promise and Tragedy* (Princeton, 2007), pp. 8–9.

2 David Stevenson, *With Our Backs to the Wall: Victory and Defeat in 1918* (London, 2011), pp. 287–8

3 Stevenson: *With Our Backs to the Wall*, pp. 418–19.

4 For more on the split in German Social Democracy and its consequences see A. J. Ryder, *The German Revolution of 1918: A Study of German Socialism in War and Revolt* (Cambridge, 1967).

5 Erich Ludendorff, *My War Memories, 1914–1918*, Vol. 2 (London, 1919), p. 679.

6   Under this electoral system all Prussian males over the age of 24 were eligible to vote, but they were divided into three classes based on the tax bracket into which they fell. There was no secret ballot and voting took place in public with votes being cast orally. Furthermore, it was an indirect system whereby each class voted for a third of electors (*Wahlmänner*). Despite the fact that there was a vast disparity in the percentage of the population that each class represented (when the system was introduced in 1849 the first class, representing those paying the top rate of income tax, was made up of 4.7 per cent of the population as opposed to the 82.6 per cent of the population represented by the third class who paid little or no tax) each class elected the same number of *Wahlmänner*, meaning that a first-class vote was worth nearly 18 times more than a third-class vote.

7   Philip Scheidemann, *Memoirs of a Social Democrat* (J. E. Mitchell, trans), Vol. 2 (London, 1929), p. 582.

8   Ibid.

9   Conan Fischer, '"A very German revolution"? The post-1918 settlement re-evaluated', *Bulletin of the German Historical Institute*, Vol. 28, No. 2 (2006), p. 15.

10 Quoted Sebastian Haffner, *Failure of a Revolution: Germany 1918–19* (London, 1973), p. 66.

11 Alan Farmer and Andrina Stiles, *The Unification of Germany, 1815–1919 (3rd ed)* (London, 2007), p. 201.

12 Nigel Jones, *A Brief History of the Birth of the Nazis*, (London, 2004), p. 48.

13 Richard Bessel, 'The Great War in German memory: The soldiers of the First World War, demobilisation, and Weimar political culture', *German History*, Vol. 6, No. 1 (1988), p. 26.

14 F. L. Carsten, *The Reichswehr in Politics*, (Cambridge, 1972), pp. 16–17.

15 See Michael Geyer, 'Insurrectionary warfare: The German debate about a *levée en masse* in October 1918', *The Journal of Modern History*, Vol. 73, No. 3 (September 2001), pp. 459–527; F. L. Carsten, *The Reichswehr in Politics* (Cambridge, 1972), pp. 17–21; David Clay Large, *The Politics of Law and Order: A History of the Bavarian* Einwohnerwehr, *1918–1921* (Philidelphia, 1980); and Dirk Schumann, *Political Violence in the Weimar Republic, 1918–1933* (Thomas Dunlap, trans) (New York, 2009), p. 24.

16 Robert Gerwarth, 'The Central European counter-revolution: paramilitary violence in Germany, Austria and Hungary after the Great War', *Past and Present*, No. 200 (2008), p. 176.

17 Ibid, p. 180.

18 For comparative studies on paramilitary violence in the interwar period see the special issue of *Contemporary European History* (Vol. 19, No.3,

2010) dedicated to the subject, as well as Donald Bloxham and Robert Gerwarth (eds), *Political Violence in Twentieth Century Europe* (Cambridge, 2011); Ian Kershaw, 'War and political violence in the twentieth century', *Contemporary European History*, Vol. 14, No. 1 (2005), pp. 107–23; and Anthony Read, *The World on Fire: 1919 and the Battle with Bolshevism* (London, 2008).

19 Richard Grunberger, *Red Rising in Bavaria* (London, 1973), p. 104.

20 Jones: *Birth of the Nazis*, p. 157.

21 William Mulligan, 'The Reichswehr and the Weimar Republic' in Anthony McElligott (ed.), *Weimar Germany* (Oxford, 2009), p. 85.

22 Carsten: *Reichswehr in Politics*, p. 79.

23 'Appeal of the Social Democratic Party for a general strike', in Anton Kaes, Martin Jay and Edward Dimendberg (eds), *The Weimar Republic Sourcebook* (Berkeley, 1994), p. 16.

24 Richard Bessel, 'Germany from war to dictatorship' in Mary Fulbrook (ed.), *German History Since 1800* (London, 1997), p. 245.

25 See, for example, Schumann: *Political Violence in the Weimar Republic*, p. 24.

26 Fischer: 'A very German revolution?', pp. 20–23.

27 See Jones: *Birth of the Nazis*, p 216 and Gerwarth: Central European counter-revolution, pp. 183–84.

28 See Manuela Achilles, 'Reforming the Reich: democratic symbols and rituals in the Weimar Republic' in Kathleen Canning, Kerstin Brandt and Kristin McGuire (eds), *Weimar Publics/Weimar Subjects: Rethinking the Political Culture of Germany in the 1920s* (Oxford, 2010), and Manuela Achilles, 'Nationalist violence and republican identity in Weimar Germany: the murder of Walter Rathenau' in Christian Emden and David Midgley (eds), *German Literature, History and the Nation: Papers from the Conference 'The Fragile Tradition'*, Cambridge 2002, Vol. 2 (Bern, 2004).

29 Richard J. Evans, *The Coming of the Third Reich* (London, 2003), p. 196.

30 Emil Julius Gumbel, *Vier Jahre politischer Mord* (Berlin, 1922), pp. 78–80.

Chapter Two

1 Anthony McElligott, 'Political Culture' in Anthony McElligott (ed.), *Weimar Germany* (Oxford, 2009), p. 30.

2 Paul Bookbinder, *Weimar Germany: The Republic of the Reasonable* (Manchester, 1996), p. 42.

3 'The Constitution of the German Republic' in Anton Kaes, Martin Jay and Edward Dimendberg (eds), *The Weimar Republic Sourcebook* (Berkeley, 1994), p. 48.

4   Geoff Layton, *From Bismarck to Hitler: Germany 1890–1933* (London, 1995), p. 79.

5   Conan Fischer, '"A very German revolution"? The post-1918 settlement re-evaluated', *Bulletin of the German Historical Institute*, Vol. 28, No. 2 (2006), p. 19.

6   McElligott: Political Culture, p. 28.

7   Friedrich Meinecke, *Die Deutsche Katastrophe* (Berlin, 1947), p. 88.

8   John Hiden, *The Weimar Republic (2nd ed)* (Harlow, 1996), p. 39.

9   Stephen E. Hanson, *Post-Imperial Democracies: Ideology and Party Formation in Third Republic France, Weimar Germany and Post-Soviet Russia* (Cambridge, 2010), pp. 144–45.

10 See Larry Eugene Jones, 'German Conservatism at the crossroads: Count Kuno von Westarp and the struggle for control of the DNVP, 1928–30', *Contemporary European History*, Vol. 18, No. 2 (2009), pp. 147–77.

11 Peter Fritzsche, 'The NSDAP 1919–1934: From Fringe Politics to the Seizure of Power' in Jane Caplan, *Nazi Germany* (Oxford, 2008), p. 54.

12 'The Twenty-five Points' in Anton Kaes, Martin Jay and Edward Dimendberg (eds), *The Weimar Republic Sourcebook* (Berkeley, 1994), pp. 124–26.

13 Fritzsche:, The NSDAP 1919–1934, p. 130.

14 See Dirk Schumann, *Political Violence in the Weimar Republic, 1918–1933* (Thomas Dunlap, trans) (New York, 2009); Robert Gerwarth, 'The Central European counter-revolution: paramilitary violence in Germany, Austria and Hungary after the Great War', *Past and Present*, No. 200 (2008), p. 181; Richard Bessel, 'The "Front Generation" and the Politics of Weimar Germany' in Roseman, M. (ed.), *Generations in Conflict; Youth Revolt and Generation Formation in Germany 1770–1968* (Cambridge, 1995); and Dirk Schumann, 'Political Violence, Contested Public Space, and Reasserted Masculinity in Weimar Germany' in Kathleen Canning, Kerstin Brandt and Kristin McGuire (eds), *Weimar Publics/Weimar Subjects: Rethinking the Political Culture of Germany in the 1920s* (Oxford, 2010).

15 Schumann: *Political Violence in the Weimar Republic*, p. 152.

16 See McElligott, 'Political Culture', pp. 36–7.

17 Anthony McElligott, 'Introduction' in Anthony McElligott (ed.), *Weimar Germany* (Oxford, 2009), p. 2.

18 Count Harry Kessler, *The Diaries of a Cosmopolitan, 1918–1937* (Charles Kessler, trans) (London, 2000), p. 184.

19 See Eric D. Weitz, *Weimar Germany: Promise and Tragedy* (Princeton, 2007), pp. 92–101 and Robert Gerwarth, 'The Past in Weimar History', *Contemporary European History*, Vol. 15. No. 1 (2006), pp. 8–10.

20 Eric Bryden, 'Heroes and martyrs of the Republic: Reichsbanner

Geschichtspolitik in Weimar Germany', *Central European History*, Vol. 43, No. 4 (2010), pp. 646, 663.

21 Nadine Rossol, *Performing the Nation in Interwar Germany: Sport, Spectacle and Political Symbolism, 1926–1936* (Basingstoke, 2010), p. 81.

22 For the history of Germany's national anthem and the controversies surrounding this and other national symbols, see Michael E. Geisler, 'In the Shadow of Exceptionalism: Germany's National Symbols and Public Memory after 1989' in Michael E. Geisler (ed.), *National Symbols, Fractured Identities: Contesting the National Narrative* (Lebanon, New Hampshire, 2005).

23 Nadine Rossol, 'Performing the Nation: Sports, Spectacles, and Aesthetics in Germany, 1926-1936', *Central European History*, Vol. 43, No. 4 (2010), p. 630.

24 Manuela Achilles, 'With a passion for reason: celebrating the Constitution in Weimar Germany', *Central European History*, Vol. 43, No. 4 (2010), p. 670.

25 Rossol: 'Performing the Nation', p. 630.

26 See Achilles: 'With a passion for reason', p. 684 and Rossol: *Performing the Nation,* pp. 66–71.

27 Achilles: 'With a passion for reason', p. 679.

28 Hanson, *Post-Imperial Democracies*, p. 128.

29 McElligott, 'Political Culture', p. 29.

Chapter Three

1 Ecclesiastes 1:9.

2 See Bernd Widding, *Culture and Inflation in Weimar Germany* (Berkeley, 2001), pp. 5–6.

3 Brett Fairbairn, 'Economic and Social Developments' in James Retallack, *Imperial Germany, 1871–1918* (Oxford, 2008), p. 62.

4 Niall Ferguson, 'The German Inter-War Economy: Political Choice Versus Economic Determinism' in Mary Fulbrook (ed.), *Germany Since 1800* (London, 1997), pp. 270–71.

5 H. W. V. Temperley (ed.), *The German Treaty Text* (London, 1920), p. 116.

6 Eberhard Kolb, *The Weimar Republic (2nd ed)* (P. S. Falla and R. J. Park, trans), (Abingdon, 2005), p. 181.

7 See John Hiden, *Republican and Fascist Germany* (Harlow, 1996), p. 113. For the ongoing debate on Germany's capacity to pay, see Gerald D. Feldman, 'The reparations debate', *Diplomacy and Statecraft*, Vol. 16, No. 3 (2005), pp. 487–98.

8 See Gerald D. Feldman, *The Great Disorder: Politics, Economics and Society in the German Inflation, 1914–24* (New York, 1997), p. 837–39,

and Niall Ferguson, *Paper and Iron: Hamburg Business and German Politics in the Era of Inflation* (Oxford, 1995), pp. 408–19.

9   See Carl-Ludwig Holtferich, *The German Inflation 1914–1923: Causes and Effects in International Perspective* (Berlin, 1986). Holtferich's thesis has been criticized for making an artificial distinction between 'good inflation' that stimulated growth until 1922 and hyperinflation which led to economic chaos thereafter, and for taking an overly narrow approach based purely on the economic data that ignores the social and psychological aspects of the inflation.

10 Richard Bessel, 'Germany from War to Dictatorship' in Mary Fulbrook (ed.) *German History Since 1800* (London, 1997), p. 238.

11 Ibid., p. 238.

12 Adam Fergusson, *When Money Dies: The Nightmare of the Weimar Hyper–Inflation* (London, 2010), p. 180.

13 Conan Fischer, 'Continuity and Change in Post-Wilhelmine Germany: From the 1918 Revolution to the Ruhr Crisis' in Geoff Eley and James Retallack (eds), *Wilhelminism and its Legacies* (New York, 2003), p. 213.

14 Fergusson: *When Money Dies*, p. 109.

15 Kolb: *The Weimar Republic*, p. 185.

16 See Conan Fischer, '"A very German revolution"? The post-1918 settlement re-evaluated', *Bulletin of the German Historical Institute*, Vol. 28, No. 2 (2006), p. 28.

17 Matthew Stibbe, *Germany 1914–1933: Politics, Society and Culture* (Harlow, 2010), p. 118.

18 Geoff Layton, *From Bismarck to Hitler: Germany 1890–1933* (London, 1995), p. 94.

19 Kolb: *The Weimar Republic*, p. 185.

20 Fergusson: *When Money Dies*, p. 236.

21 Ibid. p. 211.

22 Fischer: 'Continuity and Change in Post-Wilhelmine Germany', p. 211.

23 Fergusson: *When Money Dies*, p. 235

24 Theo Balderston, *Politics and Economics in the Weimar Republic* (Cambridge, 2002), p. 69.

25 For more on Weimar 'organizationalism' and economic institutions and interest groups, see Harold James, 'The Weimar Economy' in Anthony McElligott (ed.), *Weimar Germany* (Oxford, 2009), p. 106, and Ferguson: 'The German Inter-War Economy', pp. 269–70.

26 See Albrecht Ritschl, *Deutschlands Krise und Konjunktur 1924–1934: Binnenkonjunktur, Auslandsverschuldung und Reparationsproblem zweichen Dawes-Plan und Transferperre* (Berlin, 2002).

27 James, 'The Weimar Economy', pp. 106–7

28 Balderston: *Politics and Economics*, p. 82.

29   William L. Patch, *Heinrich Brüning and the Dissolution of the Weimar Republic* (Cambridge, 1998), p. 143.
30   Layton: *From Bismarck to Hitler*, p. 132.
31   See Adam Tooze, 'The Economic History of the Nazi Regime' in Jane Caplan (ed.), *Nazi Germany* (Oxford, 2008), pp. 170–71; Adam Tooze, *Wages of Destruction: The Making and Breaking of the Nazi Economy* (London, 2006); Dan P. Silverman, *Hitler's Economy: Nazi Work Creation Programs, 1933–1936* (Cambridge, Mass., 1998); Richard Overy, *The Nazi Economic Recovery 1932–1938* (Cambridge, 1996); Harold James, *The German Slump: Politics and Economics 1924–1936* (Oxford, 1986), Chapter 10; Harold James, 'Innovation and Conservatism in Economic Recovery: The Alleged "Nazi Recovery" of the 1930s' in Thomas Childers and Jane Caplan (eds), *Re-evaluating the Third Reich* (New York, 1993); and Raymond L. Cohen, 'Fiscal Policy in Germany During the Great Depression', *Explorations in Economic History*, Vol. 29 (1992), pp. 318–42.
32   For a detailed examination of the main theories, see Balderston: *Politics and Economics*, pp. 36–53.

Chapter Four

1   Imanuel Geiss, 'German Foreign Policy in the Weimar Republic and the Third Reich, 1919–1945' in Panikos Panayi (ed.), *Weimar and Nazi Germany: Continuities and Discontinuities* (Harlow, 2001), p. 144.
2   Wolfgang Elz, 'Foreign Policy' in Anthony McElligott (ed.), *Weimar Germany* (Oxford, 2009), p. 50.
3   See H. W. V. Temperley (ed.), *The German Treaty Text* (London: Henry Frowde/Hodder & Stoughton, 1920), pp. 97–99.
4   Ibid., p. 116.
5   Paul von Hindenburg, 'The Stab in the Back' in Anton Kaes, Martin Jay and Edward Dimendberg (eds), *The Weimar Republic Sourcebook* (Berkeley: University of California Press, 1994), p. 15.
6   Gregor Dallas, *1918: War and Peace* (London, 2000), p. 168.
7   The Fourteen Points were the moral principles for which the United States entered the First World War, as outlined in a speech given to Congress by President Woodrow Wilson on 18 January 1918, which amounted to a statement of American war aims. They included freedom of the seas, free trade, the withdrawal of German and Austrian troops from all occupied territory, the creation of an independent Polish state and an end to the system of secret treaties and alliances that had dominated pre-war diplomacy. A full text of Wilson's speech and commentary can be found at http://www.ourdocuments.gov/doc.php?flash=true&doc=62 (accessed 11/02/11).
8   Elz: 'Foreign Policy', p. 53.

9 'President Wilson's Fourteen Points', quoted in Harry Harmer, *Friedrich Ebert* (London, 2008), pp. 50–51.

10 Vejas Gabriel Liulevicius, *The German Myth of the East: 1800 to the Present* (Oxford, 2009), p. 137.

11 R. Butler and J. Bury (eds), *Documents in British Foreign Policy (First Series)*, Vol. XV (1954), pp. 258–59.

12 Alan Sharp, *Consequences of the Peace – The Versailles Settlement: Aftermath and Legacy, 1919–2010* (London, 2010), p. 6.

13 Elz: 'Foreign Policy', p. 23.

14 Peter Krüger, 'The European East and Weimar Germany' in Eduard Mühle (ed.), *Germany and the European East in the Twentieth Century* (Oxford, 2003), p. 12.

15 See Conan Fischer, *The Ruhr Crisis, 1923–1924* (Oxford, 2003), pp. 7–9, 22.

16 Jonathan Wright, *Gustav Stresemann: Weimar's Greatest Statesman* (Oxford, 2002), p. 165.

17 Zara Steiner, *The Lights That Failed: European International History, 1919–1933* (Oxford, 2005), p. 387.

18 Jonathan Wright, 'Stresemann and Locarno', *Contemporary European History*, Vol. 4, No. 2 (1995), p. 121.

19 Wright: *Gustav Stresemann*, p. 270.

20 Wright: 'Stresemann and Locarno', pp. 123–24.

21 See David Cameron and Anthony Heywood, 'Germany, Russia and Locarno: The German–Soviet Trade Treaty of 12 October 1925' in Gaynor Johnson (ed.), *Locarno Revisited: European Diplomacy 1920–29* (London, 2004).

22 Steiner: *The Lights That Failed*, p. 573.

23 Wright: *Gustav Stresemann*, p. 493.

24 *The Times*, 4 October 1929.

25 Count Harry Kessler, *The Diaries of a Cosmopolitan 1918–1937* (London, 2000), p. 368.

26 Wolfgang J. Helbich, 'Between Stresemann and Hitler: The foreign policy of the Brüning government', *World Politics*, Vol. 12, No. 1 (1959), p. 26.

27 William L. Patch, *Heinrich Brüning and the Dissolution of the Weimar Republic* (Cambridge, 1998), p. 151.

Chapter Five

1 David Clay Large, *Berlin: A Modern History* (London, 2001), p. 158.

2 F. L. Carsten, *A History of the Prussian Junker* (Aldershot, 1989), pp. 155–58.

3 See Karl Demeter, *The German Officer-Corps in Society and State 1650–1945* (Angus Malcolm, trans) (London, 1965), pp. 47–58; G. A.

Craig, *The Politics of the Prussian Army 1645–1945* (New York, 1964), pp. 393–6; Carsten: *A History of the Prussian Junker*, pp. 161–62; and David Stone, *Fighting for the Fatherland: The Story of the German Soldier from 1648 to the Present Day* (London, 2006), p. 308.

4   Matthew Stibbe, *Germany 1914–1933* (Harlow, 2010), p. 119.

5   David B. Southern, 'The Impact of the Inflation: Inflation, the Courts and Revaluation' in Richard Bessel and E. J. Feuchtwanger (eds), *Social Change and Political Development in Weimar Germany* (London, 1981), p. 55.

6   See Bernd Widdig, 'Cultural Capital in Decline: Inflation and the Distress of Intellectuals' in Kathleen Canning, Kerstin Brandt and Kristin McGuire (eds), *Weimar Publics/Weimar Subjects: Rethinking the Political Culture of Germany in the 1920s* (Oxford, 2010).

7   Stibbe: *Germany*, p. 114.

8   See Siegfried Kracauer, *The Salaried Masses* (Quintin Hoare, trans.) (London, 1998).

9   Stibbe: *Germany*, p. 112.

10 Paul Bookbinder, *Weimar Germany: The Republic of the Reasonable* (Manchester, 1996), p. 158.

11 Kathleen Canning, 'Women and the Politics of Gender', in Anthony McElligott (ed.), *Weimar Germany* (Oxford, 2009), pp. 147–48.

12 Ibid. p. 153.

13 Katherina von Ankum (ed.), *Women in the Metropolis: Gender and Modernity in Weimar Culture* (Berkeley, 1997), p. 6.

14 Eric Weitz, *Weimar Germany: Promise and Tragedy* (Princeton, 2007), p. 56.

15 Tim Mason, 'Women in Germany, 1925–1940: family, welfare, work', *History Workshop Journal*, Vol. 1 (1976), pp. 78–80.

16 Dagmar Reese, *Growing Up Female in Nazi Germany* (Ann Arbor, 2006), pp. 48, 192.

17 For a comparative perspective on issues of gender and sexuality during this period, see Alys Eve Winterbaum, Lynn M. Thomas, Priti Ramamurthy, Ura G. Poger and Tani E. Barlow (eds) *The Modern Girl Around the World: Consumption, Modernity and Globalization* (North Carolina, 2008); Virginia Nicholson, *Singled Out* (Oxford, 2008); Martin Pugh, *We Danced All Night: A Social History of Britain Between the Wars* (London, 2008), pp. 124–70; and Richard Overy, *The Morbid Age: Britain between the Wars* (London, 2009), pp. 93–135.

18 Julia Roos, *Weimar Through the Lens of Gender: Prostitution Reform, Woman's Emancipation, and German Democracy, 1919–33* (Ann Arbor, 2010), p. 4.

19 See Paul Weindling, *Health, Race and German Politics between National Unification and Nazism, 1870–1945* (Cambridge, 1989).

20 See Laurie Marhofer, 'Degeneration, sexual freedom, and the politics

of the Weimar Republic', *German Studies Review*, Vol. 34, No. 3 (2011), p. 532.

21 See Mel Gordon, *Voluptuous Panic: The Erotic World of Weimar Berlin* (Los Angeles, 2001), pp. 92–94.

22 See John Chancellor, *How to be Happy in Berlin* (London, 1929), pp. 136-7. For more on British 'sex tourism' see Colin Storer, *Britain and the Weimar Republic: The History of a Cultural Relationship* (London, 2010), Chapter 1.

23 See James Kollenbroich, *Our Hour Has Come: The Homosexual Rights Movement in the Weimar Republic* (Saarbrücken, 2007) and Marhofer: 'Degeneration, sexual freedom, and politics', pp. 538–39.

24 John Bingham, 'The "Urban Republic"' in Anthony McElligott (ed.), *Weimar Germany* (Oxford, 2009), p. 127.

25 Weitz: *Weimar Germany*, p. 41.

26 Adelheid von Saldern, '"Neues Wohnen": Housing and Reform' in Anthony McElligott (ed.), *Weimar Germany*, (Oxford, 2009), p. 210.

27 Weitz: *Weimar Germany*, p. 43.

28 Julia Sneeringer, 'The shopper as voter: women, advertising and politics in post-inflation Germany', *German Studies Review* (2004), Vol. 27, No. 3, p. 478.

29 Bingham: 'The "Urban Republic"', p. 129.

30 Giles MacDonough, *Berlin* (London, 1997), p. 214.

31 Detlev Peukert, *The Weimar Republic* (London, 1993), p. 150. See also Richard Wetzell, *Inventing the Criminal: A History of German Criminology, 1880–1945* (Chapel Hill, 2000), pp. 109–20.

32 Victoria Harris, *Selling Sex in the Reich: Prostitutes in German Society, 1914–1945* (Oxford, 2010), p. 55.

33 Sace Elder, *Murder Scenes: Normality, Deviance and Criminal Violence in Weimar Berlin* (Ann Arbor, 2010), p. 7.

34 Ibid., p. 3.

35 For a comparative perspective on Weimar crime and detection rates see Eric A. Johnson and Eric H. Monkkonen (eds), *The Civilization of Crime: Violence in Town and Country Since the Middle Ages* (Urbana, 1997); James F. Richardson, 'Berlin Police in the Weimar Republic: A Comparison With Police Forces in Cities of the United States' in George L. Mosse (ed.), *Police Forces in History* (London, 1975), p. 82; and Hsi-huey Liang, *The Berlin Police Force of the Weimar Republic* (Berkeley, 1970), especially Chapters 3 and 4.

36 Todd Herzog, *Crime Stories: Criminalistic Fantasy and the Culture of Crisis in Weimar Germany* (New York, 2009), pp. 2–3.

37 Peter Watson, *The German Genius* (London, 2010), p. 568.

38 Ibid. p. 35.

39 Ibid. p. 604.

40 Peter Gay, *Weimar Culture: The Outsider as Insider* (London, 1992), p. 6.
41 Lotte H. Eisner, *The Haunted Screen* (London, 1969), p. 51.
42 Siegfried Kracauer, *From Caligari to Hitler: A Psychological History of the German Film* (Princeton, 1947), p. 71.
43 Eberhard Kolb, *The Weimar Republic* (*2nd ed*) (P. S. Falla and R. J. Park, trans), (Abingdon, 2005), p. 88.
44 Sergiusz Michalski, *New Objectivity: Painting, Graphic Art and Photography in Weimar Germany 1919–1933* (Michael Claridge, trans.) (Cologne, 2003), p. 20.
45 Mary Nolan, *Visions of Modernity: American Business and the Modernisation of Germany* (New York, 1994), pp. 50–51.
46 Joseph Roth, *What I Saw* (London, 2003), p. 41.
47 Elizabeth Harvey, 'Culture and Society in Weimar Germany: The Impact of Modernism and Mass Culture' in Mary Fulbrook (ed.), *Twentieth Century Germany* (London, 2001), p. 63.
48 Rüdiger Graf, 'Anticipating the future in the present: "new women" and other beings of the future in Weimar Germany', *Central European History*, Vol. 42, No. 4 (2009), pp. 650–51.

Chapter Six

1 See Anna von der Goltz, *Hindenburg: Power, Myth and the Rise of the Nazis* (Oxford, 2009), pp. 84–93, 96–102.
2 Ibid., p. 126.
3 Eberhard Kolb, *The Weimar Republic* (*2nd ed*) (P. S. Falla and R. J. Park, trans.), (Abingdon, 2005), p. 76.
4 William L. Patch, *Heinrich Brüning and the Dissolution of the Weimar Republic* (Cambridge, 1998), p. 73.
5 Ibid., p. 83.
6 Matthew Stibbe, *Germany 1914–1933* (Harlow, 2010), p. 172.
7 Patch: *Heinrich Brüning*, p. 221.
8 Peter Fritzsche, 'The NSDAP 1919–1934: From Fringe Politics to the Seizure of Power' in Jane Caplan, *Nazi Germany* (Oxford, 2008), p. 51.
9 Ibid. pp. 60–66.
10 Ian Kershaw, *Hitler 1889–1936* (London, 1998), p. 201.
11 Fritzsche: 'The NSDAP 1919–1934', p. 56.
12 Dirk Schumann, *Political Violence in the Weimar Republic, 1918–1933* (Thomas Dunlap, trans) (New York, 2009), pp. 223, 252, 312.
13 See Larry Eugene Jones, 'Nationalists, Nazis, and the assault against Weimar: revisiting the Harzburg rally of October 1931', *German Studies Review*, Vol. 29, No. 3 (2006), pp. 483–94.
14 See Anna von der Goltz, *Hindenburg*, pp. 144–46 and Jürgen W. Falter, 'The two Hindenburg elections of 1925 and 1932: a total reversal of

voter coalitions', *Central European History*, Vol. 23, No. 2–3 (1990), pp. 225–41.

15 Geoff Layton, *Germany: The Third Reich, 1933–1945* (Trowbridge, 1992), p. 40.

16 Thomas Childers, *The Nazi Voter: The Social Foundations of Fascism in Germany 1919–1933* (Chapel Hill, 1983), p. 266.

17 Ibid. pp. 264–65.

18 Jürgen Falter, *Hitler's Wähler* (Munich, 1991), pp. 220–29.

19 Childers: *The Nazi Voter*, p. 268.

20 Peter Fritzsche, 'Did Weimar fail?', *The Journal of Modern History*, Vol. 68, No. 3 (1996), p. 642.

21 Richard J. Evans, *The Coming of the Third Reich* (London, 2003), pp. 264–65.

22 Ibid. p. 270.

23 Schumann: *Political Violence in the Weimar Republic*, p. 256.

24 Larry Eugene Jones, 'Franz von Papen, the German Centre Party, and the failure of Catholic Conservatism in the Weimar Republic', *Central European History*, Vol. 38, No. 2 (2005), p. 206.

25 Patch: *Heinrich Brüning*, p. 276.

26 Evans: *The Coming of the Third Reich*, p. 270.

27 Gordon Craig, *The Politics of the Prussian Army 1650–1945* (New York, 1964), p. 456.

28 Henry Ashby Turner, *Hitler's Thirty Days to Power* (London, 1996), pp. 15–16.

29 Ibid., p. 19.

30 Peter Hayes, '"A question mark with epaulettes"? Kurt von Schleicher and Weimar Politics', *The Journal of Modern History*, Vol. 52, No. 1 (1980), pp. 37–38. See also Henry Ashby Turner, *Hitler's Thirty Days to Power*, pp. 20–21.

31 Layton: *Germany*, p. 48.

32 von der Goltz: *Hindenburg*, p. 142.

Conclusion

1 Eric D. Weitz, 'Weimar Germany and its histories', *Central European History*, Vol. 43, No. 4 (2010), p. 582.

2 Eric D. Weitz, *Weimar Germany: Promise and Tragedy* (Princeton, 2007), p. 364.

3 Ibid., p. 364.

4 Weitz: 'Weimar Germany and its histories', p. 582.

5 Peter Fritzsche, 'Did Weimar fail?', *The Journal of Modern History*, Vol. 68, No. 3 (1996), p. 630.

Further Reading

The literature on the Weimar Republic in English alone is vast. What follows is therefore not intended to be an exhaustive list of all the works consulted in the writing of this book, let alone of the literature in its entirety. Rather it is intended as a guide to further reading for Anglophone readers.

GENERAL WORKS

Bookbinder, P., *Weimar Germany: The Republic of the Reasonable* (1996) Manchester University Press: Manchester.

Fritzsche, P., 'Did Weimar fail?', *The Journal of Modern History*, Vol. 68, No. 3 (1996), pp. 629–56.

Hung, J., Weiss-Sussex, G. and Wilkes, G. (eds), *Beyond Glitter and Doom: The Contingency of the Weimar Republic* (2012) Iudicium Verlag: Munich.

Kolb, E., *The Weimar Republic (Second Edition)* (P. S. Falla and R. J. Park, trans.) (2005) Routledge: Abingdon.

Layton, G., *From Bismarck to Hitler: Germany 1890–1933* (1995) Hodder & Stoughton: London.

McElligott, A. (ed.), *Weimar Germany* (2009) OUP: Oxford.

Mommsen, H., *The Rise and Fall of Weimar Democracy* (E. Foster and L. E. Jones, trans.) (1996) University of North Carolina Press: Chapel Hill.

Peukert, D. J. K., *The Weimar Republic: The Crisis of Classical Modernity* (Richard Deveson, trans.) (1993) Penguin Books: London.

Stibbe, M., *Germany 1914–1933: Politics, Society and Culture* (2010) Pearson Education: Harlow.

Vincent, C. P., *A Historical Dictionary of Germany's Weimar Republic, 1918–1933* (1997) Greenwood Press: Westport, Connecticut.
Weitz, E. D., *Weimar Germany: Promise and Tragedy* (2007) Princeton University Press: Princeton.

DOCUMENTS AND EYE-WITNESS ACCOUNTS

Kaes, A., Jay, M., & Dimendberg, E. (eds), *The Weimar Republic Sourcebook* (1994) University of California Press: Berkeley, California.
Kessler, Count H., *The Diaries of a Cosmopolitan, 1918–1937* (Charles Kessler, trans.) (2000) Phoenix Publishing: London.
Palmer, T. and Neubauer, H. (eds), *The Weimar Republic Through the Lens of the Press* (2000) Könemann Verlagsgesellschaft: Cologne.
Price, M. P., *Dispatches from the Weimar Republic* (Tania Rose, ed) (1999) Pluto Press: London.
Roth, J., *What I Saw: Reports From Berlin 1920–33* (Michael Hoffman, trans.) (2003) Granta Books: London.

IMPERIAL GERMANY AND THE FIRST WORLD WAR

Chickering, R., *Imperial Germany and the Great War* (*2nd ed*) (2004) Cambridge University Press: Cambridge.
Davies, B. J., *Home Fires Burning: Food, Politics, and Everyday Life in World War I Berlin* (2000) University of North Carolina Press: Chapel Hill.
Eley, G. and Retallack, J. (eds), *Wilhelminism and its Legacies: German Modernities, Imperialism, and the Meanings of Reform, 1890–1930* (2003) Berghahn Books: Oxford.
Gross, S., 'Confidence and gold: German war finance 1914–1918', *Central European History* (2009), Vol. 42, No. 2, pp. 223–52.
Retallack, J. (ed.), *Imperial Germany 1871–1918* (2008) OUP: Oxford.
Stevenson, D., *With Our Backs to the Wall: Victory and Defeat in 1918* (2011) Allen Lane: London.

THE YEARS OF CRISIS

Bessel, R., *Germany After the First World War* (1993) Clarendon Press: Oxford.

Broué, P., *The German Revolution 1917–1923* (John Archer, trans.) (2006) The Merlin Press: London.

Carsten, F. L., *Revolution in Central Europe* (1972) Maurice Temple Smith: London.

Fischer, C., '"A very German revolution"? The post-1918 settlement re-evaluated', *Bulletin of the German Historical Institute*, Vol. 28, No. 2 (2006).

Gerwarth, R., 'The Central European counter-revolution: paramilitary violence in Germany, Austria and Hungary after the Great War', *Past and Present*, No. 200 (2008), pp. 175–209.

Grunberger, R., *Red Rising in Bavaria* (1973) Arthur Barker: London.

Haffner, S., *Failure of a Revolution: Germany 1918/19* (1973) Andre Deutsch: London.

Jones, N., *A Brief History of the Birth of the Nazis: How the Freikorps Blazed a Trail for Hitler* (2004) Constable and Robinson: London.

Read, A., *The World on Fire: 1919 and the Battle with Bolshevism* (2008) Jonathan Cape: London.

POLITICAL CULTURE

Canning, K., Brandt, K. and McGuire, K. (eds), *Weimar Publics/Weimar Subjects: Rethinking the Political Culture of Germany in the 1920s* (2010) Berghahn Books: Oxford.

Hanson, S. E., *Post-Imperial Democracies: Ideology and Party Formation in Third Republic France, Weimar Germany and Post-Soviet Russia* (2010) Cambridge University Press: Cambridge.

Schumann, D., *Political Violence in the Weimar Republic, 1918–1933* (Thomas Dunlap, trans.) (2009) Berghahn Books: New York.

THE GREAT INFLATION AND WEIMAR ECONOMY

Baldeson, T., *Politics and Economics in the Weimar Republic* (2002) Cambridge University Press: Cambridge.

Feldman, G. D., *The Great Disorder: Politics, Economics and Society in the German Inflation, 1914–24* (1997) OUP: New York.

Ferguson, N., 'The German Inter-War Economy: Political Choice Versus Economic Determinism' in Fulbrook, M. (ed.) *German History Since 1800* (1997) Arnold: London.

Fergusson, A., *When Money Dies: The Nightmare of the Weimar Hyper-Inflation* (2010) Old Street Publishing: London.

Widding, B., *Culture and Inflation in Weimar Germany* (2001) University of California Press: Berkeley.

SOCIETY AND CULTURE

Bridenthal, R., Grossmann, A. & Kaplan, M. (eds), *When Biology Became Destiny: Women in Weimar and Nazi Germany* (1984) Monthly Review Press: New York.

Gay, P., *Weimar Culture: The Outsider as Insider* (1992) Penguin Books: London.

Harris, V., *Selling Sex in the Reich: Prostitutes in German Society, 1914–1945* (2010) OUP: Oxford.

Isenberg, N. (ed.) *Weimar Cinema* (2009) Columbia University Press: New York.

Jelavich, P., *Berlin Cabaret* (1993) Harvard University Press: Cambridge, Massachusetts.

Kolinsky, E. & van der Will, W. (eds) *The Cambridge Companion to Modern German Culture* (1998) Cambridge University Press: Cambridge.

Kollenbroich, J., *Our Hour Has Come: The Homosexual Rights Movement in the Weimar Republic* (2007) VDM Verlag: Saarbrücken.

Laqueur, W., *Weimar, A Cultural History 1918–1933* (2000) Phoenix Press: London.

Leydecker, K. (ed.), *German Novelists of the Weimar Republic: Intersections of Literature and Politics* (2006) Camden House: New York.

von Ankum, K.(ed.), *Women in the Metropolis: Gender and Modernity in Weimar Culture* (1997) University of California Press: Berkeley.

Further Reading

Williams, J. A. (ed.), *Weimar Culture Revisited* (2011) Palgrave: Basingstoke.

Fischer, C., *The Ruhr Crisis, 1923–1924* (2003) OUP: Oxford.
Hindon, J. W., *Germany and Europe 1919–1939* (1977) Longman: Harlow.
Krüger, P., 'The European East and Weimar Germany' in Mühle, E. (ed.), *Germany and the European East in the Twentieth Century* (2003) Berg: Oxford.
Lee, M. M. and Michalka, W., *German Foreign Policy 1917–1933: Continuity or Break?* (1987) Berg: Leamington Spa.
Wright, J., *Gustav Stresemann: Weimar's Greatest Statesman* (2002) OUP: Oxford.
Wright, J., 'Stresemann and Locarno', *Contemporary European History*, Vol. 4, No. 2 (1995), pp. 109–31.

THE END OF THE REPUBLIC

Evans, R. J., *The Coming of the Third Reich* (2004) Penguin: London.
Kershaw, I. (ed.), *Weimar: Why did German Democracy Fail?* (1990) Weidenfeld and Nicolson: London.
Patch, W. L., *Heinrich Brüning and the Dissolution of the Weimar Republic* (1998) Cambridge University Press: Cambridge.
Turner, H. A., *Hitler's Thirty Days to Power* (1996) Addison-Wesley Publishing: Reading, Massachusetts.
von der Goltz, A., *Hindenburg: Power, Myth and the Rise of the Nazis* (2009) OUP: Oxford.

WEIMAR GERMANY IN FICTION

Döblin, A., *Berlin Alexanderplatz* (Eugene Jorlas, trans.) (2004) Continuum: London.
Isherwood, C., *The Berlin Novels* (1999) Vintage: London.
Keun, I., *The Artificial Silk Girl* (Katherine von Ankum, trans.) (2002) Other Press: London.

231

Krajewski, M., *The End of the World in Breslau* (Danusia Stok, trans.) (2010) Quercus: London.
Lutes, J., *Berlin: City of Stones* (2004) Drawn & Quarterly: Montreal.
Spender, S., *The Temple* (1988) Faber & Faber: London.

ONLINE RESOURCES

Bauhaus Online (http://www.bauhaus-online.de/en)
German History in Documents and Images (http://www.germanhistorydocs.ghi-dc.org/section.cfm?section_id=12)
The Weimar Studies Network (http://www.weimarstudies.wordpress.com)

Index

A Short History of . . .

the American Civil War	Paul Anderson (Clemson University)
the American Revolutionary War	Stephen Conway (University College London)
Ancient Greece	P J Rhodes, FBA (University of Durham)
Ancient Rome	Andrew Wallace-Hadrill (University of Cambridge)
the Anglo-Saxons	Henrietta Leyser (University of Oxford)
the Byzantine Empire	Dionysios Stathakopoulos (King's College London)
the Celts	Alex Woolf (University of St Andrews)
the Crimean War	Trudi Tate (University of Cambridge)
the English Renaissance Drama	Helen Hackett (University College, London)
the English Revolution and the Civil Wars	David J Appleby (University of Nottingham)
the Etruscans	Corinna Riva (University College London)
Imperial Egypt	Robert Morkot (University of Exeter)
Italian Renaissance	Virginia Cox (New York University)
the Korean War	Allan R Millett (University of New Orleans)
Medieval English Mysticism	Vincent Gillespie (University of Oxford)
the Minoans	John Bennet (University of Sheffield)
the Mongols	George Lane (SOAS, University of London)
the Mughal Empire	Michael Fisher (Oberlin College)
Muslim Spain	Alex J Novikoff (Rhodes College, Memphis)
the New Testament	Halvor Moxnes (University of Oslo)
Nineteenth-Century Philosophy	Joel Rasmussen (University of Oxford)
the Normans	Leonie Hicks (University of Southampton)
the Phoenicians	Glenn E Markoe